LANGUAGE LEARNING

Language Learning: A Special Case For Developmental Psychology?

Christine J. Howe

Department of Psychology
University of Strathclyde
Glasgow, UK

LAWRENCE ERLBAUM ASSOCIATES, PUBLISHERS
Hove (UK)   Hillsdale (USA)

Lawrence Erlbaum Associates Ltd., Publishers
27 Palmeira Mansions
Church Road
Hove
East Sussex, BN3 2FA
U.K.

British Library Cataloguing in Publication Data

Howe, Christine
   Language Learning: Special Case for
   Developmental Psychology?. —
   I. Title II. Series
   401

   ISBN 0-86377-230-7 (Hbk)
   ISSN 0959-3977 (Essays in Developmental Psychology)

Printed and bound in the United Kingdom by BPCC Wheatons Ltd., Exeter.

Contents

Preface

The starting place for my essay is the notion, current in the literature for around thirty years, that children could not learn their native language without substantial innate knowledge of its grammatical form. The notion is of crucial importance for developmental psychology, but it has also attracted the attention of biologists, linguists, and philosophers. As a result, it could be one of the most widely discussed themes in contemporary academia, raising the question of what an essay at this point in time could hope to contribute. As I began to read with the essay in mind, I became convinced that there was, in fact, a great deal still to be achieved. In particular, it struck me that no-one had spelled out the assumptions on which the innateness hypothesis depends, let alone subjected them to rigorous appraisal. This, then, was the line that I decided to take.

As I followed it, I found myself persuaded of two central points. The first was that proponents of the innateness hypothesis have been too ready to treat children as miniature linguists, concerned with the representation of sentences as an end in itself. Like many before me, I felt that a more realistic approach would be to regard children as communication engineers, storing sentences to optimise the production and retrieval of meaning. The second point was that even when the communication analogy is adopted, it has been glibly assumed that the meanings children impute will be the ones adults intend. My research activities in the late 1970s had taught me to be wary, and as I read more widely I felt that this was probably wise. The strategies children use to ascribe meaning provide many opportunities for misunderstanding. Moreover, although the misunderstanding should pass unnoticed in the course of conversation, it must to some extent occur.

This said, the precise degree of misunderstanding is hard to gauge from the literature as it stands. All that is possible is the formulation of tentative hypotheses, and doing something better is, in my view, of the utmost importance. There is no hope, I feel, of seeing where the communication analogy leads without knowing what children's meanings are like, and I hope that, whatever else, my essay persuades its readers that this is correct. If it does, it means that empirical work with children has a key role to play in the innateness debate, and may therefore give a new impetus to relevant research. This is much needed. As my essay should make clear, there is up-to-date material on children's grammatical knowledge. Every time I returned to a draft I found new work to include! However, research on meaning specifically has largely fizzled out, and there is little more recent than the early 1980s.

Taking what I could from existing material, I have formulated hypotheses about the meanings children impute. Having done so, I have tried also to look at the consequences for the learning of language. I have attempted to be as rigorous as possible. I have been impressed by the quasi-mathematical work of the so-called "learnability theorists". As my essay will explain, their proofs are not directly relevant to the issues at stake, but their analytic "tightness" is, and I have tried to learn from it. What my essay does is imagine children without innate knowledge of grammar processing sentences and their putative meanings along communication lines. Detailed predictions are made about the course and time-scale of learning, and these predictions are then pitted against known empirical facts. I believe that the facts are not unduly troubling.

Having said this, I am not presenting my essay as an attempt to disprove innateness. Apart from the uncertainties over meaning, the status of "communicative processing" is not above question. Thus, disproving innateness is not currently deliverable (I say "currently" because in contrast to some theorists, I see rejection as in principle attainable). What is deliverable is the following: a convincing argument as to why innate knowledge of grammar should not be taken as read and a clear strategy for further clarification. It is in this spirit that the essay is offered.

The essay has one author, but it is not of course an individual product. My ideas have been formulated through discussions with colleagues at Strathclyde University, particularly members of the "Developmental and Educational Research Group". My text has been improved through comments from Mike Forrester, Roger Goodwin, Elena Lieven, and

David Messer. I owe all these people a great debt of gratitude. However, it is not just my academic colleagues that I wish to thank. I should like also to acknowledge the patience of my secretary Jean Cuthill, who worked uncomplainingly on the numerous drafts. Moreover, there is in addition my family. I did the research for the essay while my children were very small, and it is an unfortunate feature of contemporary society that women with small children need extensive support to produce book-length reports. This is particularly true in my case, and I should like to thank the people who have provided this support: my husband Willie Robertson, my mother-in-law Grace Robertson, and, above all, my children's nanny Fiona Kennedy, whose devoted service for over seven years has been the basis for everything.

As for my children, Miriam and Jeremy, I have never achieved the detachment of some linguistically-trained parents and managed to make systematic recordings of their natural behaviour. However, as will become clear, I have noted a few features of relevance to the themes of the essay. Thus, my children are more than a background presence in what will follow. For that reason, it is to Miriam and Jeremy that I wish the essay to be dedicated. They may have slowed its production down, but not for a moment have I minded!

Christine Howe
University of Strathclyde, 1992

CHAPTER ONE

The Case for Innate Knowledge

Until about thirty years ago, the concerns of linguists and psychologists of language differed markedly. Linguists were primarily interested in the criteria by which they could specify the sentences of given natural languages, criteria that they assumed would amount to a "grammar". Even those whose study ended with English Language at school will have a passing acquaintance with what specification via a grammar would involve. Whatever else, it would mean the categorisation of "lexical items" (that is, words plus inflections) into various "form classes", and the utilisation of rules that showed how form class members could be combined to produce sentences. Psychologists on the other hand, tended to concentrate on what was called "verbal learning". They performed countless experiments on memory for words or, even, memory for nonsense syllables. Sometimes, a list would be presented and the subject asked to recall as many items as possible. At other times, the task would be "paired associate learning" where pairs of items were presented and the subject asked to recall one member in response to the other. Through such experiments, psychologists investigated the effects of varying the number of items, the time between items and the relatedness of items. The journals of the day carried the results of these experiments in endless permutations.

The lack of overlap between linguistic and psychological concerns certainly did not lead to sterile research. The work done in both disciplines has relevance today, and will be used to some extent in this essay. Nevertheless, around 1960 the work done in linguistics was felt by its authors to be overly limited. A broadening of perspective took place, which led eventually not just to a deep interest in psychological issues but also to a fresh approach to them. The broadening was precipitated by the conviction, amongst linguists, that the notion of a grammar must be psychologically real. In other words, when ordinary speakers produce sentences, they too are demonstrating an awareness of form classes and the rules that order them. Initially the significance of this conclusion was felt to lie in a new criterion for theoretical adequacy. Amongst linguists it had long been realised that there are numerous ways in which form classes and rules of ordering can be arranged to specify sentences. Thus, what is sometimes called "observational adequacy" is not sufficient to establish one grammar over others and further criteria are required. Traditionally, these criteria have related to elegance and simplicity but once the psychological reality of form classes and rules of ordering was postulated, a new possibility was raised. Perhaps only a small number of potential grammars corresponds to ordinary human knowledge. Perhaps only one does. In which case, it (or they) might reasonably be taken as the best representation.

Having recognised psychological reality as a constraint on their activities, it was inevitable that linguists would take an interest in psychology itself. Discovering that, applied to language, psychology was coextensive with verbal learning, they perceived a gap. After all, if ordinary humans really do have knowledge of a grammar, they must, somehow, acquire it. However, as the grammar will not be told to them, they will not acquire it by memorising the linguistic output of other speakers. As the verbal learning experiments were focused on the memorising of this kind of output, they clearly could not bear on the acquisition of ordinary human grammar, raising the question of precisely how it is acquired. Intrigued, a number of linguists began to reflect on the issue, and they soon came to the conclusion that it could not even be inferred from linguistic experiences alone. Obviously these experiences must be playing some part. The differences between the world's languages are such that their speakers must acquire different grammars. These differences have to result from differing experiences. However, the linguists were convinced that linguistic experiences could not be the whole story. On the contrary, they believed that acquisition must involve the reconciliation of linguistic experiences with innate knowledge of the grammar's basic form. This, as the linguists were quick to realise, would make grammar more than an omission from the psychological study of language. It would elevate grammar into a major challenge to psychological theory.

The challenge would arise not so much from the denial of the "blank slate" approach. By the 1960s, most psychologists concerned with language had already abandoned this idea. Indeed, they would probably have welcomed a strengthening of the case against behaviourism. The challenge would not even be from the idea of innate knowledge *per se*. Innate "schemas" were being advocated in the field of perceptual development with relatively little controversy. The problem would be the sheer complexity of the innate knowledge being proposed for grammar. If true, it would amount to an *a priori* categorial structure, and this would be quite unlike what was being suggested elsewhere. Hence, it would be hard to reconcile with the general learning theory which, in the mid-1960s, was presupposed by most psychological researchers.

Have things now changed? Yes and no. It is no longer true that a general learning theory is presupposed by most psychological researchers. The problem of grammar has become too well known. Rather, the possibility of a general theory is now hotly debated, with uncertainties over empirical research that wait on a resolution. What is still true, however, is the continued centrality of accounting for grammar, with protagonists of all sides of the argument accepting that consensus here would be a major step forward.

Thus, there can be little doubt that the idea of innate knowledge of grammar is of contemporary theoretical relevance. How, then, does the idea stand? Is there really no alternative if learning is to be explained? These questions will underpin the discussion of much of this essay. By way of introduction, the present chapter will examine the reasoning that led to the idea in the first place. It will start with the logic underlying the decision to ask how grammar is acquired. It will find nothing remotely suspect. It will then turn to the considerations that produced the controversial answer and argue that they included two assumptions that might, in principle, be challenged. Recognising this, the chapter will ask whether the force of the considerations would be weakened, should either assumption be rejected. For one of the assumptions, the chapter will give a clear and categorical answer: rejecting it would do nothing to weaken the case for innateness. For the other, the chapter will discuss it only to the extent of identifying the most promising approach to an appraisal. As it raises issues of enormous complexity, following the approach will have to wait for the chapters to come.

FIRST STEPS TO INNATE KNOWLEDGE

Moving then to the origins of the innateness hypothesis, it will have been noted that it followed from what can be construed as two discrete developments in the field of linguistics. The first was the shift of emphasis from the ability of grammars to represent sentences to the ability of humans to produce them. The second was the conviction that the ability of humans to produce sentences implies at least one of the grammars capable of representation. As a result the first task will be to scrutinise these developments closely, to ask, for example, whether people really can be said to "produce sentences" in any meaningful sense of the term, and if they can, whether their productions really do guarantee knowledge of a grammar. Both questions will be discussed in the early part of the section. Finding no reason to answer in the negative, the section will turn to the innateness hypothesis itself, and ask why it followed so straightforwardly from the acceptance of psychological reality. As will become clear, a main reason was the coincidence in time between the acceptance of psychological reality and new insights into observationally adequate grammar.

The Knowledge Behind Sentence Production

Having followed the arguments so far, those previously unacquainted with the thinking of linguists might be tempted to raise a simple objection. Surely, they might say, there is no need to invoke grammar to explain how ordinary speakers produce sentences because ordinary speakers seldom produce sentences. Sentences are rarefied commodities beloved by school teachers, but rarely found in everyday usage. In particular, sentences are divorced from the vagaries of dialect, while spontaneous productions manifest these features in abundance. The objection would have to be accepted if linguists were concerned with the notion of a "sentence" that underpins explicit judgements. There is plenty of evidence that when asked to pick out the sentences in a set of utterances, people will veer towards school standards and away from their own vernacular. Thus, they will accept "I have not done it" and reject "I ain't done it" even when they themselves sometimes use the latter.

Interestingly, however, intuitive judgements only approximate school standards. They do not, as Hill (1961) and MacLay and Sleator (1960) found when they asked speakers to judge strings like "Send one to Harry and I", exactly mirror them. Hence, there is some compromise with actual usage but nevertheless, the general point holds good: the concept of a sentence underpinning explicit judgements precludes much that is produced spontaneously. However, when these precluded productions occur in ordinary discourse, the covert response is seldom rejecting. Moreover, even when it is, it still acknowledges the string as part of the language and for linguists this is enough. The linguistic concept of a sentence amounts to those strings that would be implicitly accepted as exemplars of a language. Given this concept "I ain't done it" and "I have not done it" would both pass as sentences, but "Ain't I it done" and "Have I done not it" would fail. Given this concept also, it should be clear that the vast majority of adult utterances must be viewed as sentences and thus, from the linguistic perspective, the ability to produce sentences is not the prerogative of an educated elite. It is a virtually universal property of adult behaviour.

However, if we accept this point about sentences, do we also have to accept that it implies knowledge of a grammar? Why can't we just say that when people produce sentences, they retrieve the ones they have already heard from a list in their memory? In the early 1960s several reasons were advanced for rejecting this possibility. One was that there are an infinite number of sentences and, for that matter, non-sentences open to mature speakers of every natural language. Hence, the sentences could never be specified in a list. The theorist most responsible for highlighting this point was Noam Chomsky (especially Chomsky, 1957). The flavour of Chomsky's thesis can be grasped quite simply via embedded relative clauses. No doubt, the product eventually becomes hard to understand. Nevertheless, we can embed relative clauses *ad infinitum* with each additional clause producing a new sentence. The point is beautifully illustrated by the verses of "I know an old lady who swallowed a horse ... to catch a fly".

More concrete evidence against the listing of sentences was obtained from the speech of children. It was recognised that the notion of a list implies that sentences are treated as unanalysable wholes, meaning that children's utterances should be full or, at worst, truncated versions of adults'. Data reported in the early 1960s showed this not to be the case. For instance, through his work into the earliest word combinations of three young boys, Braine (1963a) reported many strings that look decidedly unadultlike. The best known is "All gone sticky", which, it must be admitted, could be an abbreviation of something like "The cake's all gone and now your hands are sticky" but that almost certainly does not mirror a simple sentence. Working with slightly older subjects, Ervin (1964) reported even more compelling evidence against children's speech replicating adults'. Ervin and, later, other researchers, observed systematic overgeneralisation of the inflections when, for example, the plural "—s" is applied to "foot" and "mouse" and the past "—ed" to "come" and "break". Forms like "foots", "mouses", "comed", and "breaked" most definitely do not appear in adult speech. Likewise, the juxtaposition of noun and pronoun in (1.1) could not reflect anything used by more mature speakers.[1]

(Melanie (20.6) takes cup)   (1.1)
     Melanie: Milk
                    Drink it. Drink it
                    Drink it milk

Yet such strings, which appear frequently in data that I have collected, have also been documented by such writers as Bloom, Lightbown, and Hood (1975).

Thus, theoretical studies of adults' speech and empirical studies of children's pointed to the same conclusion. Our knowledge of what constitutes a sentence is not represented in the form of a list. However, besides showing this, the studies were also thought to clarify just how our knowledge is represented. It was recognised that an open-ended set of sentences could only be represented in a finite manner if experienced sentences were treated as composites, made up of units like lexical items. However, compositionality implied a mechanism whereby the components can be successfully reordered, a mechanism that in other words allows "I can run" but not "can run I" to be constructed from "I", "can", and "run". It was concluded that the only mechanisms that could do this while guaranteeing the open-endedness of sentences would be ones that called upon rules. However, it was also concluded that not just any rules would do. It became clear from the likes of "All gone sticky", "foots" and "Drink it milk" that humans can juxtapose lexical items that they have never actually experienced in adjacent positions. It was realised that they would not be able to do this if they were learning rules that order individual items. Rather, they must be categorising the lexical items in some way and learning rules that order categories. However, once this was accepted, the outcome was rules that order form classes, which amounted of course to grammar as a psychologically real phenomenon.

For twenty years after the studies were subject to this kind of analysis, the psychological reality of grammar was never questioned. However, there has recently been an upsurge of support for a "parallel distributed" approach to human knowledge, and this approach denies both rules and, in any relevant sense, form classes. As summarised by McClelland, Rumelhart, and Hinton (1986), the parallel distributed approach construes human knowledge as a vast array of units interconnected in excitatory or inhibitory fashions. The activation of one unit is supposed to lead to the activation of all excitatorily interconnected units, with the strength of activation determined by the strength of the connection. Strength of activation is supposed, in turn, to determine the combinatorial properties of the units, thereby dispensing with rules as a matter of inherent principle. Form classes are eliminated from the combinatorial process as a matter of practice, for the units are never larger than lexical items and are typically (e.g. Rumelhart & McClelland, 1987) far more microscopic. Thus, although form classes may be implied by the connections between units, they are epiphenomenal as regards knowledge.

At first sight, the parallel distributed approach seems to have much in its favour. Evidence from computer simulations has suggested that it can represent the knowledge underpinning behaviour as varied as skilled typing, stereoscopic vision, and cued memory, not to mention aspects of language of concern to this essay. On closer analysis, however, the achievements are far less impressive. Commenting on a parallel distributed simulation (Rumelhart & McClelland, 1987), which acquired the past tense of English, Pinker and Prince (1988) show how the output failed in many cases to approximate the known facts about learning. Moreover, when approximation was achieved, it was, in part at least, by virtue of features in the simulation that are ancillary to parallel distributed processing. Taking up the story, Lachter and Bever (1988) show that some of the ancillary features can only be construed as accommodations to the rule-bound nature of language. Thus, rules are excluded in an explicit sense, as a result of being implicitly acknowledged by constraints on the learning context. Even worse, however, Fodor and Pylyshyn (1988) return to the very facts that motivated the psychological reality of grammar in the first place, the open-endedness of sentences and the creativity of lexical juxtapositions. They demonstrate not only that the parallel distributed approach fails to account for these facts, but also that its advocates tacitly accept the failure. Hence, there is a strong suggestion that they have overlooked the facts as truths about language. Whatever the case, the parallel distributed approach is clearly no challenge at present to the reality of grammar. Moreover, the force of Fodor and Pylyshyn's paper is to show that, in resisting the challenge, the arguments in favour of reality are even more compelling now than they were in the past. Probably, then, there is no alternative at this point in time to conceding grammar as psychologically real, and addressing the issues that reality has raised.

The Constraints on Grammatical Rules

The issue of present concern is whether the psychological reality of grammar means that humans are imbued with partially innate knowledge. As mentioned earlier, the innateness hypothesis emerged because the acceptance of psychological reality coincided with new insights into observational adequacy and, significantly, a major source of these insights was Chomsky's (1957) book. Having demonstrated the infinite number of sentences open to the mature speakers of any natural language, Chomsky turned to the question of what kinds of grammar could specify them. In other words, his question was what kinds of grammar could achieve "observational adequacy". Chomsky concluded that there are essentially two kinds, the first of which he called "phrase structure" grammars. The central strategy of the phrase structure approach is to define every sentence by a set of rules of the kind illustrated in (1.2).[2]

$$
\begin{array}{lll}
\text{S} & \dashrightarrow & \text{NP} \; + \; \text{VP} \qquad\qquad (1.2)\\[4pt]
\text{NP} & \dashrightarrow & \text{Det} \; + \; \text{N}\\[4pt]
\text{VP} & \dashrightarrow & \text{Verb} \; + \; \text{NP}\\[4pt]
\text{Det} & \dashrightarrow & \text{the}\\[4pt]
\text{N} & \dashrightarrow & \left\{ \begin{array}{l}\text{dog}\\\text{cat}\end{array}\right\}\\[10pt]
\text{Verb} & \dashrightarrow & \left\{ \begin{array}{l}\text{bit}\\\text{chased}\end{array}\right\}
\end{array}
$$

The rules in (1.2) use symbols similar to the ones deployed by Chomsky (1957), with NP indicating "noun phrase", VP "verb phrase", DET "determiner", and N "noun". The effect of the rules is to translate the symbols to the left of the arrows into the symbols to the right. There is never more than one symbol to the left and it always indicates a category. There can, however, be more than one symbol to the right, and each symbol can indicate either a category or a lexical item. Not surprisingly, the rules illustrated in (1.2) are termed "phrase structure" rules. Applied sequentially as in (1.3), they produce what is called a "phrase marker" whose "terminal string" is an English sentence, in this case "The dog bit the cat".

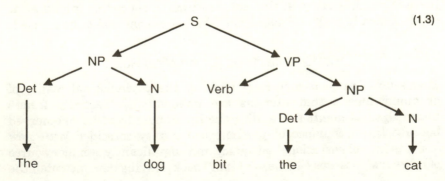

(1.3)

Although phrase structure grammars deal straightforwardly with sentences like "The dog bit the cat", they do, however, encounter problems with examples that are only slightly more complicated. These problems relate to elegance for, to use one of Chomsky's examples, we would need an extremely elaborate set of rules to account for the so-called "auxiliaries", that is words like "could", "has", and "being". Hence, Chomsky decided to supplement the phrase structure approach with what he called "transformational" rules. This produced his second kind of observationally adequate grammar, whose exemplars were, of course, called "transformational" grammars.

To appreciate what he had in mind, delete the bottom rule from (1.2) and add the rules in (1.4) to the remainder.

$$
\begin{array}{lll}
\text{Verb} & \dashrightarrow & \text{Aux } + \text{ V} \\[2mm]
\text{V} & \dashrightarrow & \left\{ \begin{array}{l} \text{bite} \\ \text{chase} \end{array} \right\} \\[4mm]
\text{Aux} & \dashrightarrow & \text{C (M) (have } + \text{ en) (be } + \text{ ing) (be } + \text{ en)} \\[2mm]
\text{M} & \dashrightarrow & \left\{ \begin{array}{l} \text{can} \\ \text{must} \end{array} \right\} \\[4mm]
\text{C} & \dashrightarrow & \left\{ \begin{array}{l} \text{s in the context NP sing.} \\ \text{ø in the context NP pl.} \\ \text{past} \end{array} \right\}
\end{array}
$$

(1.4)

Then apply the rules as in (1.5).

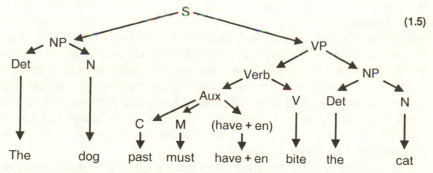

(1.5)

The terminal string of (1.5) is not, of course, an English sentence but it can readily be made into one. By deleting "past" and changing the position of "+en", we can create "The dog must have bite+en (= bitten) the cat". Other sentences containing auxiliaries can be created in an analogous fashion. It is these operations of deletion and permutation that constitute Chomsky's conception of transformational rules.

Clearly, insofar as transformational rules take complete phrase markers and delete/permute items in their terminal strings they simplify the grammar quite considerably but, equally clearly, they differ from phrase structure rules. It is true that, as specified by Chomsky, both phrase structure and transformational rules are defined as operations on categories. In the case of phrase structure rules, this is because the left-hand symbol always indicates a category. In the case of transformational, it is because their specification always refers to the preterminal symbols, and not to the individual lexical items. However, apart from this, the two kinds of rules are notable for their differences. It is particularly striking that while transformational rules operate to alter the terminal strings, which already exist, phrase structure rules operate to bring the terminal strings into existence.

Thus, Chomsky's conclusion was that observational adequacy with respect to the natural languages implies either a phrase structure or a transformational grammar, and amongst linguists this was hailed as a major breakthrough. Were they right? Scrutinising the linguistics of thirty years later, it is easy to imagine that they must have thought again. The grammars of today differ profoundly from what Chomsky was presenting in 1957, and two departures, both motivated by Chomsky (1970), might seem crucial. The first is a preference for so-called "X-bar (X')" symbols over phrasal ones, thus N' → Det + N in (1.2) rather than NP → Det + N.[3] This was precipitated, amongst other things, by the discovery that more than one level would have to intervene between S and N to specify the sentences of English. Thus, by translating S into N" (or N'" or whatever), N" into N' and N' into Det + N, extra levels could be added without losing the centrality of nouns to noun phrases. The second departure is a tendency for preterminal categories to be specified by features, thus [−V+N] for nouns and [−V−N] for prepositions. This allows the straightforward specification of facts about language that apply "cross-categorially", that is to two or more grammatical categories. For instance, it is a cross-categorial fact that both noun phrases and prepositional phrases can appear in so-called "cleft sentences", as witnessed by "It is (a cross-categorial fact/in Chomsky's writings) that ...". The fact can be elegantly specified by predicating cleft usage on the −V feature.

For Radford (1981), the departures were such as to create rules that contrast with the ones that Chomsky initially proposed. Thus, he writes of phrase structure versus X-bar rules. However, he seems to be in a minority, for Gazdar, Klein, Pullum, and Sag (1985) use features when expounding what they call a "generalised phrase structure grammar" and van Riemsdijk and Williams (1986) have a section entitled "the X-bar theory of phrase structure rules". Moreover, in a comprehensive overview of recent developments in American linguistics, Newmeyer (1986) has no doubts that the current rules are consistent with

Chomsky's original conception. Surely he has to be right. When it is remembered that what Chomsky was proposing were rules that operate on categorial symbols to translate them into strings of lexical items plus or minus rules that operate on preterminal symbols to transform the strings, it seems clear that the departures are within the framework rather than something dramatically different. Thus, thanks ultimately to Chomsky (1957), contemporary linguists do now seem in the possession of a fundamental truth. However, it is a truth about observational adequacy and this has been a concern of linguists since the time of Aristotle. Hence, Chomsky's work can be seen as the crowning glory of two thousand years of sustained enquiry and once this is recognised we can begin to appreciate why innate knowledge of grammar became, for linguists, such a compelling hypothesis.

The Introduction of Innate Knowledge

The key is, of course, that linguists were already convinced that some observationally adequate grammars must be psychologically real. Hence, it followed that the psychologically real grammars must also be of the phrase structure or transformational type, and this meant that *en route* to these grammars ordinary humans must be discovering something that defied explication for two thousand years. Even worse, ordinary humans must be making the discovery sometime in early childhood for, as even casual inspection of children's speech makes clear, learners must be well on their way to the final system by five years of age. The fact that ordinary humans operate on the tacit level can be neither here nor there, so how do they manage it? To many linguists it seemed to imply that tacit knowledge must have a substantial innate component. Indeed, the conviction of these linguists was not simply due to the poverty of what they had achieved on the explicit level in comparison with tacit human knowledge. It was also motivated by what has been established as the tacit knowledge of humans in comparison with our closest non-human relatives. As the linguists were well aware, there have been many attempts to train apes in the fundamentals of natural language. Viewed against the "dumb animal" stereotype, these attempts have revealed talents that are both surprising and challenging. However, viewed against ordinary human knowledge, the limits are clear.

To see this we should note that the training studies can be divided into two groups. The first includes the work of Fouts (1974), Gardner and Gardner (1971), Patterson (1978), and Terrace (1979). This work involved teaching the sign languages of the American Deaf to apes who were being reared in home-like environments. The second group encompasses the studies of Premack (1971), Rumbaugh (1977), and Savage-Rumbaugh (1990). Here, more artificial systems involving plastic chips and computer keyboards were taught to apes reared in laboratory conditions. The research not only demonstrated that apes are capable of learning a large number of signs (over one hundred in the case of the Gardners' Washoe). It also appeared to reveal a capacity for combining signs in a non-random fashion. For example, Terrace (1981) reports that his subject Nim produced many two-sign strings incorporating "more". In 85 per cent of these combinations, "More" appeared in a sentence-initial position. Furthermore, in addition to being non-random, some strings seemed to be novel, involving the juxtaposition of signs that had never been modelled in adjacent postions. For instance, Washoe apparently created "Water bird" to describe a swan and Patterson's Koko is reported as using "White tiger" to refer to a zebra. Remembering points made earlier in this section, all this could be symptomatic of form classes and rules of ordering.

However, even this interpretation is now regarded as controversial. Indeed, when in 1980 the New York Academy of Sciences convened a conference to review "ape grammar", the depths of academic venom must finally have been plumbed (see Wade, 1980, for a description). The basic criticism was that it is unclear whether every string containing more than one sign is in fact a true combination. On the basis of photographic evidence obtained during interaction with Nim, Terrace (1981) suggested that some so-called combinations could be isolated responses to a series of external cues. For example, the "Me" in Nim's "Me hug cat" was accompanied, and arguably cued, by the trainer's "You". The "cat" was preceded by the trainer's "Who". Like Savage-Rumbaugh (1990) I do not think that all so-called combinations can be dismissed in this fashion. Nevertheless, Terrace's evidence raises definite questions about the small number, which, if truly combinatorial, were novel. It is true that, as Lieberman (1984) reminds us, Washoe used "Water bird" on numerous occasions. However, it could still have originated as two isolated signs cued by an association between water and the swan. Koko's "White tiger" could have been something similar. We cannot be sure, but if the status of these examples is in question, the main evidence for form classes becomes doubtful.

Indeed, we can no longer be absolutely certain about rules of ordering. In the first place, the fidelity of the strings associated with Washoe is not above question, for as Premack (1985) points out, the main concern was to represent meanings, and not to preserve the signs. In addition, even when the strings can be taken as faithful, they were not, as Lieberman (1984) acknowledges, as variable as human language. A relatively small number of formats were combined with each other and used repeatedly as in "Play me", "Play me Nim", "Play me play" and "Play me Nim play". Apart from the now doubtful novel combinations, there is nothing in these strings to guarantee the existence of rules of ordering. There is, for example, no evidence of a capacity to generate an infinite set of sentences. Hence it is possible that far from using rules of ordering, the apes were randomly juxtaposing memorised strings.

Clearly, the debate on these issues is going to continue for some time to come, but in the present context, its conclusions are of limited relevance. Even if we grant form classes and rules of ordering, the grammars entailed by ape strings will be a far cry from the phrase structure and transformational grammars that were considered earlier. From the examples given in the previous paragraph, it seems unlikely that a phrase structure grammar of any kind is required. Certainly, there will be no need for phrase structure rules that measure up even to the ones in (1.2) and (1.4). As transformational grammars employ phrase structure rules, they look equally implausible. Thus, if phrase structure or transformational grammars are required for the natural languages (and it seems that they must be), they are only required for those languages, and in that sense are uniquely human.

However, if phrase structure or transformational grammars are part of human knowledge (and the psychological reality of grammar has already been conceded as a working hypothesis), they must be grasped quite readily and, to return to the original point, this is no mean achievement when measured against the history of linguistics. Yet does this imply that the case for innate knowledge has been won? At this point it must look exceedingly powerful, but nevertheless it should not be granted. The inference of innateness from the discrepancy between the explicit achievement of linguists and the tacit achievement of ordinary human beings rests on two assumptions. The first is that ordinary humans process their linguistic experiences in a fashion analogous to linguists. The second is that ordinary humans have linguistic experiences that are essentially equivalent to those of linguists. The assumptions may seem plausible but they should still be scrutinised. Hence, the next section will initiate a discussion intended to do this.

POTENTIAL ASSISTANCE FROM OTHER SPEAKERS

To impose some order, let us accept for the moment that tacit learners do process their linguistic experiences in a fashion analogous to linguists. Perhaps therefore, for ease of exposition, we can talk about them following the "linguistic" process. Taking both the process and its name for granted, let us concentrate on the input it would receive. Let us ask whether in the case of tacit learners it would, instead of being equivalent, prove superior to the genuine linguists. By way of introduction, we should note that the process followed by linguists involves taking sentences and checking their consistency with current ideas about grammar. To the extent they prove inconsistent, the grammar is revised and subsequently tested against fellow linguist feedback on specimen strings. What this means is that individuals following the linguistic process learn in response to two kinds of information—sampled sentences, which prove inconsistent with the existing grammar, and negative feedback, which demonstrates inadequacies in the output strings. As a result, demonstrating that tacit learners following the process would be more privileged would involve showing, first, that they receive both kinds of information and, second, that the exemplars of each kind are of a better quality. Can it be done? To find out, we shall need empirical research into tacit learners' experiences and, fortunately, there is plenty. Hence, the present section will review it, looking for evidence of superiority relative to *bona fide* linguists. The next section will ask whether the experiences could be so good as to answer the case for innateness.

The Significance of Motherese

Looking first at sentence samples, there can, given the concept of a sentence with which we are working, be no doubt about their occurrence. Thus, the issue we need to address is their possible superiority during the period when tacit learning is in progress. As mentioned earlier, children must master a significant proportion of adult knowledge by the time they reach five. Thus, it is reasonable to treat the tacit learning period as the preschool years, and certainly this is what is assumed in the relevant research. Does the research show superiority? It certainly shows difference. Broen (1972), Drach (1969), Newport, Gleitman, and Gleitman (1977), Remick (1976), and Sachs, Brown, and Salerno (1976) have all compared mothers' speech to children of about two years with mothers' speech to adults. The speech analysed by these researchers was obtained in similar circumstances, namely short recordings of relatively unconstrained conversation. Insofar as they used similar categories, their results were also similar. They found that speech to two-year-olds is slower, less disfluent, and more repetitious than speech to adults. It is also shorter, often more complete, and, in some respects, simpler. However, the simplicity relates only to the low proportion of so-called "complex" sentences, that is sentences with co-ordinated and subordinated clauses. As Newport et al. have pointed out, speech to two-year-olds is more complex in its range of sentence modalities. Speech to adults is swamped by declaratives. Speech to two-year-olds employs imperatives, interrogatives, and declaratives in roughly equal proportions. All these characteristics of speech to young children have been confirmed in studies by Cross (1977), Moerk (1974, 1975), Phillips (1973), and Snow (1972). In addition, these studies allow us to look at changes in mothers' speech as children mature linguistically. They show that, from about two years onwards, greater maturity is associated with a steady decline in the speech adjustments. However, even at five years, there are still marked differences between mothers' speech to children and their speech to adults.

Thus, throughout the preschool years, children experience a corpus of speech that is different from speech to adults. Is this corpus, which is normally termed "motherese", of benefit to learning? Few would question the helpfulness of strings that lack disfluencies and are largely complete. Where there is disagreement is over the value of the sentence-types that mothers choose to model. Some would argue that the selection is "finely-tuned" to the child's needs as a learner. Others would dispute this. Newport et al. (1977), for example, suggest that the relatively high use of imperatives and interrogatives impedes learning. Regarding imperatives and interrogatives as transforms of declaratives, they argue that a finely-tuned model would start with declaratives. Gleitman, Newport, and Gleitman (1984) have implicitly withdrawn the claim about modalities while still disputing the "fine-tuning" contention. The central theme of Gleitman et al.'s paper is that adult grammar is complicated and the sooner children sample its intricacies the better. Hence the problems lie not with the range of modalities but with the rarity of complex sentences.

Inspired, perhaps, by these theoretical disputes, there have been several empirical investigations into the tuitional value of motherese. The investigations have all been correlational in nature, relating the frequency with which mothers use some feature of motherese with one or more measure of grammatical development. Their authors are well aware of the dangers of drawing causal inferences from correlational data. In a sense, however, their apologies are beside the point because they rarely obtain more significant correlations than would be expected by chance. Thus, Cross (1978) compared mothers' speech to eight "accelerated" developers with mothers' speech to eight "normal" developers, rate of grammatical development being defined via the mean length of the child's spontaneous utterances (hereafter MLU) and the child's score on a comprehension test. The mothers differed on only one of the twenty-one features deemed potentially relevant to grammar: the mothers of the accelerated developers used sentences that showed less preverbal complexity. These disappointing results are reflected in the work of Gleitman et al. (1984), who correlated eleven features of motherese with five measures of grammatical development. At one or other of the age levels studied, they found that the child's ability to use auxiliaries was positively correlated with the proportion of complex sentences and Yes/No-interrogatives in their mothers' speech, and negatively correlated with the proportion of repetitions. Few other correlations reached statistical significance. More dismally still, Wells (1980) found no relations at all between the well-formedness and structural complexity of mothers' speech and children's progress in terms of MLU and verbs per utterance. Superficially, the work of Furrow, Nelson, and Benedict (1979) produced more encouraging results, containing a sizeable number of significant correlations. Indeed, one of these correlations replicates Gleitman et al.'s finding on maternal interrogatives and child auxiliaries. However, unlike the other researchers, Furrow et al. did not place adequate controls on the child's initial linguistic level. Without such controls, their results could be an artefact of motherese being more frequent at lower levels of linguistic maturity and less mature children developing more rapidly. In addition Furrow et al. used a sample of seven children, far less than the other researchers and woefully small for a correlation-style analysis.

Over all, then, empirical research into the significance of motherese has proved disappointing, though, in fairness, it is unclear whether this reflects a true non-effect or a methodological artefact. For instance, all the studies reviewed in the previous paragraph defined the frequency of motherese in scalar terms. A threshold concept might be more appropriate with variations being irrelevant above a certain minimum. All this remains to be seen. However, rather than pursue it further let us note that showing that mothers' speech to children is more helpful than mothers' speech to adults does not amount to showing that the sentences available to children are superior to the ones available to linguists. This is the case even if mothers' speech to adults is reflective of the sentences linguists work with. The reason is that whereas linguists can be assumed to process sentences in their entirety, children cannot be. It is possible (and most parents would say certain) that children ignore a proportion of the sentences addressed to them. It is also possible that they discount lexical items from the sentences they attend to. Certainly, there is a classic study by Brown and Fraser (1964) where children aged two to three were asked to repeat adult sentences. The results were strongly age-related but in some cases up to 50 per cent of the items were omitted.

Scrutinising their results, Brown and Fraser noted that the omitted items were more likely to be centrally positioned than end-placed, and more likely to be "closed class" than "open" (that is, determiners, auxiliaries, and inflections rather than nouns, verbs, and adjectives). It has to be recognised that the alignment of omission with form class could mean that, instead of discounting, children reject items that they notice but cannot process grammatically. However, this interpretation is rendered implausible by Gleitman and Wanner's (1988) demonstration that sentential stress is a better predictor of omission than the closed/open distinction. For one thing, it fits better with the omission of mid-placed items. For another, the few closed class items of English that are heavily stressed, for instance the negative particle "No" and the interrogative wh-words "What", "Who" and so on, tend to be preserved. Moreover, when the closed class items that are unstressed in English are stressed in other languages, they also tend to be preserved. A good illustration of this is Mayan where, as Pye (1983) demonstrates, the stressed inflections are more likely to be preserved by children than the unstressed open forms they append to. When a perceptual feature like stress turns out to be the best predictor, the interpretation of omission as discounting is hard to resist. For the purposes of this essay, I certainly feel that I must accept it and this, as mentioned already, is bad news when the issue is the sentences sampled by children versus the sentences sampled by linguists.

The Relevance of Conversational Replies

Having drawn far from encouraging conclusions from the analysis of sentence samples, let us turn now to the question of negative feedback. Let us ask whether tacit learners experience it and, if they do, whether it is in a particularly helpful form. At first sight even the first question seems to receive a disappointing answer for, with children in the preschool age group, there are virtually no signs of explicit negative feedback. Children of this age certainly do not receive it in answer to questions from themselves about well-formedness. However, they also seem not to receive it in response to their spontaneous speech. Hirsh-Pasek, Treiman, and Schneiderman (1984), Moerk (1978), and Penner (1987) have all computed the frequency of "verbal disapproval" or "verbal rejection" in mothers' responses to children. Their results were consistently in the range of 2 to 3 per cent. It is true that in my own work I have observed mothers repeating overgeneralisations with heavy irony. Assuming children appreciate the irony (which, for reasons developed in Chapter 2, is doubtful), this could be interpreted as negative feedback of a relatively straightforward kind. However, my impression is that such responses are even rarer than "verbal disapproval".

This said, perhaps we are being overly restrictive in looking for such unembellished instances of negative feedback. Earlier in the section, it was emphasised that adult speech to children consists largely of complete sentences. To the extent that these sentences incorporate some preceding and ill-formed remark of the child's, might they not also, as far as the child is concerned, have the force of negative feedback? If this seems reasonable (and it certainly does to Moerk, 1991), it will be gratifying to hear that the rules of conversation permit at least three kinds of reply that allow the incorporation of preceding remarks. The first is associated with contexts where the first speaker's remark is being evaluated. Evaluations can be given via some stock phrase like "Yes", "No" and "Uh-huh". However, they can also be given via reduced, exact, or expanded imitation of the first speaker's remark, as (1.6) makes clear.

(Eileen (23.8) points puppet towards television)   (1.6)
    Eileen: Skippy o' telly
    Mother: That's Skippy on the telly

A second kind of reply, which would also allow incorporation, is the correction of ill-formed strings as in (1.7).

(Ian (23.24) looks at book)   (1.7)
    Ian: He doing teeth
    Mother: You mean 'He's doing his teeth'

Finally, it is legitimate, within the course of conversation, to extend the previous speaker's remark by partially changing either its topic or its informational content. Extensions can, as (1.8) shows, also incorporate the previous speaker's remark.

(Nicola (23.9) draws picture)   (1.8)
    Nicola: Nose
    Mother: He's got a pointed nose, hasn't he?

Although expansion, correction, and extension all have the potential to incorporate ill-formed speech in well-formed, one can be dismissed from consideration very quickly. Whatever its potential, the correction of ill-formed strings has little value in practice simply because, like explicit negative feedback, it almost never occurs. Brown and Hanlon (1970) were the first to make this point and, since their paper, no-one has come forward with conflicting data. Even Moerk (1991), who reports several hundred supposedly corrective exchanges, has very few instances where a child's remark is both amplified and said to be wrong.

I certainly cannot oblige in this respect. For a study that was reported in Howe (1981a), I analysed 1711 maternal replies, of which 12 per cent were corrections. However, only one of these corrections, the example given in (1.7), was concerned with well-formedness. The remainder related to the appropriateness of individual items as in (1.9) or their pronunciation as in (1.10).

(Yvonne (22.0) looks at me)   (1.9)

      Yvonne: Girl

      Mother: It's a lady. Not girl. Not girl when you don't know them

(Sally (23.8) pours water into cup)   (1.10)

      Sally: A teatop. Teatop. Teatop. Teatop

      Mother: It's a teapot

      Sally: Teatop

      Mother: Teapot, not teatop. Teapot

      Sally: Sugar

Moving onto expansion and extension, the situation is much more hopeful. Both occur with reasonable frequency, particularly to children of about two years, and both have been positively associated with measures of grammatical development. Since Brown and Bellugi (1964) first identified expansion as a potential teaching device, there have been numerous attempts to estimate its frequency in maternal speech. The mothers of Brown and Bellugi's own subjects expanded about 30 per cent of their children's remarks but work by Cross (1978), Demetras, Post, and Snow (1986), Lieven (1978), Seitz and Stewart (1975), and Wells (1980) suggests that a figure between 10 and 20 per cent is more usual. My 1981 data support this. Reanalysing those data for comparability with other studies, I found that, on average, expansion accounted for 16 per cent of the mothers' replies when the 24 children in the sample were aged 20 to 22 months and 12 per cent when the children were three months older. However, I, like other researchers, found considerable variation, a rather fortunate state-of-affairs, should one be considering correlational analysis of teaching effect. Two researchers who have explored this possibility are Cross (1978) and Wells (1980). Both found significant positive correlations between the frequency of mothers' expansions and indices of children's grammar. Further support is to be found in the experimental work of Nelson, Carskaddon, and Bonvillian (1973), who interacted over an 11-week period with 27 children who were 32 to 40 months at the beginning of the study. The children were divided into three groups, with one group receiving expansions in reply, the second receiving well-formed sentences that were not expansions and the third acting as a control. The expansion group was superior to the others on each of five measures of grammatical development. Alas, however, Nelson et al.'s study substantially replicated earlier work by Cazden (reported in Brown, Cazden, & Bellugi-Klima, 1969). Cazden did not find expansion having any effect on grammatical development.

The work of Cazden and Nelson et al. is also relevant to the evaluation of extension. The group who experienced well-formed sentences that were not expansions must, unless the rules of conversation were drastically flouted, have received extensions in reply. In Cazden's study, this group showed faster development than both the expansion and the control groups. In Nelson et al.'s study, it did not differ from the control group on any of the five measures! Again, more consistent, though less controlled, results come from correlational studies. The research reported by Barnes, Gutfreund, Satterly, and Wells (1983) and Wells (1980) found strong positive correlations between the frequency of maternal extension and various measures of grammatical development. Cross (1978) found the mothers of her "accelerated" developers extending more, although her results do not quite reach statistical significance. One of the main themes of my 1981 work was the effect of maternal extension. I was fortunate to find that, when the children were 20 to 22 months old, the mothers fell into two groups by their use of extensions. Eight mothers used extensions very rarely; 16 used them for between 21 and 41 per cent of their total replies. My interest was primarily in the development of meanings. Nevertheless, one of my measures would, given the age group under consideration, relate very closely to indices of grammar. This was the percentage of utterances expressing more than one feature. To give some idea of what was meant, "Baby", "The dolly" and "A car" mention one feature. "Picture daddy", "There animal house" and "Ride a horsie" mention more than one. Using this measure to compare the children at 23 to 25 months, I found significant differences depending on the mothers' earlier use of extensions. The children whose mothers had used extensions between 21 and 41 per cent of the time did significantly better. Moreover, my statistical manipulations and *post hoc* investigations mean that these results, although correlational in nature, are strongly suggestive of a causal relation.

The Role of Misunderstanding

Reviewing the data on expansion and extension, there are undoubtedly some negative findings. Nevertheless, the balance of evidence does seem to support a special role in grammatical development. Can we infer that this is because expansion and extension provide implicit negative feedback? Unfortunately not. The association with grammatical development could arise simply because well-formed sentences in a conversational context have a strong attention value. Yet while this possibility must be acknowledged, the data on expansion and extension seem sufficiently encouraging to warrant a hunt for other sources of implicit negative feedback. Interestingly, there is something that, although hardly conversationally appropriate in the sense of expansion and extension, still seems relevant. It is occasions where other speakers misunderstand the product of immature grammars. For a time, it was very "non-U" to suggest that such occasions occur. However, both Ryan (1974) and I (Howe, 1981a) have argued the point. In my work, I found misunderstandings when the non-verbal context was inadequate to compensate for the sentence structure, as in (1.11).

(Ian (21.0) picks stacking ring up)		(1.11)
Ian:	Play that	
Mother:	You're going to play with that, eh?	
Ian:	Mummy, you play that	

However, I even found misunderstanding when the non-verbal context was perfectly clear, as in (1.12).

(Kevin (20.21) has removed xylophone notes)		(1.12)
Kevin:	Off. Off. Off. Off	
Mother:	You can't take any more off	
Kevin:	Off. Off	
Mother:	Do you want to put it on again?	
Kevin:	Off. Off	
Mother:	That goes on here	
	Look there, not off, it's on	
Kevin:	Off. Off. Off. Off	
Mother:	It's 'on' Kevin	
	Can't you say 'on'? 'On'	
Kevin:	Off. Off. Off	
	Took it off	

The mothers in (1.11) and (1.12) clearly misinterpreted their children. Moreover, the effect of these misunderstandings was to elicit clarifications that were grammatically more adequate than what had preceded. Indeed, the clarifications provided by Ian and Kevin (and they were not exceptional) were the most sophisticated remarks to be produced in the whole of a forty minute recording.

Thus, misunderstanding leads to advancement in the short term, but does it have any effect in the longer term? In other words, it clearly encourages children to use rules at the limits of their existing competence, but does it push them to acquire new rules? We cannot say on the basis of examples like (1.11) and (1.12) and unfortunately, a more systematic investigation would be exceedingly difficult. The obvious strategy would be to correlate the frequency of naturally-occurring misunderstandings at time 1 with grammatical development between time 1 and time 2. However, to do this, we would need confidence in our frequency count, and that, to me, would be unwarranted. If we focus on utterances that the context is inadequate to disambiguate, it is clear that they occur frequently in mother–child interaction. For example, when single word utterances like "Ball", "Car" and "Dolly" are used to refer to distal objects, they could always be intended either to draw attention to the object or to request it or to do both. Likewise, the use of "Up", "Push", or "Mend it" to refer to possible but non-occurring actions could be declaring either the child's own intention to act or the child's wish that somebody else should act. Studies like Greenfield and Smith (1976) have shown that utterances referring to distal objects and possible actions are amongst the most frequently used in the second year of life. Yet responses to such utterances rarely elicit the kind of corrective feedback illustrated in (1.11) and (1.12). Does this mean they are never misunderstood? This is possible but unlikely, given their inherent ambiguity. It is much more likely that a proportion are misunderstood but the mistakes are seldom made explicit. As the proportion cannot be estimated, any attempts to correlate naturally-occurring misunder- standings with grammatical development are doomed to inexactitude. It might, of course, be possible to do something with experimentally- induced misunderstandings but this has still to be attempted. Until it is, the role of misunderstanding in both the promotion of grammar and the provision of feedback must remain hypothetical.

Suppose, however, that subsequent research did show mis- understanding to be a source of negative feedback. Suppose, also, that it showed the same thing about expansion and extension. Would we be justified in thinking that the experiences of tacit learners were particularly valuable? Would we be justified in thinking that they would be so valuable as to be superior to those of genuine linguists? One point we might make in answer to the first question is that the implicit negative feedback putatively given to tacit learners may be of greater value than the explicit negative feedback withheld from them. This follows from an observation made earlier that when ordinary speakers make explicit judgements of sentencehood, they veer towards standards of correctness learned at school. Insofar as those who interact with tacit learners are nothing more than ordinary speakers, they would be expected to apply similar standards in explicit negative feedback. This might help with sentences in the school sense, but not in the linguistic sense with which we are concerned. Unfortunately, however, the linguists who make explicit judgements of their colleagues' productions suspend their everyday framework and apply the concept that their work addresses. Hence the superiority of implicit negative feedback in relation to ordinary speaker judgements by no means guarantees its superiority in relation to genuine linguists and, at the present time, we should be hard pressed to assert this.

Indeed, we might even find equivalence hard to defend, for the message children would receive from implicit feedback would be far from consistent. There have recently been a number of studies concerned with the incidence of expansion, extension and so on as a function of the ill- or well-formedness of children's speech. Examples are Bohannon and Stanowicz (1988), Demetras et al. (1986), Hirsh-Pasek et al. (1984), Morgan and Travis (1989), and Penner (1987). The studies demonstrate, without exception, that the putative sources of feedback sometimes occur with well-formed utterances. It is true that expansion, in particular, seems more frequent with ill-formed utterances than with well-formed. Nevertheless, the imperfect alignment means that even if the replies did constitute feedback the overall message to children would be that some well-formed utterances are incorrect, making for extreme inefficiency in learning.

Even worse, however, the message from feedback that incorporates children's remarks could, by definition, only bear on "sins of omission". As Bowerman (1987, 1988) points out, "sins of commission" like the inflectional overgeneralisations alluded to earlier would remain untouched, and I think that we have to accept this as a crippling problem. It is true that Moerk (1991) has tried to answer it via instances where mothers supply well-formed substitutes for children's speech, for example "You see it" for "I seed it" and "Eve bit a hole in it" for "I bite a hole in it". However, clear-cut substitutions were rare in Moerk's data (as rare perhaps as *bona fide* corrections). Moreover, they also occurred with well-formed speech. It was not, after all, only the verb that was substituted for in the above examples. It was also the "I"! Moerk does not compare the frequency of substitution to ill-formed speech with substitution to well-formed, but I doubt whether he would find much difference.

All in all then, we must surely conclude that, as regards negative feedback, tacit learners could not be privileged relative to linguists. At best, their information is no better. In fact, it is probably worse. As regards sampled sentences, the conclusions are slightly less damaging. The information presented to tacit learners is certainly no worse than what linguists experience. Given its fluency and completeness plus possibly some of its other properties, it might even be better. However, could it be so much better as to compensate for the tendency of children to ignore and discount? Moreover, could it do this to the extent of dealing with the timescale of learning? The next section will present some work which will allow us to say for certain.

FURTHER OPTIONS FOR THE ACQUISITION PROCESS

The work to be considered was done under the auspices of mathematical linguistics. It assumes the linguistic process and recognises that as learners who engaged in it without *a priori* knowledge of grammar would be completely unconstrained, their task can be construed as "guessing" which of the possible grammars would be observationally adequate. The mathematical work investigates the consequences of guessing using every conceivable strategy with, on the one hand, sentence samples alone and, on the other, sentence samples plus negative feedback. It shows that although some learners might make a lucky guess early in their careers it would take an eternity before success could be guaranteed in every case, even assuming both sentences and feedback. Moreover this is the verdict no matter what strategy is followed and no matter how valuable the data. It means, of course, that as the acquisition of an observationally adequate grammar does not take an eternity, the environmental support to tacit learners could never, on the linguistic process, be sufficiently powerful to allow learning in the absence of *a priori* knowledge. As it is inconceivable that *a priori* knowledge of grammar could be anything but innate, the case for innateness would, given the linguistic process, have to be conceded. However, are linguistic experiences really processed along linguistic lines? The section will end by raising the possibility of a negative answer.

The Power of the Linguistic Environment

To comprehend the work done in mathematical linguistics, it is important to note that when it uses the term "grammar", it means any set of rules that generates strings by translating one sequence of symbols into another. Hence, it is considering not just the observationally adequate grammars but all systems definable in translational terms, which leads, of course, to a broader conception of "language". In fact when the term "language" is used in mathematical linguistics, it encompasses finite sets of strings as well as infinite. It also includes infinite sets that are qualitatively different from the natural languages. With this in mind, we should note that the starting point for mathematical linguistics is an extrapolation from classical studies of inductive logic. This, startlingly enough, is that, regardless of language, learners who guess at grammar could never be guaranteed to hit on an observationally adequate system by experiencing sentences alone.

The extrapolation led to a paper by Gold (1967), which provided the framework for much subsequent work. In the paper, Gold proved that such learners could do somewhat better from sentences alone if they refer to a well-established taxonomy. This taxonomy is sometimes called the "Chomsky hierarchy" and it classifies languages according to their inherent properties. Thus, languages comprising finite sets of strings are placed in the "finite cardinality" category. Gold's paper presupposed that learners not only have access to the Chomsky hierarchy. They can also enumerate the grammars that could represent some language in each of the categories. The paper then shows that given any particular language in the finite cardinality category, learners who guess at grammar could be guaranteed to choose an appropriate grammar from sentences alone. Essentially, if such learners always select a grammar that can generate the sentences they have experienced there will come a time with a finite set when they will not have to change their minds.

The trouble is that Gold's paper also proved that success could not be guaranteed from sentences alone for any infinite languages. With an infinite language, negative feedback would also be required. Basically, the paper's argument was that if the learners we are considering guess a finite grammar, they will have to change their minds an infinite number of times. If they guess an infinite grammar, they will have no mechanism without additional constraints for discovering over-generalisation. This is clearly a serious problem. For one thing, no matter where they fall in the Chomsky hierarchy, natural languages are undoubtedly infinite. For another, although negative feedback may be more plausible than it once appeared, it is unlikely, as we have just seen, to be in a form that corrects overgeneralisation. Even worse, however, work reviewed by Pinker (1979) has shown that the number of grammars to be enumerated is so huge that even if sentence samples and negative feedback were available, the trials before learning could be guaranteed would reach astronomical proportions. Moreover, the work has also shown that no other strategy consistent with the linguistic process could do better than enumeration. Thus even though the systematic listing implied by enumeration sounds wildly implausible when applied to young children, nothing is to be gained by simply replacing it.

We should make no mistake about the implications of this work. When it talks about sentences, it means a flawless sample that is processed in its entirety. When it talks about negative feedback, it means responding unambiguously to every error. Thus, it is presupposing linguistic experiences far superior to what could be warranted from the data presented earlier. Yet the work shows that even in such optimal circumstances, grammar learning could not take place in the time available. Thus, we can be in no doubt about what to conclude regarding the linguistic experiences of grammar-learning children. No matter how good they are, they could not be sufficiently good to allow the guessing of grammar in its appointed time period. As guessing is what linguistic processing without *a priori* knowledge would amount to, we can also conclude that the linguistic experiences are inadequate to permit this arrangement. This means that if we continue to assume linguistic processing, we must cease to deny *a priori* knowledge. As *a priori* knowledge of grammar would be too specific to be anything but innate, we must also acknowledge the latter. However, should we continue to assume the linguistic acquisition process? Let us now consider this carefully.

The Possibility of an Alternative Process

We might begin to have doubts if we note that when children experience adult sentences, their first reaction is to imbue them with meaning. More precisely, their first reaction is to imbue them with what they take to be the speaker's intention in uttering them, a sense of meaning that is often termed "utterance" meaning or "pragmatic" meaning rather than meaning *per se*. For present purposes, such niceties need not concern us. Insofar as we are interested in the sense of meaning relevant to children we can, so long as the sense is clear, use the simple term to describe it. That meaning in the sense of speaker's intention is relevant to children should be clear from work like Huttenlocher (1974), Schaffer and Crook (1980), Schnur and Shatz (1984), and Shipley, Smith, and Gleitman (1969). This work investigated the responses of children aged around 21 months to such well-formed imperatives as "Throw me the ball" and "Show Mummy the baby's bottle". Its main finding was that with minimal delay, the children reacted by performing actions on the denoted entities, reactions that could not have been given without attention to meaning. The point should also be clear from work like Camaioni (1979), Ervin-Tripp (1970), Ninio and Bruner (1978), Savic

(1978), and myself (Howe, 1981a) on 21-month-old children's reactions to well-formed interrogatives. Here, sentences like "What's that?", "Where's the baby?" and "Which book do you want?" typically elicited information about their topics as the more or less immediate responses. Once more, such responses could not have been made without attention to meaning.

In view of this, the central point cannot surely be doubted: when children experience adult sentences, their first concern, by 21 months at the latest, is the derivation of meaning. The point would certainly not be disputed by the linguists who advocated innate knowledge of grammar but, in making the concession, they seem to lay themselves open to a simple question. Why, they might be asked, would children whose first reaction is to imbue sentences with meaning ever want, as the linguistic process assumes, to specify them as autonomous entities? When children have already displayed a primary interest in understanding, surely they would be more likely to specify sentences as a function of their meanings so that they could be interpreted as swiftly as possible should communication require it.

Once raised, the possibility sounds only too plausible and yet, in acknowledging it, we should be introducing a language acquisition process profoundly different from the linguistic one with which we have been dealing. It would involve a cycle whereby sentences (or rather the fragments that remain after the discounting we have already discussed) are first checked for their interpretability, and not for their consistency with ideas about grammar. To the extent that the sentence fragments prove interpretable, all well and good. To the extent that they partially or wholly do not, their meanings are completed from external sources, and then both the fragments and their meanings are used to revise the specification. This would constitute a second departure from the linguistic process in that the input would derive from sentence-meaning pairings, and not from sentences alone. A third departure would arise because children would undoubtedly use their specification to create expressive devices. Hence, to the extent that the specification allowed more than one device for any given meaning, they would attempt to discover how each should be used. Certainly, they would respond to negative feedback should it be available. However, they would also turn to subsequent sentence samples, looking for adults' preferences, contextual constraints and so on.

All in all, the process under consideration would make children more like communication engineers than miniature linguists, suggesting that it might, again for succinctness, be termed the "communicative" process. Faced with it, the first question must be whether it really does sound plausible as the process of learning. I suspect many would accept that it does for the literature of the past fifteen years has repeatedly depicted children as "trying" or "wanting" or "being motivated" to subordinate language to their communicative ends. The trouble is that some of the most ardent advocates of the imagery have already anticipated what must be the second question, whether innate knowledge would be required to allow children following the communicative process to acquire an observationally adequate grammar in a reasonable time period. The theorists I am thinking of are Pinker (1984) and Wexler and Culicover (1980). Both would, I think, see children of 21 months plus as attempting to fit linguistic input for communicative ends. However, far from asserting that in doing so children could attain an observationally adequate grammar in its appointed time span, they add a sizeable chunk of *a priori* grammatical knowledge to speed things on their way! In the case of Pinker, this amounts to the basic principles of Kaplan and Bresnan's (1982) "lexical functional grammar". In the case of Wexler and Culicover, it is a full-fledged system of phrase structure rules that, for illustration but non-crucially, are taken to be those proposed by Chomsky (1965). This goes way beyond the "parameterised templates" that Chomsky (1981) as a contemporary advocate of the linguistic process seems to be suggesting.

The warning of Pinker and Wexler and Culicover's work needs to be taken seriously. We certainly should not assume that the communicative process would automatically deal with the problem at hand, but yet nothing we have considered so far entails we deny it. In the first place, the fact that the input would derive from sentence-meaning pairings and not from sentences alone means that the grounds already advanced for pessimism about relevant experiences would not necessarily apply. To ascertain the appropriate attitude, the exercise of the previous section would have to be repeated, with the focus on meaning. Thus, it would be necessary to ask what meanings are expressed to grammar learners, and what sense is made of them. In addition, the fact that the input would be organised in accordance with retrievability means that learners would no longer be unconstrained in what they did with the data. Although, as Anderson (1975) points out, there can be no *a priori* guarantee that the constraints would help, their existence implies that learners would not have to be construed as guessing at grammar. Hence, the points raised by mathematical linguistics would no longer apply. Finally, the fact that learners would attempt to delimit the use of apparent synonyms means that overgeneralisations of one kind could be excluded without negative feedback. These are overgeneralisations caused by the treatment of two mutually exclusive rules as if they were alternatives. It follows because rescrutiny of sentence samples to establish adult preferences would suffice to exclude the ill-formed "option". The point is well-rehearsed in the literature because the delimitation envisaged here is similar (perhaps even terminologically equivalent) to what Clark (1987) presents as a "principle of contrast" and Pinker (1984) as a "unique entry" principle. Both writers emphasise the power of their principles to deal with the overgeneralisations in question.

The power is far from empty. As Fletcher (1985) and Kuczaj (1977) have documented, children come to use well-formed pasts such as "came" and "broke" as alternatives to the likes of "comed" and "breaked". Hence, the inflectional overgeneralisations mentioned on several occasions already can be viewed as instances where two mutually exclusive rules are treated as alternatives. Given their prevalence in children's speech, the capacity of the communicative process to deal with them without negative feedback is clearly a strength. However, we should need evidence of other strengths before we could draw encouraging conclusions as regards our present question. In particular, to conclude that the communicative process would allow an observationally adequate grammar in a reasonable time-scale without requiring innate knowledge, we should need evidence that children following the process without innate knowledge would acquire a grammar whose only shortcoming was overgeneralistions of the kind we are considering. Moreover, we should need evidence that the grammar would be acquired sufficiently quickly to allow both its rules to be finalised and its overgeneralisations to be eliminated in the time this normally takes.

The trouble is that to produce such evidence we should be obliged to proceed on a language-by-language basis, specifying the sentence-meaning input and imagining its integration one language at a time. Precisely because learners would be constrained rather than construable as guessing, the option of universal proof would not be available. However, proceeding on a language-by-language basis through all the natural languages can scarcely be contemplated, meaning that sampling is required. This is the crux of the problem because it is far from clear *a priori* what a representative sample would be like. We could only hope to define its parameters in the course of studying one specific exemplar. This is the basis on which the essay will proceed, choosing as its exemplar the English language. Being the language that has been most extensively researched over the past thirty years, English is likely to provide the most testing data. Thus its selection needs no apology (though I freely confess that it is also the only language I feel confident with!). Thus, the next three chapters will focus exclusively on English, leading to a concluding chapter that tries to consolidate what has been shown for cross-language research.

A Strategy for Further Research

As a first step, Chapter 2 will focus on the input that would be available to children learning English should the communicative process be followed. Taking the conclusions already drawn about sentences for granted, the chapter will concern itself with the associated meanings. It will start by outlining the meaning potential of English sentences, estimating how much of the potential is modelled in adult speech to children. It will then ask how children who find the sentences challenging will interpret them from those "external sources" that were alluded to earlier. It will assume that the external sources are located in the extralinguistic context. This seems a reasonable assumption given that children seldom ask for explicit clarifications. Making it, the chapter will draw three main conclusions. First, inference from contextual data places limits-in-principle on the attribution of certain meanings. Second, inference from contextual data allows for considerable departure from adult intention even when it does not actually require it. Third, where departure is possible, empirical research suggests that it may well take place. Thus, the overall verdict of Chapter 2 will be that the meanings on which the communicative process would operate may well be a distortion of adult intention. The question is whether it is a distortion that would prove helpful in the context we are considering.

The question will be addressed in Chapter 3, which will start by spelling out what is meant by following the communicative process without *a priori* knowledge, what, in other words, the constraints imposed by storage for retrievability would actually imply. Having done this, the chapter will imagine children following the communicative process being confronted with samples of English sentences and what are taken to be their contextually completed meanings. It will ask where organising the samples for ready retrieval would lead: a grammar consistent with observational adequacy in a reasonable time period or up the garden path? Applying what consistency with observational adequacy in a reasonable time-scale has already been taken to mean, it will find no reason to deny the former. Of course, the evidence about contextually completed meaning is far from complete, and this will be acknowledged throughout. Nevertheless, the conclusion of Chapter 3 will be that if the communicative process is a plausible possibility, innate knowledge has not been necessitated to explain the time-scale of English.

However, do we have to concede innate knowledge to explain other facets of learning English? As hinted at at several points in the present chapter, a body of evidence has now been amassed about the nature of grammatical knowledge as it emerges in humans. Is the picture consistent with what, in the absence of innate knowledge, the communicative process would predict? If it is not, we may have shown that innate knowledge is unnecessary to explain the learning time-scale, but we should not have provided an affirmative answer to the question the chapter began with, whether there is an alternative to innateness if learning is to be explained. Thus, the issue of consistency with emergent knowledge is important, and Chapter 4 will initiate an attempt to probe it further. Chapter 4 will start by taking up a theme, implicit already in the discussion of discounting, that the sentence-meaning input available to children following the communicative process will change as learning progresses. It will explain what, given the communicative process devoid of innate knowledge, the changes should imply for the emergence of grammar. It will argue that they should produce two developmental periods, the first lasting until about two-and-a-half years.

During the first period, children's communicative expressions should become increasingly conventional. They should contain a higher proportion of the required lexical items, with the items placed in a sequence that is increasingly orthodox. However, the knowledge underpinning these advances should never fulfil the demands of a grammar. The lexical items should not be organised into form classes, and their sequencing should not be achieved by rules. It should not be until after two-and-a-half that a grammar is attained and, as Chapter 4 will explain, the attainment should be by a predictable route. Essentially, there should be a fairly rapid shift to a rule-bound system. Moreover, the rules that emerge around two-and-a-half should produce phrase markers equivalent in shape to those in the final system. The shift to form classes, and indeed to the categories they are dominated by, should take more time. Indeed, it should proceed in a piecemeal fashion. Armed with what amount to hypotheses about the course of development, Chapter 4 will then scrutinise the available empirical work to see if they are confounded. It will consider data amassed by both psychologists and linguists. It will look at all age groups, from adults to very young children. It will find no insurmountable problems.

By the end of Chapter 4, the essay will have said all that it intends to about the learning of English. Its conclusion will be that given the facts currently available there is an alternative to innate knowledge of grammar, namely learning on the communicative process. How, though, about other languages? As was pointed out earlier, an investigation that parallels the present one will eventually have to be carried out with a representative sample of all the natural languages. The hope has already been expressed that an in-depth analysis of one language will elucidate the parameters by which the sample should be chosen.

Chapter 5 will start by considering whether the hope has been fulfilled. It will argue affirmatively, pointing out that during the course of Chapters 2 to 4, the features of sentence-meaning input crucial to both the developmental course and the timeliness of the final system have been carefully laid out. Thus, by treating the features as values on dimensions, languages that show suitable contrasts should be easy to find. Chapter 5 will give pointers to some candidates and without pre-empting the encyclopaedic enterprise that proper investigation would entail, it will introduce some relevant data. Having done so, Chapter 5 will conclude with an altogether more general issue, the location of the communicative process in psychological theory. As was pointed out at the start of the essay, the problem with innate knowledge of grammar from the psychological perspective was, and is, that it flies in the face of a general theory of learning. However, the intricacies of the mechanisms outlined in Chapter 3 will be such as to bring the communicative process' superiority sharply into question. The mechanisms may not amount to knowledge of grammar, but they may seem equally language-specific and thus just as unwelcome. Although understandable, Chapter 5 will argue that this interpretation is, in fact, ill-founded.

En route to this conclusion, many issues will be raised and much research will be discussed. However, it is important not to forget that eventually it will all bear on the generality of psychological theories, for this concern is the essay's *raison d'être*. As such it will inform the structure plus, of course, the title. It will also influence the style for (acknowledging the relevance to psychologists in general) the deliberately "minimalist" approach to linguistic terminology adopted in this chapter, will be continued elsewhere. As a consequence, linguists and child language experts may feel that easy ideas are being laboured and difficult ones skimmed over, and for this I can only apologise and express the hope that my motives are appreciated. What I have tried very hard not to do is to take my minimalisation so far that it trivialises the ideas that have emerged in contemporary linguistics. I began the chapter by showing how the psychologists of language working prior to 1960 missed issues critical to their own concerns by ignoring linguistics. I should be disappointed to be judged to have done likewise!

NOTES

1. Some of the examples that will appear in this essay come from my own recordings of children's speech. To differentiate them from other examples, they will be presented in the format of (1.1). Within these examples, the

children's ages will be given in months and days, e.g. (20.6) = 20 months and 6 days.

2. To explain the linguistic conventions used here and elsewhere:

(a) X → Y + Z means 'X can be written as Y + Z'

(b) X → Y(Z) means 'X can be written as Y or Y + Z'

(c) $X \rightarrow \left\{ \begin{matrix} Y \\ Z \end{matrix} \right\}$ means 'X can be written as Y or Z'

3. In early formulations of the X-bar thesis, bars were printed over the symbols, thus $\bar{N}$ and $\bar{A}$. To facilitate printing, primes are now more frequently used, making for N′ and N″. Primes are the convention that this essay will follow.

CHAPTER TWO

The Contextual Completion of Meaning

Chapter 1 raised the possibility that children do not operate as miniature linguists, testing sentences for compatibility with extant grammars and changing the grammars when incompatibilities arise. Rather, driven by their communicative needs, they test sentences for direct interpretability by trying to read off meanings from sentence properties alone. To the extent they are entirely or partially unsuccessful, they complete the meanings from the context of usage and try to specify the sentences as a function of the meanings to optimise direct interpretation in the future. Finally, when their specification allows several options for any given meaning, they look to adult speech and/or the extralinguistic context to delimit their choice. In Chapter 1, this approach to sentence processing was called the "communicative process", and the question was raised as to its consequences for the time-scale of learning. In particular, it was asked whether, if children follow it, they could acquire an observationally adequate grammar in the time they normally take without requiring inbuilt knowledge. Chapter 1 suggested that what amount to two criteria would have to be fulfilled for an affirmative answer. First, the consequences of specification for ready interpretation in the absence of inbuilt knowledge would have to be a system that was either observationally adequate in its own right or removed from observational adequacy by virtue only of a specific kind of overgeneralisation. The system would, in other words, have to generate all the sentences of the children's language and, if it fell short of all and only those sentences, it would have to do so in a particular way. Second, the system would have to be achieved sufficiently quickly so that, whether or not it was observationally adequate in its own right, it could achieve observational adequacy in a reasonable period.

Accepting the criteria, all that can be said at present is that if children follow the communicative process, they will not stop specifying sentences as a function of their meanings until they possess a system that represents all their language's sentences. This would be the case whether or not they are innately primed, for until they possess such a system they will experience sentences that they cannot interpret directly. Thus, the first step towards seeing whether the criteria are fulfilled would surely be to spell out the system that specification for ready interpretation would lead to, on the assumption of no innate knowledge. This would in some sense or another involve imagining children confronted by sentences that they had not represented. It would also involve imagining them pairing whatever they could remember of the sentences with their contextually completed meanings and, without any *a priori* knowledge whatsoever, trying to store the pairing to facilitate direct interpretation in the future. However, to follow this through we should need to know what would be remembered from sentences and what the contextually completed meanings would be like.

The first issue was discussed in Chapter 1 but, as regards the second, much remains uncertain. All we can conclude at present is that contextually completed meanings are the one component of the communicative process whose status is more than hypothetical. Work summarised in Chapter 1 showed children of 21 months giving responses to adult speech that guarantee the ascription of meaning. We cannot tell whether these responses followed an attempt at direct interpretation, nor do we know that the meanings were preserved once they were given. However, we can be sure that if they did follow an attempt at direct interpretation, it will have been an attempt that failed. Data presented in Chapter 1 suggest that at 21 months children discount most of the closed class items that appear in English sentences, and some of the open. Hence, even if they make successful direct interpretations of the remaining items (and this is by no means guaranteed), they would not have enough of a meaning to make a response. By this token, direct interpretation must fail. However, when direct interpretation fails, meanings must be ascribed by external sources and for reasons outlined in Chapter 1 these external sources must involve contextual inference. Thus, if the responses given by 21-month-olds did follow an attempt at direct interpretation, they must bear witness to contextually completed meanings. However, even if they did not do this, there can, of course, be no alternative to contextual inference.

Thus, no matter what the status of the communicative process as a whole, contextually completed meanings are real. So what are they like? Looking back at the responses that, in Chapter 1, were used to demonstrate the ascription of meaning, the impression of identity with adult intention is hard to resist. On further reflection, this is hardly surprising. If children gave responses that indicated unintended interpretations, the errors would be as obvious to their conversational partners as they are to us. Hence, children would undoubtedly receive adverse feedback from those partners that, over time, would be translated into loss of faith in the contextually-based method of completing meaning. If faith was lost, the method would be abandoned. Contextually-based inference may be the speediest method of interpreting sentences that are not yet represented, but it is not the only one that children could employ. Although, as we have noted, they do not ask "What does — mean?" as a matter of practice, nothing would prevent them from doing this in principle if they felt the need. They do, after all, say "What's (a) —?" when they want to know the referents of lexical items. As direct requests for clarification carry a guarantee of reliability, children would almost certainly adopt them if contextual inference fell into disrepute. As children do not adopt them, we can assume that contextual inference does not fall into disrepute. Hence, following the argument backwards we can also conclude that children must rarely, if ever, receive adverse feedback on their interpretations of adult speech. Consequently, they must rarely, if ever, give any indication of misunderstanding.

However, does the fact that children's responses seldom suggest misunderstanding guarantee that understanding will actually take place? If it does, the issue of what contextually completed meanings are like can be readily resolved. As mentioned above, children give the responses at 21 months when they are discounting so many lexical items from their sentential experiences that, no matter what acquisition process they are following (and no matter how much innate knowledge they have), their grammatical knowledge must be extremely weak. If their contextually completed meanings correspond to adult intention at this stage, they must surely do so later when their knowledge will have reached a higher level. Thus, should we be justified in inferring understanding from the lack of observable misunderstanding, we could say that at all levels of grammatical knowledge contextually completed meanings will concur with adult intention. Helpful or not given our current concerns, this conclusion would at least be simple. The trouble is that in the absence of additional evidence it would not be warranted for it is conceivable that some aspects of adult meaning are overlooked without being displayed in the responses children give. Before we jump to conclusions, we need to consider this carefully.

Accepting the point, the present chapter will try to follow it through. It will attempt to spell out the meanings that English sentences to children are used to express. This alone will be no small undertaking, because it will implicate concepts from pragmatic theory as well as adult–child interaction. Having reviewed English sentences from the perspective of adult intention, the chapter will look more closely at the responses given by 21-month-olds, and ask whether there are areas where full understanding should not be taken for granted. It will, in fact, find plenty and hence it will try to probe them further. It will ask whether additional evidence can be mustered to guarantee understanding at 21 months. To the extent it cannot, the chapter will ask whether understanding can be guaranteed at any point after 21 months, but prior to the full representation of the sentence in question. It will appeal to both logical necessity and empirical evidence, and in the latter area it will find some gaps. Nevertheless, insofar as the evidence points anywhere, it will always be in the same direction: divergent interpretations not just at 21 months but until full representation. Moreover, as we shall see, the divergence is such that virtually no English sentences could escape contextually completed meanings that departed from adult intention. What does this mean should children be using such sentences and meanings in accordance with the communicative process? As we shall see in Chapter 3, it means a scenario that is far from discouraging when the ultimate aim is observational adequacy in its proper time span.

IMPERATIVE SENTENCES AND THE DIRECTING OF BEHAVIOUR

To proceed, the chapter will obviously require a scheme for organising the sentences whose interpretation it needs to discuss, and there are several reasons for employing the age-old distinction between imperatives, interrogatives, and declaratives. First, the one piece of evidence that will clearly be crucial is children's responses to adult speech. As hinted in Chapter 1, studies of those responses have been structured around the imperative/interrogative/declarative distinction. Second, the distinction, by intention at least, applies to the "surface" structure of sentences. Hence it should allow meaning to be discussed without precipitate decisions about phrase structure and transformational rules. On the other hand, the distinction between imperative, interrogative, and declarative sentences has one important drawback that needs to be noted. This is that even within linguistics where the distinction originated, there is disagreement about its application. Indeed, usage is often motivated by beliefs about underlying structure. Clearly, such disparities will work against a straightforward exposition. Nevertheless, in the absence of a better alternative, the present chapter will stick with the imperative/interrogative/declarative distinction. To try and minimise confusion, it will start with some non-controversial examples of each of the categories. Then it will pinpoint areas where linguists disagree and come to some (hopefully) non-arbitrary resolution. In the case of imperatives (which will be the present section's focus), delimiting the category will lead to a discussion of the contextual constraints on usage. As should become clear, this will set the scene for specifying the meanings that imperatives to young children express. Having achieved a specification, the section will then consider the responses that 21-month-olds make, arguing that from them alone full understanding cannot be inferred. Bringing further evidence to bear, the section will paint a picture of attributed meanings, which excludes aspects of both the general "function" and the specific "content". Moreover, this will not just be at 21 months, but throughout the period when imperative structure is being mastered. The section will, alas, be lengthy. Specifying the contextual constraints on imperative usage will require the introduction of a complex apparatus. Deciphering the meanings that children attribute will entail a detailed (and slightly unorthodox) selection from an extensive literature. Hopefully, the length will be forgiven when it is appreciated that points raised will simplify significantly the sections to come.

The Functions of Imperative Sentences

The chapter will start with imperatives because structurally and, I shall argue, functionally, they are the most straightforward of the three modalities. However, although straightforward in relative terms, there is more to the concept of imperatives than the simple main verb constructions of "Come in", "Sit down" and "Shut up". In the first place, it is recognised that imperatives include complex as well as simple sentences. Thus, "Write when you arrive", "Stop if the light flashes", and "Tell me what she said" would all be regarded as imperatives. In the second, it is accepted that sentences that lack main verbs altogether, like "Be kind", "Be careful" and "Don't be stupid", can also be categorised as imperatives. Moreover, even when imperatives contain main verbs it is acknowledged that they can be padded out with a range of optional extras. Thus, "Wash yourself quickly", "You wash your hands", and "Wash your hands in the basin" are all acceptable imperatives containing main verbs. Indeed, it might seem reasonable to represent the surface structure of simple imperatives containing main verbs as "(Noun phrase) + verb + (noun phrase/s) + (adverb) + (prepositional phrase/s)" where all the bracketed items are optional.

However, although the formula provides a useful summary, it turns out in practice to be overly general. It ignores the fact that no linguist would accept a string as imperative unless the first (or "subject") noun phrase of its main clause refers to the hearer/s. It also ignores the fact that, according to Lakoff (1966), no linguist should accept a simple string as imperative if its main verb is "stative". Stative verbs, which include "want", "hear", and "know", are so-called because they normally express states-of-affair. According to Lakoff, they should be perfectly acceptable in complex strings like "Want an apple and you will have one" but not in simple strings like "Want an apple". Certainly, there is something odd about "Want an apple" when taken out of context, yet there are situations where it would pass without comment. To see one, note my final contribution to (2.1), a rather stormy conversation that took place in my home a few years ago.

(My daughter Miriam (26.4) has just finished the first course of her lunch)   (2.1)

Me:	What do you want for pud?
Miriam:	Want an apple
Me:	Okay, here you are
Miriam:	Want an orange
Me:	We haven't got any oranges
Miriam:	Want an orange
(Several further exchanges and growing irritation on my part)	
Me:	You said you wanted an apple
Miriam:	Not want apple
Me:	Want an apple. Otherwise go without

Myself, I suspect that all Lakoff's exceptional cases can be "normalised" in specific discourse contexts. Consequently, I should like to go along with the linguists who, in contradiction of Lakoff, refuse to constrain the main verbs in imperative sentences and look beyond the grammar to explain the oddity of strings like "Want an apple" when they are used out of context. Sometimes they turn to the work of Searle (1969) and it will be useful for our more central concerns to see why this is. By way of introduction, it should be noted that many imperative sentences can be ascribed a general "function" of directing behaviour. This is not to say that directing behaviour is the only general function. Complex sentences like "Want an apple and you will have one" and "Vote Liberal Democrat and secure a Tory government" would be regarded as imperatives by many writers. Yet their function would normally be to express conditionality. Equally, it is not to say that directing behaviour always reduces to initiating actions. "Stop writing" could operate directively but through terminating an ongoing action rather than initiating a new one. Nevertheless, while recognising this, it is still legitimate to claim that one of the major functions of imperative sentences is to direct behaviour. It is also legitimate to claim that when presented out of context, most people would interpret imperatives structured like "Want an apple" as if they were intended to do this. Indeed, out of context most people would interpret such imperatives as attempts to direct a hearer to produce the behaviour that is specified in the sentence.

As such, imperatives structured like "Want an apple" fulfil what, in the terms of Searle (1969), is the "essential condition" on directing the specified behaviour. However, according to Searle, fulfilling the essential condition will not, even in adult conversation, guarantee this interpretation in actual usage. Doing this depends on a number of other conditions. These conditions are presented more or less verbatim from the 1969 work in (2.2), though it should be noted that Searle uses the term "action" in the broad sense we have reserved for "behaviour".

Preparatory conditions: (2.2)
1) Hearer can perform the action
2) Speaker believes that hearer can perform the action
3) Hearer is not obviously going to perform the action of his own accord
4) (?) Speaker has the right to tell hearer to perform the action

Sincerity condition:
1) Speaker wants hearer to perform the action

Propositional content condition:
1) Speaker predicates a future action of hearer

Together with the essential condition, the preparatory, sincerity, and propositional content conditions are usually called the "felicity" conditions. If we accept that they all contribute to the realisation of meaning in context, we can readily appreciate the alternative explanation of "Want an apple". It would go along the lines of wanting a particular foodstuff is not something that people can normally do at will. Hence, out of context, it is hard to see how the sentence could be used without violating the first preparatory condition. As we should usually expect fulfilment of the conditions on which meaning depends, the sentence sounds odd. In the specific example involving my daughter, the argument would be that the context suggests she could have wanted the apple if she stopped being perverse. As a result, my "Want an apple" comes across as fulfilling the first preparatory condition. It may cast aspersions on my skills as a mother but linguistically it sounds perfectly unexceptionable.

The use of Searle's felicity conditions to interpret sentences like "Want an apple" probably sounds quite plausible. Nevertheless, it is almost certainly an oversimplification. In a paper that Searle (1975) seems happy to accept, Grice (1975) makes claims that imply that violations of the felicity conditions will not always sound odd. The claims only imply this for rather than addressing the felicity conditions *per se*, Grice is ostensibly concerned with four basic "maxims". These maxims do not coincide with the felicity conditions but, as Brown and Levinson (1978) point out, they can be related to them. For example, one, the maxim of quality, exhorts speakers to avoid falsehood, with obvious parallels to the sincerity condition. Grice argues that should the maxims be flouted, sentences will normally fail to achieve their full meaning potential. However, they will not invariably sound odd. Rather, they will only sound odd if they cannot be given a different interpretation, which preserves the image of maxim (and, by implication, felicity condition) following. Thus, the oddity of "Want an apple" follows from the fact that out of context, it is hard to see, first, how it could be used without violating a felicity condition on behaviour directing and, second, what it could mean consistent with felicity condition following. It is these two features in combination that create the problem, not the first one alone.

In my view, this synthesis of Searle and Grice does constitute a more adequate explanation of simple imperatives with stative verbs than would denying their sentencehood. If the view is shared, we shall obviously have sharpened the distinction between sentences and non-sentences, a development of great relevance when the ultimate aim is a commentary on grammar. However, in invoking Grice to help us, we have also taken a few steps towards a more immediate goal—the meanings associated with sentences to children. To begin to see why, note that in his 1975 paper, Grice goes on to say that where there is a meaning which is consistent with the following of the maxims/felicity conditions, adult speakers will give it. Thus, there is an implied distinction between "literal" and "non-literal" meaning, literal meaning being the interpretation sentences will be given either out of context or in fulfilment of the maxims/felicity conditions, and non-literal being the interpretation they will be given in other circumstances to preserve the assumption of fulfilment. It is easy to think of examples that support both Grice's point and the distinction it implies. For instance, suppose that, on finding the front door left open and a gale raging through the house, I were to yell at my husband "Go on, open all the windows as well". He would hardly hear me as asking him to open the windows. His most probable interpretation would be an adverse comment on the temperature and a direction to warm things up. In making that interpretation, he would of course be preserving the general behaviour directing quality of the literal meaning, but denying the remainder in favour of something non-literal.

Of course, non-literal meanings do not always have to be at the expense of literal. It is also possible for them to be attributed in addition to literal. To see this, consider the fourth of Searle's preparatory conditions, the requirement that "speaker has the right to tell hearer to perform the action". Undoubtedly, this is a somewhat marginal condition in Searle's thinking, hence its question mark in (2.2). It appears as a footnote to Searle (1969) and is omitted from Searle (1975). Nevertheless it is interesting because it is the only felicity condition to involve social considerations. A speaker's right to tell the hearer to do something is, after all, dependent on his/her being of superior status. Moreover, when this dependency does not pertain through the speaker being of equal or inferior status there is, as Grice would predict, some impact on meaning. Yet the impact is not to undermine the literal interpretation, but to supplement it. To see this, consider a specific example, perhaps my saying "Give me some comments on this chapter by Monday" to my boss or, even, my colleagues. The remark will still be heard as a behavioural directive. However, as is clear from a recent study of mine (Howe, 1989), it will, through its abject rudeness, take on an additional meaning, namely a contemptuous attitude towards extant status.

Faced with these examples, it is obvious that humans do have the ability to infer non-literal meaning from maxim/felicity condition violation. However, it should also be obvious that maxim/felicity condition violation is not just a hypothetical possibility for theorists to contemplate. It is a strategy that ordinary speakers use to achieve communicative impact. This is what makes it relevant for us for, without doubt, it features not just in conversations between adults, but also in speech addressed to children. If evidence of the latter is required, consider teasing (for example, "Catch Mummy" as Mummy speeds away), fantasy play (for example, "Kill Daddy", as Daddy feigns death) and exasperation (for example, "Go on, burn yourself" as match play persists). Indeed, without being conclusive, studies like Hopper (1983) and Miller (1986) suggest that non-literal usage might even be more frequent in speech to children than in speech to adults. Be that as it may, children undoubtedly experience imperative sentences that are being used non-literally. Hence, given our present concerns, we shall have to address as much attention to their interpretation as we do to the interpretation of imperatives used literally.

The Sensitivity to Behaviour Direction

Starting, however, with literal usage, we should perhaps return to the studies, introduced in Chapter 1 and cited earlier in the present chapter, that are concerned with children's responses to adult speech. After all, amongst the studies was the work of Huttenlocher (1974), Schaffer and Crook (1980), Schnur and Shatz (1984), and Shipley et al. (1969) and this work was, without exception, concerned with imperatives that were literal and directive. It documented children who were around 21 months of age, responding by performing actions on the designated entities. From points made as an introduction to the present chapter, we can now say a little more about these responses and the imperatives that preceded them. Essentially, the imperatives must have been intended to produce the actions that were subsequently performed. Anything else would have given the impression that the children had misinterpreted and, as we have already established, such impressions must be rare. However, can we move from the impression of not misinterpreting to the presumption of interpreting? Can we, in other words, conclude that the children actually realised that the actions were wanted, and that they were to carry them out?

In answer, it is hard to imagine how children could have selected the desired actions from the vast number of contextually possible ones without understanding what was wanted. However, they could have selected the desired actions without understanding that they were being directed to carry them out. In theory, their responses could have resulted from an interpretation like "Behaviour X is wanted" and a decision like "I might as well perform it", and precluding this is far from easy. Nevertheless, I think it can be done, with reference, somewhat paradoxically, to children's remarks when they do not comply. If they say anything, it is usually little more than "No". However, as Garvey (1975) and McTear (1985) have shown, they sometimes, even in the age group under scrutiny, give reasons for their non-compliance along the lines of (2.3). In my view, it is difficult to reconcile the child's contribution to (2.3) with anything short of the belief that she was being directed to perform the behaviour.

(Mother watches Ursula (24.22) trying to post shapes)   (2.3)
        Mother: Pop it in
        Ursula: Can't. Can't. Can't

However, if these conclusions are to be drawn under literal usage, surely they must also be drawn where there is a non-literal substitute. When a non-literal meaning substitutes for a literal, the responses must also have involved the desired but non-specified actions. Remembering some of the examples used earlier in the section, production of the specified actions would have constituted *faux pas* of newsworthy proportions! Following the arguments of the previous paragraph, when children produce the desired actions they must at minimum be aware that this was the behaviour that was wanted and at maximum also know that they were being asked to perform it. However, if the minimal interpretation is to be excluded under literal usage, it would be most peculiar to permit it under non-literal. It would be even more peculiar to permit it for the literal component of sentences that carry a non-literal supplement, but how about these supplements themselves? When children respond by performing specified actions on specified entities they could have missed the non-literal component altogether. Do they do this? On logical grounds alone, the answer has to be "Yes". Observing imperative sentences that happen to be used with a supplementary intent, children who find them structurally challenging could in theory construct the literal component by contextual inference. However, constructing the non-literal would require seeing the sentential structure as inappropriate in its context of usage. Clearly, judging the sentential structure as inappropriate presupposes that it is known, and this is precluded by definition with the sentences we are considering.

What is being claimed then is that as a logical consequence of their inferential strategies, children will be precluded from determining the supplementary meanings associated with the sentences that are beyond their grammatical knowledge (and hence, recalling a point in Chapter 1, from appreciating contempt and irony). For certain purposes, it might be important to find out when supplementary non-literal meanings are discovered, and interesting papers by Ackerman (1978) and Mitchell-Kernan and Kernan (1977) suggest around seven or eight years at the latest. However, given our present concerns such issues are beside the point. All that matters is the unavailability while the sentences are not fully known and this matters for several reasons. It means, of course, that contextually completed meanings could at any level of grammatical knowledge depart from adult intention. Thus, it is the first evidence that a communicative process would not be operating on the meanings that adults intend. It also means that the process would treat simple imperatives as a relatively homogeneous bunch. The consequence of the arguments advanced in the last few paragraphs is to claim that when they are considered from the perspective of grammar-learning children, all simple imperatives and most complex ones will be behaviour-directing and never anything more.

Expressing this diagrammatically, we can say that the meanings children attribute to the vast majority of imperative sentences will involve the hierarchical arrangement depicted in (2.4).[1]

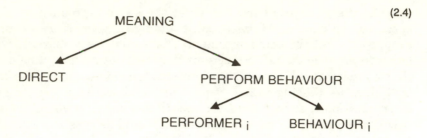

(2.4)

Yet, by using (2.4) by way of summary, we may simultaneously be suggesting too much and too little. We may be suggesting too much because the depiction of (2.4) on the printed page gives the impression that the elements are serially as well as hierarchically ordered. If anything, we ought to be viewing the elements as free floating, like the images on an infant's mobile. We may be suggesting too little because (2.4) implies limited awareness of the behavioural content. Recalling that in the studies cited earlier 21-month-old children responded by performing actions on the entities that were designated, it will seem as if further subcategorisation of the behavioural component would not come amiss. Certainly, the entities might be expected to appear and there might even be a case for including the roles that the entities were being asked to play. Nevertheless, we need to be careful. We should only be justified in doing this if other entities could have been implicated in the actions and/or other roles could have been performed. Otherwise, the children's responses could reflect strong contextual constraints rather than inferences about meaning. Closer scrutiny is clearly required.

The Awareness of Entity Roles

In the studies under consideration, the entities were generally at a distance from the child and they were not necessarily the focus of ongoing attention. Thus the fact that the designated entities were acted upon must surely mean, first, that identifiable entities were anticipated in the intentions of others and, second, that effective strategies were deployed to find out what the entities were. The nature of the strategies has, in fact, been widely discussed. Work by Bridges (1979) and Murphy (1978) suggests that children could derive assistance from adult pointing. However the conclusive evidence that Hoff-Ginsberg and Shatz (1982) and Shatz (1982) have demanded has yet to be obtained. Whatever the truth, the main point surely holds good: when children respond to directive imperatives by acting on the designated entities, they do so in the knowledge that the entities were meant. Of course, in drawing this conclusion it is not being suggested that young children acknowledge the full subtleties of adult noun phrases. It is not, for example, being suggested that such children recognise the differing intentions behind "a ball", "the ball", "this ball", "that ball", and "some balls". Indeed, it seems unlikely, from work summarised by, for example, Macnamara (1982), that they become sensitive to such niceties before about three years of age. Classic work by Brown (1973) shows that by three most children are already using the determiners in their spontaneous speech, albeit in a somewhat erroneous fashion. Hence, importantly for us, this means sometime after the constructions will have become grammatically known.

Moving onto entity roles, the attribution of full understanding is, if anything, more seductive. In the studies we are considering, children heard sentences like "Throw me the ball", "Put the penny in the cup", and "Show Mummy the baby's bottle". It is hard to think how they could have responded appropriately unless they had "read off" the roles that the entities were intended to play. It is hard but not, alas, impossible. Instead of understanding the "patient" role of "ball", "penny" and "bottle", the "recipient" role of "me" and "Mummy", the "locative" role of "cup", and the "possessor" role of "baby", they could have interpreted the sentences as requests to associate the actions and entities in some unspecified way. This is because with actions like throwing, putting, and showing, they would have been more or less obliged by the objects' physical properties to adopt those roles. Imagine, for example, throwing "me" to the ball!

The problem seems to be a general one for, glancing through the role relations in the studies as a whole, there are no cases where children would have needed to decipher specific roles to give appropriate responses. This is certainly true with the patient, recipient, locative, and possessor roles. It is also true with the agent role once we remember that there is a conceptual distinction between performance and agency, the former being of the behaviour and contrasting with witnessing and the latter being in the behaviour and contrasting with the aforementioned roles. This being the case, exchanges like (2.3) have no bearing. The problem amounts to the fact that because, with the directive imperatives addressed to young children, the behavioural roles demanded of specified entities are strongly indicated by their physical properties, there will always be two possible explanations of the appropriate responses that usually occur. One implicates the conventional interpretation and the other an interpretation along the lines of "associate X with Y".

Faced with the problem, we shall have to find other evidence, but what form should it take? Inspired by the work of Bloom (1970) many researchers have suggested looking not so much at how children respond to others but at what they themselves express. These researchers believe that children typically use contextual cues to compensate for gaps in their linguistic knowledge. Hence, although they are persuaded by work (like Brown, 1973) that conventional markers of role are absent until into the third year, they believe that speech in its context of usage may provide evidence for the much earlier expression of roles themselves. They see such evidence as useful and hence, turning the tables on what has been contemplated so far, they have taken children's speech and used contextual cues to assign it meaning. By this method, they have concluded that very young children do express behavioural roles. In the case of Greenfield and Smith (1976) and Rodgon (1976) "very young" meant children who were barely 18 months of age. Is this plausible? I am on record (Howe, 1976, 1981b) as a diehard sceptic, for nowhere have I found contextually based interpretation of children's speech being used in a way that justifies behavioural roles rather than general associations. Claims to the contrary have always turned on conceptual confusion (particularly over the performer/agent distinction), circular reasoning, and/or adultomorphic perspectives. Yet perhaps I should not have worried, for there is a more general point to be made. This is that extrapolation from expression to interpretation is in principle untenable. It is, after all, conceivable that children aspire to specificity in their own expressions, but treat the expressions of others as more open-ended.

Suppose, then, that we steer clear of contextually based interpretation of children's speech. What is the alternative? The most obvious approach would surely be to present entities whose roles relative to each other are not strongly indicated, and to ask children who are too young to make sense of the linguistic cues to use the entities in some action. If such children assume that sentences express roles, they should use the entities differentially. The exact roles they adopt, and the strategies they use to assign roles to entities would not matter. If, on the other hand, such children assume that sentences express general associations, they should feel free to fluctuate between differential and non-differential usage.

Accepting this as the obvious approach, problems arise once we look for relevant research. There have been countless studies where children have been asked to act on entities whose roles are not strongly indicated. In the majority of these studies, two animate entities are presented and, via instructions like "Make the cow chase the horse", children are asked to make one entity the agent and the other the patient. The earlier studies of this genre have been reviewed by Bridges, Sinha, and Walkerdine (1981) and Cromer (1976, see also Cromer, 1991), and both these studies and their successors will be detailed in Chapter 4. The trouble with all the studies is that their concern has typically been the age at which children make sense of the linguistic cues, in particular the lexical sequence. What is relevant in the present context is what children do when their age is such that making sense of the linguistic cues is out of the question. However, there have been a few exceptions and typically their results turn out to be more consistent with the attribution of general associations. For example, Bridges (1980), Chapman and Kohn (1977), de Villiers and de Villiers (1973), and French, Sinclair, and Bronckart (1972) have all reported both entities being made the agent and/or both entities being made the patient in addition to role differentiating responses. Moreover although Bates et al. (1984) and Slobin and Bever (1982) comment on the rarity of undifferentiating responses, the fact that they obtained some from children who were typically older than the ones in the other studies can also be seen as consistent.

Although presenting entities whose relative roles are not strongly indicated seems the obvious way forward, it is not the only strategy that could be adopted. In Howe (1981b), I suggested an alternative one, namely presenting entities in one role arrangement and training children in the conventional description, as, for example, with presenting a hat on a boy and training with "The hat's on the boy". Having established successful training, the test would be to present the entities in several role arrangements including the trained one, say a hat placed on a boy and a boy placing a hat on someone else, and see where the descriptive expression was applied. Children who, during the training phase, had taken the expression to describe the specific roles should be discriminating. They should, in other words, restrict the expression to the patient/location relation. Children who, during the training phase, had taken it to describe the non-specific association of two entities should not discriminate. I do not own the copyright on the method. Something very similar was pioneered by Braine and Wells (1978) and has subsequently been applied by Braine and Hardy (1982) and Bridges (1984). However, their usage was with children who were of an age to have mastered expressive devices for the roles being considered. What is more relevant is a study that I myself conducted employing the method (Howe, 1981b, 1982).

The study involved two groups of children, each group containing six boys and six girls. The children in one group were within 20 days of 22 months; the children in the other were within 20 days of 28 months. All 24 children were presented in their homes with three tasks, of which only the second need occupy us here. This involved two tests, one concerned with "NP_1+for+NP_2" as an expression of the patient/recipient roles and the other concerned with "NP_1+on+NP_2" as an expression of the patient/location roles. Part I of each test checked relevant vocabulary. Pictures of the four entities to be used during later parts were presented singly and the child asked "What is it?" Appropriate labels were accepted and used subsequently. Alternatives were suggested to inappropriate labels. Mastery of labels was rechecked by presenting the pictures in two pairs and asking the child to "show me" each entity in turn. Part II was the training phase. The four pictures to be presented in the third and fourth parts were shown one at a time. For NP_1+for+NP_2 they were a man giving tea/cake to a woman and vice versa. For NP_1+on+NP_2 they were a girl putting a hat/shoe on a boy and vice versa. As each picture appeared the child was given an appropriate expression and encouraged to use it. For example, at the very least the child might be told "Look, here's the man. And here's the cake. The man's giving the cake to the lady. The cake's for the lady. The cake's for the lady. Can you say that?" Sometimes (usually, in fact) the training took much longer.

In Part III the child was shown the pictures in pairs. Each pair kept the agent and recipient/location constant while varying the patient. For example, one pair consisted of a man giving tea/cake to a woman and another of a girl putting a hat/shoe on a boy. With these pairs, the child might be asked "Where's the cake for the lady?" and "Where's the hat on the boy?" Four pairs of pictures were presented during Part III of each test. Part III was not in itself a test of role understanding. Children could get the correct answer by simply locating labelled entities. Rather, Part III checked mastery of the test procedure by presenting the pictures and instructions to be used in Part IV, which constituted the role test proper. As with Part III, Part IV involved showing the pictures in four pairs, one pair at a time. This time, however, each pair kept the patient constant while alternating the agent and recipient/location. For instance, one pair consisted of a man giving cake to a woman and a woman giving cake to a man. Another consisted of a girl putting a hat on a boy and a boy putting a hat on a girl. The child would again be presented with questions like "Where's the cake for the lady?" and "Where's the hat on the boy?" Half the children received the NP_1+for+NP_2 test first and half the NP_1+on+NP_2. The order of pictures in each part was varied across children.

To analyse the results, the children were given one point if they touched the correct picture, making a maximum score of four points for each of Parts I, III, and IV. (2.5) presents the results averaged across children.

	Part I	Part III	Part IV	(2.5)
22-month-olds				
NP_1+for+NP_2	4.00	3.50	1.83	
NP_1+on+NP_2	4.00	3.58	1.75	
Combined	8.00	7.08	3.58	
28-month-olds				
NP_1+for+NP_2	4.00	3.67	2.33	
NP_1+on+NP_2	4.00	3.75	2.83	
Combined	8.00	7.42	5.16	

From (2.5) it can be inferred that all the children in both age groups obtained maximum scores on Part I. Although some of the children did not obtain maximum scores on Part III, the overall performance in both age groups was significantly better than would be expected by chance.[2] On Part IV, however, statistical analysis showed the performance of the 28-month-olds to be significantly better than would be expected by chance, but the performance of the 22-month-olds to be more or less at chance level.

To draw some conclusions, remember what we have noted already about children's mastery of conventional role markers. The implication is that by 28 months most children will have some idea of the relevant constructions. At 22 months they will mainly have none. Thus, if it indicates anything, my study must suggest that children who find the constructions challenging will not treat them as expressing the patient/recipient roles nor will they treat them as expressing the patient/location roles. Rather they will regard them as expressing non-specific associations between two entities, implying two general points. First, the compliance with directive imperatives, which motivated the present discussion results, in part at least, from the entities' physical properties. Second, insofar as it involves contextual inference, the interpretation of countless simple imperatives, be they literal or non-literal, will depart from adult intention. This means, of course, something of considerable consequence.

Because the implications are of consequence, it would be gratifying to find them endorsed by other research that deploys an equivalent procedure, but this is easier said than done. There is a study by Corrigan and Odya-Weis (1985). However, the results of this study (which in any event makes debatable assumptions about chance responding) confound awareness of agency with awareness of performing. Clearly, then, the customary plea for further research is nowhere more apt than in the context of behavioural roles. Yet some conclusions can certainly be drawn. In particular we can say that research inspired by responses to directive imperatives contains nothing that necessitates behavioural roles and a few shreds that tentatively deny them. It seems to me that the wisest course of action at this point in time is to accept the shreds, inconclusive though they are, and see where they lead. Hence, from now on it will be assumed that behavioural roles can never be part of contextually completed meanings. This means that until role marking expressions are acquired, the meanings attributed to directive imperatives will, given simple surface structure and at least one post-verbal noun phrase, be limited to the hierarchical arrangement shown in (2.6).

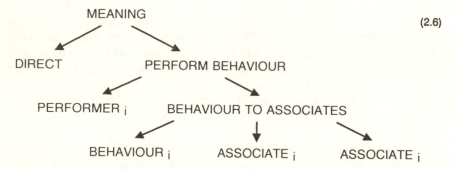

(2.6)

Since, as we have seen, virtually all imperatives will be read by grammar learners as directives, (2.6) also approximates the meanings that will be attributed to imperatives in general.

INTERROGATIVE SENTENCES AND THE ASKING OF QUESTIONS

Armed with these verdicts on imperatives we shall turn now to the interrogative modality, noting at the outset how the discussion can be eased by what has preceded. The conclusions about behavioural roles can be extrapolated forward, and there is in addition little point in looking at non-literal meanings that are supplementary in nature. Thus, even though the meanings undoubtedly occur (as witnessed by "What time is it?" during a very boring party) they will not be discussed further. On the other hand, we shall need to consider non-literal meanings that play a substitutive role, and this will be one of the main themes of the section. It will soon become clear that their relation to literal meaning differs in several interesting ways from what was observed with imperatives. However, in mentioning this point, the analysis is getting ahead of itself because there is another more basic difference between imperatives and interrogatives, which lies squarely on the level of structure. Unlike imperatives (and indeed, declaratives), interrogatives have traditionally been divided into two broad categories, the members being termed yes/no- and wh-interrogatives. Moreover, although defined with respect to structure, the distinction has implications for literal meaning that we shall need to make clear. Having made the implications clear, we shall be well poised to discuss the attribution of literal and non-literal meaning to challenging instances. As with imperatives, the discussion will focus first on the general functions and then on the specific content. As with imperatives also, it will find departure from adult convention in both domains.

The Subcategorisation of Interrogative Sentences

Looking at the structure of yes/no- and wh-interrogatives, we can observe further contrasts with imperatives. For example, yes/no-interrogatives are obliged by their linguistic definition to have a subject noun phrase located before their first verb. This subject noun phrase is not required to refer to the hearer, and is in fact as unbounded as any other noun phrase. Also in contrast with imperatives, the verbs that appear in yes/no-interrogatives are not allowed to be unembellished items. They must be supplemented by auxiliaries, either "modals" like "can", "must", and "should" or non-modals like "was", "does", and "has". These auxiliaries are supposed to occupy the sentence initial position, and thus are separated from the first verb by the subject noun phrase. To appreciate what this means, consider "Can you swim?", "Will he come?", "Are we ready?", and "Do they want it?", which would all pass as yes/no-interrogatives.

Wh-interrogatives can also involve an auxiliary before the subject noun phrase. However, their distinguishing feature is the presence of a wh-word like "what", "who", "when", "where" and, inconsistently, "how". These wh-words normally occur in the sentence initial position as in "What's that?", "Where can the cat be?", and "When are you coming home?". Nevertheless, exceptions are, as Brown (1968) has pointed out, permitted as conversational replies. For instance, in the course of conversation, "You heard what?" and "He's coming when?" are perfectly acceptable.

Despite the structural differences between yes/no- and wh-interrogatives, it is common to find them described collectively as devices for asking questions of the hearer. This is not wrong as an expression of their adult literal meaning, though even here it could be accused of minimising some important differences. It arguably misses the point that yes/no-interrogatives express topics plus information about those topics. Thus, to the extent that they can be conceptualised as asking questions, it is for evaluative feedback on the information provided. Wh-interrogatives, on the other hand, do not provide information. Thus, to the extent that they can be conceptualised as asking questions, it is, by contrast, for information that permits completion. In my view, it would be useful to find a terminology that makes the distinction clear, but unfortunately the literature is less than helpful. Although the distinction has frequently been drawn, it has yet to generate concise conventionally accepted labels. Dore (1977a), for example, talks of yes/no-interrogatives as "soliciting the hearer to affirm, negate or confirm the proposition" and wh-interrogatives as "soliciting information about the identity, location or property of an object, event or situation"! Given this absence of usable precedents, I should like to propose "asking for feedback" as the literal meaning of yes/no-interrogatives and "asking for completion" as the literal meaning of wh-interrogatives.

Having done so, I should like to distance myself from certain widely espoused implications of the "asking" concept. In particular, I should like to emphasise that my use of "asking" is not supposed to suggest a requirement for an overt, verbal response. As I have argued elsewhere (Howe, 1983) it is the social context and not the grammatical structure that determines whether such a response should be given. In contexts like lectures and sermons, where conversation is prohibited, no remark, albeit interrogative or declarative, should receive an overt, verbal response. On the contrary, the expectation is covertness. In contexts where conversation is allowed there is, according to Sacks, Schegloff and Jefferson (1974) an implicit norm that hearers make a contribution at any possible "transition point". As the completion of a sentence is always a potential transition point, every sentence should receive an overt, verbal response, again regardless of its inherent structure.

Of course, it may be the case that in contexts where conversation is allowed, interrogatives do, in practice, receive more overt responses. Indeed, it would be surprising if things were different. Interrogatives are normally spoken with a rising intonation and rising intonation appears to have attention value from the first months of life. Sullivan and Horowitz (1983) found that, under laboratory conditions, rising intonation had an effect on attention at two months of age. Working in the more naturalistic context of a baby clinic, Ryan (1978) found that 12-month-olds were more likely to shift gaze and/or vocalise after maternal speech on a rising tone. Given this attention value, it is also possible that when conversation is allowed, speakers frame their remarks in interrogative form to maximise the chance of an overt response. Nevertheless, the point raised in the previous paragraph still holds good: it is not the case that literally used interrogatives always require overt responses and, when such responses are in order, the requirement is by no means specific to the interrogative category.

The Deployment in Indirect Speech Acts

The contextual factors that constrain overt responding do not, of course, influence the literal meaning of yes/no- and wh-interrogatives. They lead, however, up to the point that for Searle (1969, 1975) interrogatives are just as subject to felicity conditions as imperatives. Moreover, violations of these felicity conditions do not simply diminish the probability of a literal interpretation. They also increase the probability of a non-literal. As mentioned earlier, the non-literal meaning can sometimes be attributed in addition to the literal. However, it can also be attributed in contradiction of the literal, and this is where the real interest lies. Focusing on the latter, one is immediately struck by the enormous scope for non-literalness. With imperatives, it was concluded that non-literal meanings that deny the literal tend nevertheless to preserve the general behaviour directing function. With interrogatives, the parallel restrictions seem not to occur.

For example, there is a class of interrogatives that may, in denial of their literal function, become non-literally behaviour directing. They include yes/no- structures like "Can you come tomorrow?", "Will you leave on Saturday?", and "Do you want to go now?", and wh-structures like "Why don't you get here for lunch?". As Gordon and Lakoff (1971) have pointed out, they are distinguished by the fact that on a literal reading, they ask for feedback or completion of the felicity conditions on directing behaviour. They are interesting in contexts where they not only violate the felicity conditions on their literal interpretation but also fulfil the felicity conditions on directing behaviour. Here, according to Ross (1975) and Sadock (1974), they become behavioural directives at the expense of asking.

Is this correct? Searle (1975) demurs, arguing that the behavioural directiveness is in addition to the literal force, but I suspect he is mistaken. To see why, consider an interrogative where the behaviour-directing is most definitely in supplement, say "What time is it?" as a hint to leave. Here it would be quite unacceptable to respond to the hint alone, either by leaving or by saying, for example, "I'm enjoying myself too much". To fulfil the rules of conversation, the response must, at the very least, acknowledge the literal meaning and it need, in fact, do little more. This is obviously the reason why children are never confronted with their failure to infer supplementary non-literal meanings. Consider now interrogatives like "Can you come tomorrow?" and "Why don't you get here for lunch?". When they are used to direct behaviour the hearer is perfectly free to give a response that, like "Okay" and "I'll try", recognises this function alone. Moreover, should he/she give a response that recognises the literal meaning, the outcome will, as Green (1975) has pointed out be "smart alecky".

Because of their unique properties, the directive meanings of interrogatives like "Can you come tomorrow?" and "Why don't you get here for lunch?" have been granted a distinguishing label, namely "indirect speech acts". The question we need to consider is whether adult speakers regard them as too indirect to be used with children. The answer turns out to be categorically "No", for the developmental literature contains many reports of interrogatives being used as indirect speech acts. Such interrogatives have been observed in speech to two-year-olds by Shatz (1978), speech to 18-month-olds by Schneiderman (1983) and speech to 12-month-olds by Bellinger (1979). Schneiderman found that they constituted a steady 30 to 40 per cent of the "action-directives" addressed to children in the age range 18 to 36 months. Using a slightly different method of classification, Bellinger found a peaking of 45 per cent at 18 months with a decline to 14 per cent by five years. Obviously, the discrepancies need explaining, but whatever we make of them, the studies as a whole show that interrogatives used as indirect speech acts figure prominently in the young child's experience.

This being the case, interrogatives used as indirect speech acts must, given the presumable non-obviousness of misunderstanding, typically receive appropriate responses, and this is well documented in Shatz (1978). In her main study with two-year-olds, Shatz found that 52 per cent of the responses to interrogatives used as indirect speech acts involved the specified actions on the designated entities. In a follow-up with younger children, the figure was 34 per cent. To appreciate the strength of these findings, it should be noted that with imperatives only 40 per cent of the responses given by two-year-olds involved the specified actions. With the younger children the figure was 38 per cent. Given the findings, the conclusions for interrogatives used as indirect speech acts has to be contextually completed meanings, which also include (2.4).

The Implication of Literal Meaning

How about interrogatives used literally? Strangely enough, they have rarely constituted a category in the motherese literature. However, of those studies concerned with interrogatives in general, Broen (1972), Remick (1976), and Savic (1975) provide sufficient data to show that literal usage must be prevalent during the child's second year. Taking Broen's study as an example, it is clear that wh-interrogatives used to ask for completion amounted to at least 15 per cent of the speech addressed to children in the age range 18 to 26 months. It is also clear that when such wh-interrogatives are addressed to children they elicit responses. In Chapter 1, mention was made of research by Camaioni (1979), Ervin-Tripp (1970), Ninio and Bruner (1978), Savic (1978), and myself (Howe, 1981a), which showed children of 21 months and under responding to wh-interrogatives by providing information about the sentences' topics. As all the research, apart from Ervin-Tripp's, was based on naturally occurring conversations, our recurring assumption about obvious misunderstanding permits two immediate inferences. First the wh-interrogatives that the information-providing responses succeeded must have been literal ones, in other words intended to ask the hearer for completion. Second, the information that they provided must normally have seemed appropriate.

That is not to say that errors never occur. Scrutinising the literature, it is clear that the vast majority of wh-interrogatives addressed to small children are variants on the theme of "What is it?" and "Where is the —?". However, there are exceptions and when they occur children's responses are far from conventional. This is clear from the aforementioned work by Ervin-Tripp (1970), together with the other experimental studies of Cairns and Hsu (1978) and Tyack and Ingram (1977). It is also apparent from the exchanges in (2.7), which were recorded by Savic (1978).

(1) Adult: But whose is it? (2.7)
    Child: Rub
(2) Adult: What colour are the gloves?
    Child: Jasmina's
(3) Adult: What kind of ball is this?
    Child: Jasmina's

However, although unconventional, the responses in (2.7) would still create the impression that the general "asking hearer for completion" function was well understood. Is this just an illusion? Surely not as regards the "wanting completion" component but how about the "asking hearer"? Here we are faced with problems that parallel those mentioned with behavioural directives. Fortunately, they can be resolved by appealing to analogous evidence. Occasionally, though admittedly rarely in the age range we are considering, children offer explanations such as (2.8) for their failure to give answers.

(Nazma (23.11) takes pieces of felt from mother)   (2.8)

    Mother: What are they?

    Nazma: I don't quite know them

(2.8) is a relatively (and perhaps precociously) clear example, though I have also recorded "Don't know" and "Won't tell" from 21-month-olds. Taken as a whole, these responses surely constitute evidence that from 21 months (if not earlier) children understand the functions of literal wh-interrogatives in their entirety. Yet no-one has ever challenged the claim first made by Klima and Bellugi (1966) that at 21 months the only part of the wh-interrogative structure that will be known to children is that a wh-word is required. Hence sentence interpretation will be very largely a matter of contextually-based inference. If we can guarantee the intended meaning at this stage, we can surely guarantee it later when less will be unknown.

However, is it just the general function that 21-month-olds understand? Obviously not. Insofar as they normally respond by providing information about the sentences' topics, they must be identifying those topics. Insofar as the information they provide is normally appropriate, they must be understanding something of what the speaker has in mind. Must they be understanding everything? If they must, we shall have to modify our conclusions about behavioural roles for, "Where is it?" is, of course, concerned with location. Fortunately, despite its locative intention, it would be possible to respond appropriately by treating "Where is it?" as "What is the identity of that entity's associate?" This is the interpretation our earlier conclusions will oblige us to take, implying that the contextually completed meaning of "Where is it?" will include the structure represented diagrammatically in (2.9).

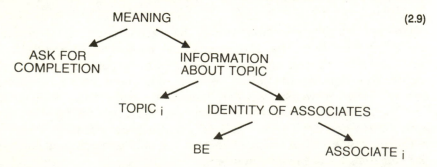

(2.9)

By a simple substitution of IDENTITY OF ATTRIBUTE for IDENTITY OF ASSOCIATE and COLOUR$_i$, SHAPE$_i$, and SIZE$_i$ for ASSOCIATE$_i$, we will have the meanings of "What colour/shape/size is it?" when unlike (2.7(2)) children manage to deal appropriately with such strings. Early work by Piaget (1929) suggests that throughout the preschool period, children treat names as attributes, seeing them just as much parts of phenomena as their physical properties. In which case, the implication is IDENTITY OF ATTRIBUTE in the meaning of "What is it?" with ATTRIBUTE$_i$ realised as NAME$_i$. This is somewhat more complex than adult thinking would imply.

With these conclusions on wh-interrogatives, we can perhaps move onto yes/no-interrogatives. Doing so, it will be recalled that the literal function of yes/no-interrogatives is to ask hearers for feedback and, as (2.10) shows, hearers have several options if they wish to be seen to supply it.

(1) (Wayne (20.6) picks up lorry)   (2.10)

      Mother: Is that the door for the car?

      Wayne: A door

(2) (Mother shows crayon to Ian (21.0))

      Mother: Is that one for me?

      Ian: Yes

(3) (Yvonne (25.4) picks doll's brush up)

      Mother: Isn't that a nice one?

      Yvonne: No

(4) (Richard (25.9) touches toes)

      Mother: Are they your piggies?

      Richard: No, toes

However, although all the responses in (2.10) would allow the speaker to be construed as giving feedback, it is clear that with very young children the imitative rejoinders of (2.10(1)) are by far the most common. The point can be inferred from the negligible number of studies concerned with non-imitative replies in contrast with the vast number concerned with imitative, of which investigations by Brown and Bellugi (1964), Moerk (1972, 1974, 1975, 1976), Nelson (1973), Rodd and Braine (1970), and Seitz and Stewart (1975) constitute a small proportion. The point can also be seen in my 1981a work. Here, there were roughly four times as many imitations as yes/no and corrective responses combined when the children were aged 20 to 22 months and still over three times as many when they were three months older. Yet from the present perspective, the predominance of imitation seems rather unfortunate. What we want to know of course is whether the responses young children give guarantee that the asking for feedback function has been properly understood. Remembering that parrots can mimic, it is conceivable that children could be giving imitative replies without intending them as feedback let alone as feedback, in response to being asked.

On the issue of the intention to give feedback, the yes/no responses of (2.10(2)) and (2.10(3)) look slightly more promising. Nevertheless we should be wary. A study reported by Steffenson (1978) warns against ascribing a conventional interpretation to "yes" and "no" from their usage alone. On the other hand, the corrective response of (2.10(4)) does seem to give the guarantee we are looking for and, somewhat surprisingly, given the status relation between adults and children, it is not a one-off phenomenon. In my 1981a work, responses where children correct adults accounted for 8 per cent of a total based on imitative, yes/no and corrective responses combined when the children were between 20 and 22 months, and 15 per cent when they were three months older. Although these percentages are not staggeringly high, they are hopefully sufficient to establish the point,
children correct and, ergo, intend feedback on the information provided by yes/no-interrogatives. Moreover, having established feedback from corrective responses, we are probably now safe to assume it for imitative ones plus, of course, "yes" and "no".

If we do all of this, it follows that we must recognise feedback as the prevailing response-type with literally used yes/no-interrogatives. Research by Dore (1977b), Ervin-Tripp and Miller (1977), and Horgan (1978) provides evidence on total responses to yes/no-interrogatives throughout the period 15 to 42 months. Its message is that at least 80 per cent of the responses immediately following yes/no-interrogatives are imitative, yes/no or corrective. Yet by accepting the frequency with which children give feedback, we cannot automatically assume they see feedback as asked for. Paralleling the dilemma identified earlier, they could be thinking "Information is being provided and I may as well appraise it". To preclude this we need further evidence and, as with imperatives and wh-interrogatives, the most promising source would seem to be children's excuses when they fail to comply. Given that feedback occupies such a high proportion of the total responses, excuses will obviously be rare. Nevertheless, the literature, including the work of Dore (1977b), contains reports of their occasional usage. Thus, once more there are grounds for assuming a conventional interpretation of the general function.

With this verdict on yes/no-interrogatives three general functions have now been identified: directing behaviour, asking for completion and asking for feedback. Directing behaviour seems to be virtually the only function that grammar-learning children associate with imperative sentences. However, in the context of indirect speech acts, such children also associate the function with yes/no- and wh-interrogatives. Where interrogatives appear unique is over the "asking for" functions, with yes/no-interrogatives aligned with asking for feedback and wh-interrogatives with asking for completion. We shall need to recall these conclusions when in the final section of the chapter, we turn to declaratives. However, we shall also need to consider what has been inferred on the level of content. Here, the conclusions have been more tentative but they amount to two main claims. The first is that grammar-learning children attribute a topic and/or performer element plus a behavioural or identificational element. The second is that the behavioural element can be accompanied by one or more associates while the identificational must be accompanied by an associate or an attribute.

DECLARATIVE SENTENCES AND THE PROVIDING OF INFORMATION

Those whose primary interest is adult grammar must be wondering why declaratives have been left until last. After all, as we saw in Chapter 1, declaratives are by far the most frequent of the modalities used by adults addressing adults. Moreover, there is also a powerful tradition, dating from early transformational grammar (and represented, it will be recalled, in the work of Newport et al., 1977), which regards declaratives as structurally the most basic. Nevertheless, declaratives are no more frequent than imperatives or interrogatives in the speech addressed to children and, on the theoretical side, not every linguist would treat them as basic. More importantly, there are, for present purposes, clear-cut advantages in leaving them until last. To see why, note that, like interrogatives, declaratives can be used as indirect speech acts with behaviour directing force. For illustration, consider the potential meanings of "You will go upstairs immediately", "You can do it if you try", "Officers will wear uniform", and "Dogs must be kept off the grass". Given this potential, it would be hard to make sense of declaratives without first discussing imperatives. Thus, imperatives had to come first. In addition, most theoretical analyses of indirect speech acts, not to mention developmental studies, have focused on interrogatives. Thus, to avoid glaring gaps, interrogatives had to come second. By being left until last, the discussion of declaratives can be much simplified. After all, extrapolating from imperatives, we can conclude that if declaratives carry non-literal meanings, which are supplementary in character, they will be treated as literal until after their structure has been mastered. Extrapolating from interrogatives, we can also conclude that if declaratives operate as indirect speech acts, they will be interpreted non-literally. Taken as a whole, these extrapolations do not quite amount to discounting non-literal meaning altogether. There are, after all, possibilities for substitutive non-literal meaning, which do not involve indirect speech acts. Nevertheless, the extrapolations do permit some de-emphasising of non-literal meaning, and this will prove invaluable in the section to follow. This is because, even when they are used literally, declaratives have complexities peculiar to them. It will be much easier to do justice to these complexities if we can minimise for the moment the issue of non-literalness.

The Differentiation of Information Providing

Despite the interest in meaning, we cannot discuss declaratives without first defining them, and this requires a brief sortie into the domain of grammar. Accepting this we find that, like the other modalities, declaratives can take a number of forms. They can be simple or complex, verbal or adjectival, and positive or negative. Moreover, like interrogatives, though not imperatives, declaratives are obliged by their linguistic definition to have a subject noun phrase before their first verb. Also like interrogatives the first verbs to appear in declaratives can be embellished by a range of auxiliaries, both modal and, in the case of main verb declaratives, non-modal. The chief difference between interrogatives and declaratives lies in the fact that, with the latter, auxiliaries are optional, and when they occur they must follow the subject noun phrase. This suggests that to exemplify well-formed declaratives, we could list "The people agree", "A ball is round", "Some lions are chasing the zebra", "Their house has not been painted", and "I may have seen a fat tabby cat in the henhouse". Indeed, these are all examples of simple declaratives. If we move on to complex sentences, we could also mention "I've fed the cat who is sitting over there", "The fact of the matter is that our neighbour has contacted her solicitor", and "It's too high to reach".

From the examples it should be clear that on literal usage the general function of many declaratives is to provide information. Moreover, it should also be clear that this is just as true of speech to children as it is of speech to adults. Nevertheless, while accepting this it is likely that declarative sentences to children are restricted in the way they provide information. Reading the literature on adult speech to children, I have the impression that not only is the subject noun phrase almost invariably reserved for the topic. The topic when the information is behavioural is almost invariably the performer. With English speakers, this is, as Bates and MacWhinney (1979, 1982) point out, a strong tendency in adult speech to adults but, as Slobin and Bever (1982) have also noted, it seems virtually exceptionless in adult speech to children.

Whether it aids comprehension is hard to establish, but comprehension can certainly be assumed. After all, when we observe children responding to declaratives in the fashion of (2.11) it seems clear, given that the previous section established the responses as feedback giving, that both the topic and something of the information must have been grasped.

(1) (Mother indicates a doll to Caroline (21.3))   (2.11)

     Mother: There's your dolly

     Caroline: Dolly

(2) (Barry (21.18) picks up feet of model fireman)

     Mother: There's his feet

     Barry: Not

                   It's not

                   Not feet

(3) (Ian (21.0) pushes red car)

     Mother: That's red

     Ian: That yellow

The trouble is that although the responses in (2.11) do guarantee some grasp of topic and information, they do not guarantee any grasp of the overall function. They are imitative, yes/no, and corrective and hence identical to the replies given to yes/no-interrogatives. Furthermore, work like Moerk's (1976) shows that imitative, yes/no and corrective responses dominate the total with declaratives just as they did with interrogatives. Recognising this we must face the question of whether, instead of being interpreted by children as providing information, declaratives are rather viewed as asking for feedback. To give a negative answer it might, in lieu of any qualitative differences in predominant responses, seem tempting to cite quantitative ones. Certainly Olsen-Fulero and Conforti (1983) have shown that information providing declaratives receive proportionately fewer responses than feedback soliciting interrogatives. Unfortunately, from points raised earlier, this need not reflect differences in interpretation. It could simply result from the rising intonation of the interrogatives in comparison with the falling intonation of the declaratives. On another tack, it might also seem tempting to cite non-habitual qualitative differences, in particular the fact that although, as we have seen, children will excuse themselves from complying with feedback soliciting interrogatives, they have never been reported as doing this with information providing declaratives. The trouble is that as such excuses are rare with interrogatives, their non-occurrence with declaratives could be a sampling artifact rather than a real difference.

Yet while bearing all this in mind, I think we can argue for the differentiation of declaratives and yes/no-interrogatives when they are both used literally. Moreover, I think we can do this with reference to the replies children make. To see why, let us reiterate once more that when young children produce imitative, yes/no, and corrective replies, it is legitimate to see them as intending feedback. Let us next note that giving feedback is an instance of providing information, albeit information of a rather specific kind. At the present time there is, as far as I know, no comprehensive review of the structural properties of imitative and corrective replies. Nevertheless, the examples offered by Bloom (1970), Halliday (1975), Keenan (1974), McTear (1985), and myself (Howe, 1981a) suggest falling intonation plus or minus an emergent declarative structure. They most definitely do not suggest rising intonation and/or the interrogative format, indicating that it is the declarative structure and not the interrogative that very young children associate with the provision of information. I stand to be corrected in the light of further research but I should like to assume this in what will follow.

At least, this is what I should like to assume while discussing interpretation on the level of sentences. In adult discourse relative clauses as in "The girl who was running" provide information just as surely as simple declaratives, yet linguists would treat relative clauses as having interrogative structure. Thus, for adults, information-providing is aligned in the context of relative clauses with the interrogative structure, and the question is whether this also applies for grammar-learning children. I think that it probably does. According to Bowerman (1979), Hsu, Cairns, and Fiengo (1985), and Limber (1973) the acquisition of relativisation is a protracted affair, starting in the middle of the third year but taking up to two years to complete. Yet there is evidence in such work as Brown (1971), Cook (1973), Sheldon (1974), Smith (1974), and Tavakolian (1981) that when children as young as two-and-a-half are presented with sentences like "The gorilla that bumped the elephant kissed the sheep", they will act out both main and relative clauses. This suggests parallels in the functions attributed to main and relative clauses. Thus, as the previous paragraph established, independently of acting out, that the main clauses will be treated as providing information, we can probably assume the same for relatives. This means that even before they are specified grammatically, declarative and relative structures will be assigned interpretations, which include (2.12).

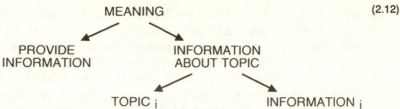

(2.12)

Of course, saying that children see main and relative clauses as providing information before their structure is known does not amount to saying that they see these clauses as providing information throughout early childhood. On the contrary, work by Bever (1970) shows that before two-and-a-half the typical response to sentences like "The gorilla that bumped the elephant kissed the sheep" is to make the gorilla bump the elephant while omitting the remainder. From the perspective of avoiding observable misunderstandings, it is just as well that, as Chapter 1 made clear, relative clauses are rarely addressed to very young children. Equally, saying that children see main and relative clauses as providing information before their structure is known does not amount to saying that they see these clauses in a fully adult fashion. In adult usage, the information provided by relative clauses is different from the information provided by main, in that the former is subordinated to the latter (hence the term subordinated clauses for relatives). Tavakolian has, however, suggested that up to five years, children miss the subordination, treating sentences with relative clauses as containing two co-ordinated elements. Thus "The gorilla that bumped the elephant kissed the sheep" would be given an interpretation closer to the literal meaning of "The gorilla bumped the elephant and kissed the sheep". I must confess that I do not find Tavakolian's argument entirely convincing. It presupposes a high level of errors with sentences like "The gorilla bumped the elephant that kissed the sheep" and although this squares with Tavakolian's own results, it was replicated only by Sheldon in the other studies cited above. Indeed, a subsequent paper by Goodluck and Tavakolian (1982) showed the errors to be significantly reduced when the final noun phrase was inanimate, as would be the case with sentences like "The gorilla bumped the elephant that kicked the fence". In addition, research by Tager-Flusberg, de Villiers, and Hakuta (1982) reveals that when children are actually given co-ordinated sentences akin to "The gorilla bumped the elephant and kissed the sheep", they tend to act out the two clauses simultaneously. This is not the case with "The gorilla that bumped the elephant kissed the sheep".

Interestingly, simultaneity is equally not the case with sentences containing verb phrases with complemental clauses. Examples of such sentences include "I told him that you had gone" and "I told him to go", and here too Tavakolian would argue for a "co-ordinated" interpretation for the two-and-a-half to five age group, implying for the first example the literal meaning of "I told him and you had gone". Tavakolian presents data consistent with her argument, yet there is a problem. To argue a line for complemented sentences that paralleled the claims for relative clauses, Tavakolian would have to present evidence of examplars like "I told him to go" being interpreted as "I told him and I went". Unfortunately, it is a celebrated observation of child language research, first reported by Chomsky (1969) and replicated on numerous occasions thereafter, that such sentences are typically interpreted with the second noun phrase of the main clause as the subject of the complement. Indeed, so strong is this tendency that sentences like "I promised him to go" are interpreted erroneously as "I promised him that he would go". Of course, the tendency could be co-ordination along the lines of "I told/promised him and he went" but being different from what is proposed for relative clauses this would raise more questions than it would answer. Acknowledging these questions and acknowledging also the different acting out of co-ordinated and complemented sentences, there do seem grounds for crediting a grasp of complementation at least by the age of two-and-a-half. Thus, it will be my assumption for the duration of this essay that from the middle of their third year children do understand that the content of relative clauses and clausal complements is subordinated to the sentence as a whole. It will also be my assumption, remembering the work of Bever (1970) that they do this after a period when they fail to interpret more than one clause.

The Exclusion Of Performative Clauses

The brief discussion of sentences with co-ordinated and subordinated clauses means that all the major types of sentence have now been mentioned. We have after all looked at the imperative, interrogative, and declarative modalities, and we have now introduced a simple versus complex dimension. Throughout, we have repeatedly encountered a small number of extremely general functions, suggesting that with contextually completed meanings the form–function relation is fairly straightforward. However, is this really the case? Work by Austin (1962) urges caution, for in that work Austin not only identifies a kind of declarative whose general function is not, despite literal usage, always to provide information. He also shows that in talking about these declaratives in terms of general functions alone, we should be missing crucial points about their literal, adult meanings.

To appreciate Austin's argument, consider first such ritualistic formulae as "I name this ship the Jolly Roger", "I pronounce you man and wife", "I sentence you to six months imprisonment", and "I dub thee Sir Francis". Not only would it take an enormous contortion of everyday thinking to describe these sentences as providing information, declarative though they undoubtedly are. It would also be wrong to think of them purely in terms of general functions. If the sentences are doing anything, they are performing the specific functions designated by their verbs, respectively, the acts of naming, marrying, sentencing, and conferring knighthood. Obviously, the sentences are not, in their own right, of enormous consequence, particularly from the developmental perspective adopted in this essay. By their very nature they will not figure prominently in the young child's experience. However, they are, as Austin realised, symptomatic of a wider phenomenon that is not so obviously irrelevant. Take verbs like "bet", "warn", "command", and "promise" and it will be easy to think of instances where the "I + verb + —" structure could be used naturally and non-ritualistically for a range of specific functions. Moreover, some of these everyday uses, say "I promise you some chocolate", "I warn you not to touch", and "I bet you a million pounds you can't reach that apple" do not seem in the least alien from the world of young children.

Unfortunately, there may, according to Austin, be more than ten thousand verbs that can be slotted into "I + verb —" structure, each with some impact on specific function. Austin used the term "performative" to characterise these verbs. Hence, the clauses they appear in are called, correspondingly, "performative clauses". In some cases, the performative clause will create a declarative, which, while having any one of the numerous specific functions, can still be characterised as providing information. In other cases, it will not, and *a priori*, there seems no reason to exclude either type from the young child's experience. Indeed, there seems no reason to restrict the specific functions associated with each type, meaning that we need to consider their consequences. More precisely, we need to imagine young children trying to interpret the functions from the context of usage, and the immediate conclusion seems to be failure to appreciate the specific ones. To see why, think of the contexts in which "I promise you some chocolate" and "I warn you not to touch" could occur plausibly. These contexts might, given their non-verbal properties, suggest the offer of some chocolate and the direction not to touch. However, why should they suggest a promise or a warning? Insofar as "I promise you" and "I warn you" are integral parts of the functions they perform, it is hard to see how contextual information could render their specific meanings. Thus, to express the point differently, contextual inference should lead to "I warn you/I suggest you/I entreat you (etc., etc.) —" being assigned some general behaviour directing function but not their specific nuances, making them, in effect, synonymous.

Encouragingly, this conclusion does not fly in the face of one of the recurrent themes of the chapter, that young children cannot observably misinterpret the speech they hear. Taking, say, "I warn you not to touch" as a general directive, children will either go ahead and touch or compliantly fail to touch. In both cases their behaviour would be perfectly compatible with the more specific interpretation that adults intend. Thus, there is nothing inconsistent in assuming a general analysis of performative clauses and there is, in fact, good reason (see Astington, 1988) for taking it for granted. Indeed, I myself can add anecdotal support, because my daughter Miriam, whose socialisation, I am afraid, involved a wide range of directive performatives, found fit to acquire just one of them. This was "I tell you —" which around the age of three, she not only transformed into "I tell what —" but also combined, to the point of tedium, with a large number of quasi-imperative structures. These included "I tell what sit there/go outside/get me some beenie (= Ribena)/buy me some sweeties". Interestingly, when her intention was non-performative, Miriam used the "I — you" structure with a wide range of verbs. Hence, her restricted use in performative contexts must surely suggest the presumption of synonymy as outlined above.

If this verdict on performatives can be taken as read it means that, consistent with adult convention, young children do not treat all literally used declaratives as providing information. However, in violation of adult convention, they do restrict all literally used declaratives to the general functions mentioned already. There are four of these functions—directing behaviour, asking for completion, asking for feedback and providing information—and, for brevity, let's call them DIR, ASK(C), ASK(F), and INF respectively. Taking them as the limits for declaratives means that they are also the limits for all well-formed English sentences, literal or non-literal, simple or complex until after the sentences have been specified. This means that we can now draw the straightforward conclusion about contextually completed meanings intimated earlier.

Indeed, bearing the limits in mind, and recalling what the chapter has established about supplementary non-literalness, indirect speech acts, and now performative clauses, we can also draw some conclusions about particular sentence–meaning relations. First, all the sentence modalities might, in certain circumstances, be assigned the DIR function: imperatives when used literally, interrogatives when used as indirect speech acts, and declaratives when used as indirect speech acts or with directive performatives. It is not the case that all the modalities could be assigned the ASK(C), ASK(F), and INF functions. Second, all the functions might, again in certain circumstances, be assigned to declaratives: DIR as intimated above, ASK(C) and ASK(F) with appropriate performatives, and INF with appropriate performatives or with literal non-performative usage. It is not the case that all the functions could be assigned to interrogatives and imperatives. These conclusions about contextually completed meanings constitute a departure from adult convention for there, thanks to supplementary non-literalness, every modality could be associated with every function. Whether this is a useful departure must wait on Chapter 3.

Some Conclusions on Specific Content

Clarification must also wait on further discussion of literally used declaratives because so far most of our discussion has been on the level of function. Declaratives also carry a specific content that under literal, non-performative usage, amounts to a topic and the information provided about that topic. It was mentioned earlier that from the responses very young children give we can infer that contextually completed meanings will contain the intended topic and some part of the intended information. However, will it contain every part? We have yet to see, but once we remember the verdict on imperatives and interrogatives we must surely say "No". Declaratives like "She danced", "She sang an aria", "She collapsed on stage", "She was carried by stretcher to the hospital", express behavioural roles, and they have already been excluded from contextually completed meanings. This suggests that when declaratives express such roles their contextually completed meanings will include (2.13).

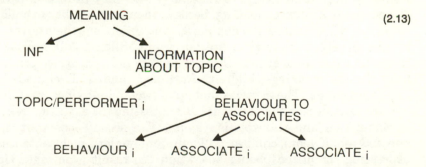

(2.13)

(2.13), it will be noticed, incorporates part of (2.6) and all of (2.12). It will not, however, be a universal feature of information providing meanings for, as with "That is a ball", "The ball is under the table", and

"A table is a piece of furniture", we can find instances where behavioural roles are not even being expressed. With "That is a —" sentences we can, in recalling the discussion of wh-interrogatives, anticipate a contextually completed meaning including (2.14).

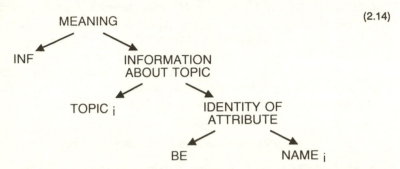

(2.14)

As children probably interpret phrases like "A piece of furniture", "A pair of shoes" and "A cup of tea" in a wholistic fashion, (2.14) would most likely feature in the contextually completed meanings of sentences like "A table is a piece of furniture". "The ball is under the table" would require a few changes to (2.14) but refer to the discussion of wh-interrogatives, and it will be clear what they would involve.

Thus, by bringing earlier points to bear, a great deal can be concluded about the informational content of declarative sentences. Yet a great deal might also be missed because, unlike the other modalities, the majority of declaratives contain auxiliaries and verb inflections. These auxiliaries and verb inflections mark a wide range of modal and temporal distinctions. Although the modal and temporal distinctions are implicit in the content of imperatives and interrogatives, their lack of explicit marking means we could easily have overlooked them. This would be unfortunate for two reasons. First, they are an important component of sentence meaning. Second, their accessibility to children who have still to master the auxiliaries and inflections themselves has, thanks largely to the work of Antinucci and Miller (1976), become the subject of widespread debate. Using observational data drawn primarily from Italian-speaking children, Antinucci and Miller made two important claims. The first was that up to two-and-a-half years children will see sentences in the past tense as expressing the aspectual relation of completion and this relation alone. The second was that up to two-and-a-half years, children will only contemplate such sentences as expressing completed phenomena when the result is in view. Up to two-and-a-half, Italian children will, remembering the discounting discussed in Chapter 1, scarcely even notice the auxiliaries and inflections in adult speech, let alone use them themselves. Thus,

Antinucci and Miller are clearly talking about meaning prior to mastery of the linguistic forms. The question is whether their claims are correct particularly, in the present context, when applied to English.

The claims have certainly attracted considerable research, yet much of the research is not really relevant First, it is mainly concerned with the modal and temporal notions that children express. As noted in the discussion of behavioural roles, the meanings children express cannot be assumed to correspond to the meanings they attribute to others. Second, the research focuses primarily on the notions children express once the auxiliaries and inflections have begun to be mastered. Nevertheless, despite these shortcomings, the research is probably adequate to reject the second of Antinucci and Miller's claims. The only apparent support appears in an experimental study by Bronckart and Sinclair (1973). Here French-speaking children of six years and under were thought to reserve the only past tense they consistently used, the passé composé, for completed phenomena with clear results. Yet even that supposition was not strictly true, for the passé composé was also used with enduring sounds. Moreover, the experimental procedure was such that even adults would probably have avoided the passé composé in the contexts where the children did this. Discounting Bronckart and Sinclair's study, the research has produced very little to support Antinucci and Miller's second claim and much to counter it. As Weist's (1986) review makes clear, children learning Turkish, Greek, Polish, Serbo-Croatian, Russian, Hebrew, Spanish, Japanese, Finnish, and, indeed, Italian and English treat sentences in the past tense as referring to events that either do not produce a result or whose result is not in view. Moreover, they will do this well before two-and-a-half years of age.

Rejecting Antinucci and Miller's second claim does not, however, entail rejecting their first, and as regards the first claim the research turns out to be reasonably encouraging. Both Smith (1980) and Weist (1986) have noted that children have considerable difficulty with sentences that, like "I went into labour last night" and "I started slimming two months ago", refer to actions that began in the past but are still ongoing. A specific example of this is the difficulty American children below about four have in producing (see Cromer, 1974, 1991) and processing (see Nussbaum & Naremore, 1975) sentences containing the "have been —ing" present perfect tense. As Cromer points out, the difficulty cannot be structural because American children use "have", "been" and "—ing" in other tenses long before the full present perfect. Thus, it more or less has to reflect the restriction of the present perfect in American usage to ongoing actions that began in the past, a conclusion that is strongly endorsed by Gathercole (1986). Noting Fletcher's (1981) observation that British children do not experience the equivalent difficulty, Gathercole demonstrates that British speakers are allowed to use the present perfect for completed actions so long as the completion was recent and/or the outcome salient. She then shows that the usage of the present perfect by British children aged three to six-and-a-half is tied to completed actions of precisely this kind. This being the case, Antinucci and Miller's first claim, that sentences in the past tense express completion, can surely be said to have some plausibility. For present purposes, I think that we should tentatively accept it.

Of course, if we accept that young children do see sentences in the past as describing completion, we are fairly constrained in our possibilities for sentences in the present and future. Essentially the implied unidimensionality leaves us with three alternatives: (i) no differentiation from sentences in the past tense; (ii) a two-way contrast between completed and not completed; and (iii) a three-way contrast between completed, in progress, and possible. It is my contention that studies by Harner (1976, 1980) and Herriott (1969) not only give overwhelming support to the third alternative but that they also show that it is sentences in the present tense which are associated with being in progress and sentences in the future which are associated with being possible. I hope that the authors would agree with me, though I should perhaps point out that these conclusions have not been drawn by the authors themselves. I think this is because they have not, by and large, related their data to the research mentioned in the previous paragraph. If they did this, I am fairly confident that they would be led to the same conclusion. Indeed, they would probably also be led there by Harner's (1976, 1982) and Sachs' (1983) observations that the future tense is more readily applied to the immediate than to the remote future, and Pea and Mawby's (1981), Shields' (1974), and Wells' (1979) observation that the modal auxiliaries have a predictive rather than a truth function during the first four years.

It is obvious that if we accept the above points we shall have a straightforward system in our contextually completed meanings that fuses the adult notions of temporality and modality. It is less obvious but nevertheless true that we shall also have a much simplified concept of negation. To see why consider "That could bite me" and "That might bite me", two English sentences that are salient to me because my daughter once used them almost ritualistically in response to pictured animals. For most speakers of English, they are virtually synonymous. Yet consider them with "not" inserted after "could" and "might". "That could not bite me" provides information that denies the affirmative but "That might not bite me" certainly does not do this. At least, it does not do this for adult speakers, but how about children? We can assume from research by Barrett (1979), Greenfield and Smith (1976), McShane

DECLARATIVE SENTENCES AND INFORMATION 73

(1980), and Pea (1982) that sentences with "not" are seen as negating from a very early stage, but what kind of negating? Surely, from points raised in the previous paragraph, we must assume that while the auxiliaries are still being mastered "That might not bite me" will be glossed as "That cannot possibly bite me". This, of course, gives it the conventional meaning of "That could not bite me".

This reduction of "might not" to "could not" also makes for the reduction of what modal logicians would call "external" denial to what they would call "internal", and I wonder if this is general with sentences that are not fully specified. It is certainly possible to think of other instances where the external interpretation is precluded and, as an example, consider "The target was not hit by many arrows" and "Many arrows did not hit the target". The sentences were discussed for quite different reasons by Jackendoff (1969), and the second is, for adults, an instance of external denial. Now take the perspective of a young child and imagine "The target was not hit by many arrows" being interpreted from its context of usage. For simplicity, imagine also that "target", "not", "hit", and "many arrows" are independently interpretable. In these circumstances, the sentence's meaning could, in principle, be constructed from the context. Now take "Many arrows did not hit the target" and imagine the same amount of pre-existing knowledge. If few arrows adhere to the target, how is the child to know from one context that the meaning does not preclude many? If many arrows adhere, how is the child to know that the meaning does not preclude few? It is impossible. The best that could be done is to assign the meaning conventionally associated with "The target was not hit by many arrows", implying once more the preclusion of external denial.

The Nature of Contextually Completed Meaning

Assuming that there is something general about the preclusion of external denial, the discussion of the preceding paragraphs implies some considerable simplification of adult meaning. Summarising adult meaning, polarity, that is the affirmative–negative distinction, interacts with modality, which in turn is independent of temporality. What the preceding paragraphs have suggested is that until the expressive devices are fully specified, modality and temporality will be fused into a single dimension, and this dimension will be orthogonal to polarity. Thinking what this implies for contextually completed meanings as a whole, flick back over the hierarchical diagrams that have appeared in the chapter, that is (2.4), (2.6), (2.9), (2.12), (2.13), and (2.14). Each of them shows that meaning comprises a function element and a content.

Each also shows that the content comprises a topic and/or performer element[3] and what is being predicated on that element. It is on this second level that polarity and modality will need representing implying, if we remember that the serial order is arbitrary, that something representable by (2.15) will appear in the contextually completed meaning of every English sentence.

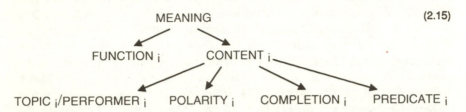

(2.15)

(2.15) is not, however, merely a "universal" of the meanings attributed to English sentences. Remembering the brief discussion of complex sentences it should be clear that, during the period when auxiliaries and verb inflections are being mastered, (2.15) should appear in the contextually completed meanings of every clause in an English sentence. This is important because, thanks to the restricted options for $FUNCTION_i$ and $COMPLETION_i$ relative to adult usage, it means that any clause of any sentence could be given a contextually completed interpretation that departs from adult intention. However, it is not just on the universal level that departures can occur. Reviewing the diagrams that have appeared in the chapter, it will be clear that the predicate is being assumed to comprise a behavioural or identificational element. This does not in itself diverge from adult convention but note that the behavioural element is being assumed to be unembellished or to be accompanied by one or more "associates". Note also that the identificational element is being assumed to take an associate or an attribute This concept of an "associate" is, as the chapter has emphasised, a departure from adult usage for adults differentiate a number of behavioural roles. Moreover, it is a departure that does not only have implications for the predicate. The topics of "Daddy's tea is cold" and "The tea on the tray is cold" are associated with elements in specific behavioural roles. However, it would be inconsistent to see these roles as contextually interpretable if we are assuming that associates are the limit for the predicate. If we are, we must assume the same for the topic.

Are we likely to be correct? I hope my own uncertainties came across when the issue was first discussed. As I tried to point out then, the limitation of contextually completed meanings to non-specific associates was motivated by a few encouraging studies in a sea of inconclusiveness.

How about other areas where the verdict on contextually completed meanings was departure from adult intention? Like non-specific associates, the decisions about completion and, as a corollary, polarity, were empirically based and thus limited by the current state of the art, and here again I hope my tentativeness was clear. With the functions, however, where the departure was in the small number of possible ones, the verdict was a logical consequence of the contextually-based method of completing sentence meaning. Here, then, there is hardly room for debate, impying of course that contextually completed meanings depart from adult intention to some degree at least. The only question is the extent of the departure and further studies along the lines implied by the chapter would be helpful. However, can such studies be expected? Surely only to the extent that the present conclusions bear interestingly on our underlying theme. This, it will be recalled, is whether children following the communicative process could formulate an observationally adequate grammar in a relatively short period without needing innate knowledge to help them. Drawing what conclusions we can about contextually completed meaning, we are now in a position to pursue the theme directly.

NOTES

1. The tree diagrams in this chapter and its successors will use upper-case letters to signify elements of meaning. When lexical items are represented in diagrams, it will be via lower-case letters.
2. As analysed by the randomisation test (Siegel, 1956).
3. From now on "topic and/or performer" will be abbreviated (without the intention of implying synonymy) to "topic/performer".

CHAPTER THREE

The Time-scale to Observational Adequacy

Underlying the discussion in Chapter 2 were three simple but undeniable facts. The first was that when young children experience adult sentences, their primary concern is to attribute meaning. The second was that the strategy young children use to make attributions to sentences that are beyond them is not direct questioning of the speaker but rather tacit inference from the context of usage. The third was that the use of contextually-based inference allows for the possibility of distortion in the meanings attributed, and it was this third fact which became the central theme of Chapter 2. It led to one overriding conclusion for English-speaking children, namely that no matter how it proceeds, contextual inference both allows distortion and in some cases actually entails it. In particular, it restricts the interpretation of each clause in an English sentence to a functional element and a content. It also limits the functions that can be attributed to four global elements. Contextual inference is not inherently restrictive as regards the internal structure of the content. However, it does allow for interpretations that are less discriminatory than adult convention, and Chapter 2 discussed this possibility at length, drawing two conclusions from the research as it stands. The first was that the content comprises a topic/performer element, a polarity element, a completion element, and a predicate. The second was that the predicate comprises a behavioural element plus optionally one or more associates or an identificational element plus an associate or attribute. The

77

topic/performer can also be linked with associates and/or attributes. If true (and the research was not deemed to be decisive) these conclusions mean that a significant proportion of English sentences stand to have contextually completed meanings which depart from conventional usage.

Faced with departure, numerous questions will spring to mind. For the present, there is, however, only one that needs pursuing, and this is the consequences for learning under what in Chapter 1 was termed the "communicative process". Under this process, children would attempt to store contextually completed meanings with their associated sentences to optimise the retrieval of the former as a function of the latter. As the nature of the store would depend partly on the input meanings, departure along the lines being considered would clearly have some consequences. What is unclear is whether the consequences would be beneficial and, if they would, whether they would be so beneficial that children following the communicative process could acquire an observationally adequate grammar of English in the time they normally take without needing innate knowledge to help them. There is only one way to shed some light, and it would be laborious. Essentially, it would involve imagining children following the communicative process without *a priori* knowledge, and asking where storage under the envisaged circumstances would lead. It became clear in Chapter 1 that, for a positive result, storage would have to lead relatively quickly to a system that not only generates all English sentences. To the extent that it fails to generate all and only, its sole overgeneralisations would be sentences that treat mutually exclusive rules as if they were alternatives. As Chapter 1 pointed out, such overgeneralisations could be corrected as children following the communicative process seek to constrain the options for expression that their system allows. Other overgeneralisations would require a form of negative feedback that, even under the most optimistic of Chapter 1's scenarios, could not occur. Thus, the conditions for a positive result are severely constrained, and the question is whether they are fulfilled. The aim of the present chapter is to discover what can be said by way of an answer.

To proceed, a further issue will have to be addressed, how children following the communicative process without *a priori* grammatical knowledge would actually learn. So far, little has been said on the issue, because claiming that children would specify sentences so that their meanings could be efficiently read off in the future is only a skeleton. We need some flesh, and the present chapter will start by trying to supply it. Essentially, the chapter will identify two approaches to language learning that have appeared in the literature and that might be construed as the detailed model we are seeking. Hence, it will discuss both at length. Its conclusion will be that despite appearances to the contrary, neither does, in fact, amount to the communicative process devoid of *a priori* knowledge. However, far from being disappointing, this conclusion should, if subsequent arguments are accepted, be the occasion for some relief. It turns out that when the implied processes stand a chance of fulfilling our conditions for observational adequacy to a reasonable time-scale, *a priori* knowledge has crept in inadvertently. When *a priori* knowledge is precluded, fulfilling the conditions is manifestly impossible. Yet in reaching the verdict, the chapter will not have gone round in a circle, for the shortcomings of the published approaches will not only have helped to clarify how children following the communicative process without *a priori* knowledge would really learn, they will also have pinpointed the facts about English most likely to inhibit an acceptable outcome. These facts will prove invaluable when, in its concluding section, the chapter will commit itself to an alternative model and attempt an evaluation of the likely result. The details of the approach to evaluation will become apparent as the chapter unfolds. Its conclusions can, however, be summarised quite briefly. They will be that, given that sentences are associated with the meanings we are supposing, observational adequacy in a reasonable time-scale cannot, for English, be denied.

ASSIMILATION TO EXTRALINGUISTIC STRUCTURES

With the finale in mind, let us return to the beginning and consider the two published approaches that are going to help us scene set. Of the approaches, the first is by far the best known to child language specialists. It postulates that, independently of their linguistic experiences, children elaborate structures by which they categorise reality. For illustration, let us imagine that one of these structures is analogous to (3.1).

(3.1)

When children subsequently encounter sentences that are challenging to them, they are supposed to access structures whose categories contain the elements of the contextually completed meanings. This implies that the structure in (3.1) would be accessed given experience with "The dog chased the cat". Having accessed a structure, children then, according to the approach, try to map the lexical items in the sentence on to the appropriate categories. Assuming they are successful, this would, in the case of our example, result in something like (3.2).

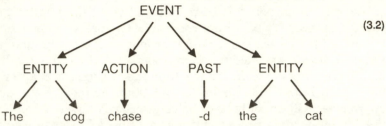

(3.2)

Finally, children are supposed to abstract what is specific to the elements in the mapping and express the remainder as grammatical rules that, given (3.2), should produce something along the lines of (3.3).

EVENT	- - - ➔	ENTITY + ACTION + PAST + ENTITY	(3.3)
ENTITY	- - - ➔	The + entity word	
ACTION	- - - ➔	action word	
PAST	- - - ➔	past marker	
Entity word	- - - ➔	{ dog / cat }	
Action word	- - - ➔	chase	
Past marker	- - - ➔	-d	

Clearly the essence of the approach is the "assimilation" of sentences to extralinguistic structures. Consequently I should like to refer to it as the "assimilation approach" for future discussion. However, it should be emphasised that this is my term and not the one employed by the vast number of researchers who, in one form or another, have espoused the approach. Indeed, amongst such researchers, the preferred label is the "cognitive theory" but I want to avoid this for one simple reason. It seems to miss the point that all theories concerned with grammatical knowledge must, in some sense, be "cognitive". Thus, taking the assimilation term as read, I shall start by explaining how the approach came to such prominence in the field of interest. Then, I shall discuss its consistency with observational adequacy in a reasonable time-scale, drawing a somewhat pessimistic conclusion. Finally, I shall ask whether the assimilation approach can really be regarded as the communicative process without *a priori* knowledge.

The Emergence of the Assimilation Approach

The assimilation approach can be viewed as an indirect consequence of studies by Braine (1963a), Brown and Fraser (1964), and Miller and Ervin (1964). Using longitudinal data recorded in more or less natural circumstances, these studies began by classifying the lexical items occurring in children's earliest combinatorial utterances by frequency and distribution. They identified two discrete classes. Nowadays, the first class is called the "pivot" class, following terminology originally employed by Braine. In terms of frequency, pivot items were those items that were few in number but frequent in usage. In terms of distribution they were those items that occupy fixed positions in combinatorial utterances and that never occur in isolation or in combination with each other. Pivot items were contrasted with items in the "open" class. Amounting to the class identified as "open" in Chapter 1, open items were those items that were numerous in quantity but low in frequency. They were those items that were not tied to particular positions in combinatorial utterances and that could occur in isolation and, in some cases, in combination with each other. As a concrete example of the pivot-open distinction, consider (3.4).

(Eileen (22.0) kisses her doll)   (3.4)

        Eileen: Bye

                       Oh. A baba. A baba

                       A man. A man

                       Baba. Daddy

                       Oh

                       Oh

                       A me

                       A me

                       Daddy

                       Chair

Within (3.4) and, indeed, throughout the forty minute recording it derives from, "A" was used with very high frequency. Moreover, it was always restricted to the first position of two-item strings. Thus "A" (which was pronounced like the vowel in "cat") would have been classed as a pivot. "A" was about three times as frequent as the second most frequent word. Of the remaining words, most were used less than five times. The five that were used with moderate frequency could appear in both single- and two-item utterances. Thus, all of Eileen's words apart from "A" would have been classed as open.

Faced with speech like Eileen's the validity of the pivot-open distinction as a classificatory device cannot be denied. At least, it cannot be denied for some children at some stages because, as Bloom (1970) and Bowerman (1973) have pointed out, there are other children for whom it never seems to fit. For the moment we can ignore these children. The crucial point is that faced with speech like Eileen's where the pivot-open distinction does fit, Braine (1963a) and his contemporaries would have argued for more than a classificatory device. They would have advocated grammatical rules along the lines of (3.5):

$$S \dashrightarrow \left\{ \begin{array}{l} P_1 + O \\ O + P_2 \\ O\ (+\ O) \end{array} \right\} \qquad (3.5)$$

The rules in (3.5) are essentially linear and this, for McNeill (1966), was their weakness. Using a complex series of arguments, McNeill tried to show that even those sentences describable by (3.5) must reflect grammatical rules, which are hierarchical in structure.

McNeill began by pointing out that children at the start of combinatorial speech occasionally produce three-item utterances. From an adult point of view, these utterances manifest two distinct surface structures: determiner plus noun or pronoun plus noun, and verb plus noun or pronoun plus noun. Examples with the first structure would include "Here my dolly" and "It man hat". Examples with the second would be "Draw pu'cat eyes" and "Comb baby hair". McNeill took it as self-evident that these utterances contain possessive noun phrases. Realising that possessive noun phrases required hierarchical derivation in all extant grammars, McNeill believed he had shown hierarchy at the very beginnings of combinatorial speech, and he proposed new rules accordingly. These rules would have produced the phrase markers in (3.6).

(3.6)

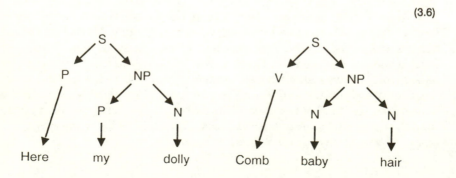

In these rules, McNeill is retaining the pivot class (P) but calling the open class (N) for nouns. This is because he felt few items apart from nouns appeared in the open class. Verbs (V) are specific to three-item utterances. Having presented these rules as both necessary and sufficient to represent three-item utterances, McNeill realised that he was faced with a paradox. Using the P and N terminology, he accepted that two-item utterances could be generated by $S \rightarrow P_1 + N$, $S \rightarrow N + P_2$ and $S \rightarrow N + N$. However, that would mean that P + N and N + N were governed by S in some contexts and NP in others. This would be most peculiar and McNeill resolved the dilemma by suggesting that all utterances are hierarchically derived, with items being optionally deleted to produce two- or even one-item utterances.

Bloom (1970) arrived at very similar conclusions, though contrary to McNeill she believed that the deletion mechanism (which she termed a "reduction transformation") was obligatory rather than optional. In the early 1970s, the case for and against obligatory deletion was hotly debated. Paradoxically, although Bloom had the worst of the argument, her work as a whole turned out to be the more influential. Unlike McNeill, Bloom was completely explicit about the procedures by which she moved from recorded utterances to underlying structures. Essentially these procedures involved four steps: (i) specifying the utterances' meanings when used by children; (ii) thinking of the utterances used with those meanings as part of well-formed sentences; (iii) seeing how those well-formed sentences would be derived by the version of transformational grammar popular at the time; and (iv) attributing children with knowledge of the grammar sufficient to produce the recorded utterances. The important point about the procedures was that they resulted in similar phrase markers being assigned to utterances whose putative meanings had much in common. Thus, the procedures led to similar phrase markers being assigned to "I fit", "Girl write", and "Mommy busy", utterances which, given Bloom's interpretations, were related in meaning. Because Bloom was completely explicit about her procedures, this consequence was apparent to all who read her. Hence it soon inspired other researchers to a more radical possibility than Bloom was proposing.

The version of transformational grammar that Bloom's work invoked was the one outlined by Chomsky (1965). Building on the ideas developed in Chomsky (1957), it deployed the categories that we encountered in Chapter 1—form classes like nouns, verbs, determiners, and auxiliaries dominated by phrasal categories like noun phrases and verb phrases. Such categories are defined purely by the distributional properties of lexical items/strings within sentences as a whole and are usually called "syntactic" categories. They imply phrase markers like

(3.7) for "I fit" with analogous solutions for "Girl write" and "Mommy busy".

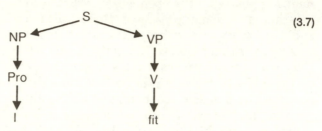

(3.7)

However, the fact that Bloom's work was attributing analogous phrase markers to meaning-related utterances led researchers like Bowerman (1973), Brown (1973), Edwards (1973), Kernan (1970), and Schlesinger (1971) to question the need for syntactic categories. Surely, they argued, the categories in very young children's phrase markers could reflect the meaning relation between utterances with, for example, ACTION replacing VP and "Action-Word" replacing V in the likes of (3.7). Having made the point, the researchers tried to formulate the grammars that, given meaning-based categories, young children must be using. Interestingly, despite differing in their child subjects, their empirical methods, and their analytic techniques, they came to very similar conclusions. They all, for example, envisaged ACTION/Action-Word categories and STATE/State-Word. Insofar as they discussed the issue at all, they also envisaged temporal categories similar to Chapter 2.

It must be stressed that in no sense did the work of Bowerman and her contemporaries establish the grammars they were presenting as real. At best they showed what the grammars would look like if meaning-based categories could be taken for granted. At worst they did not even do this, for the conception of children's meanings from which the categories were derived would be hard to square with everything in Chapter 2. In any event, the empirical status of the work was limited, but, despite the warnings of its authors, in the early 1970s this was hardly noticed. The consensus was sufficiently uplifting for some theorists to accept the grammars as real. Having done so, they were moved to contemplate the further question of how the grammars had originated. They were led by the work of Piaget (1955) to the assimilation approach with which we began. To see why, it should be noted that in his 1955 work Piaget argued that through extralinguistic interaction children build up structures for categorising reality. He was vague about the precise requirements of extralinguistic interaction, particularly over the need for intrinsically social experiences. Bruner (1975) and Lock (1980) have taken him to task on the point. He was, in my view, also vague about the precise nature of the categorising structures, but this view was not shared by the theorists we are considering. They saw in Piaget's work evidence for extralinguistically derived categories identical to the ones their grammars were using. They also saw evidence for the categories being structured in a fashion that was isomorphic to the putative phrase markers. From then on, convergence on the assimilation approach waited on two simple ideas: (i) contextually-completed meanings are used to access the categorising structures supposedly documented by Piaget; and (ii) once accessed, categorising structures provide pegs onto (and across) which lexical items are mapped. These ideas were not long in coming!

An Appraisal of the Initial Model

It is important to note that the version of the assimilation approach that appeared in the early 1970s, the first as we shall see, of a number, was always advanced as a hypothetical possibility. It is true, as mentioned above, that its proponents treated the parallels between grammatical and extralinguistic structures as proven facts. Nevertheless, even supposing this was justified, the parallels could not in their own right guarantee the developmental procedures that assimilation presumes, and this was widely recognised. Yet, it was also felt that the first assimilation model could not be precluded by data available at the time. Was this valid? Alas not. The first model cannot be reconciled with the one fact of concern to the chapter, the acquisition of an observationally adequate grammar in a relatively short period.

To appreciate why, note once more that the first model differentiated ACTION and STATE in both phrase markers and, by implication, extralinguistic structures. It also, when the issue was discussed, differentiated temporal categories along lines consistent with Chapter 2. Taken together, these points imply that a heterogeneous collection of strings would be mapped onto the categories in any given structure. To see this let us focus on the structures involving ACTION and note, first, that references to actions need not involve verbs. They can involve adjectives like "busy", "playful", and "fretful" and nouns like "departure", "arrival", and "donation". Having registered the point let us note, second, that references to actions in the presence of children almost certainly involve all three form classes. They definitely involve action verbs and action adjectives, for both have been recorded in children's own speech. Virtually all the studies cited earlier in the section carry reports of children using action verbs, and both Maratsos and Chalkley (1980) and Nelson (1976) have commented on the occurrence of action adjectives during the second and third years.

All in all then, we can safely assume that sooner or later children following the first assimilation model would be mapping sentences as varied as "The children danced", "The baby was fretful", and "The arrival was triumphant" onto structures involving ACTION. Recognising this let us now, for the sake of argument, imagine that the structures fix PAST after ACTION. In these circumstances the consequences of mapping would be along the lines of (3.8).

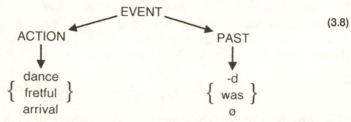

(3.8)

Thus the consequence of abstracting the specifics and expressing the remainder as rules would be phrase structure rules like (3.9) plus, of course, transformations that moved action words into the sentence positions of adjectives and nouns.

EVENT   - - - ➔   . . . . . . + ACTION + PAST + ...   (3.9)

ACTION   - - - ➔   Action word

PAST   - - - ➔   Past marker

Action word   - - - ➔   { dance fretful arrival }

Time marker   - - - ➔   { -d was ø }

The trouble with these rules is that they not only permit "... danced", "... was fretful", and "The arrival ..." but also "... arrivalled", "... was dance", and "The fretful ...". Moreover, these travesties would occur even if we fixed PAST after ACTION in the action structures or, alternatively, treated them as unfixed.

Thus, we seem to have hit on a serious problem. It amounts to the fact that, given what all advocates of the first assimilation approach would assume about extralinguistic structures, the outcome would be a grammar that overgeneralises to the extent of allowing every action word to operate as a noun, verb, or adjective. However, serious though it would be, the problem would not be insuperable in principle. The grammar would obviously provide children with a great deal of choice for the expression of any given action and, when choice exists, children following the communicative process would seek to constrain it. In their efforts to do this they could, as we have seen, rid themselves of overgeneralisations of the kind we are discussing. Accepting this as a matter of principle, the question is whether the problem could be solved in a reasonable time period. To see why the answer has to be negative, note first that every illegitimate noun, verb, and adjective would have to be explored separately and the time involved would, though finite, be mind-boggling. Probably no-one knows exactly how many action words feature in the English language, but it is clearly a lot. After all, recall Austin's (1962) estimate of over ten thousand performative verbs, and there are on the one hand many action verbs that cannot operate performatively and on the other, many action words that are not verbs. Hence, we are talking about an enormous number of "trials to learning". Making the implausible assumption that every overgeneralisation could be eliminated on a single trial, even one hundred thousand trials would seem a conservative estimate!

Moreover, these trials would only resolve the problem with actions. It is easy to see that all the points raised in the previous paragraphs with respect to action words apply equally to states. Superficially, expressing states seems to be the province of adjectives, but here, too, the reality is more complex. Some adjectives have verb equivalents and others have noun. Thus, there are close relations between, on the one hand "The road was icy" and "The road had iced up" and, on the other, "She was astoundingly beautiful" and "Her beauty was astounding". Given these relations, the first assimilation model would be condemned to a common underlying structure for state adjectives, verbs, and nouns. This would, once more, lead to extensive overgeneralisation and further hundreds of thousands of corrective exchanges. Indeed, the scale of the corrective task would be only part of the problem. To produce every illegitimate noun, verb, and adjective, children would have to know every legitimate one. I do not suppose any adult would claim exhaustive knowledge in this area, and certainly no child attains it by the time grammar is mastered. Thus, even if several hundred thousand exchanges were within the range of adult–child conversation, the relevant ones could not all take place during the appointed time period. Once we recognise this, I think we have to concede the basic point: in no circumstances could children following the first assimilation model attain observational adequacy in the time they normally do.

The Implications of Sentence Assimilation

Reviewing developments after the early 1970s, one is struck by a seeming paradox. Researchers who have stayed with the first assimilation model seem more aware of its problems than researchers who have abandoned it! Thus, Schlesinger (1981, 1982, 1988) is acutely aware of the difficulties, but something equivalent to the model still appears in his writings. The reason is that Schlesinger sees the model as an empirically plausible account of early development, and believes that a subsequent process, which (confusingly for us but perfectly reasonably) he calls "semantic assimilation" can take care of the problems. Semantic assimilation is the scrutiny of lexical items categorised by assimilation in our sense to see what meaning features they share with equivalently positioned items not so categorised. To the extent features are found, the category is broadened. Thus, items like "hit", "kick", and "push", previously categorised as "action", would be scrutinised for commonalities with items like "admire", "increase", and "vanish". This is because, being verbs, these items would be equivalently positioned. Arguing that all verbs have something in common, Schlesinger posits the eventual derivation of the verb category. It might be possible to accept his view if all action words were verbs but, as we have seen, they are not. The action-word category includes adjectives and nouns, and hence the logical conclusion of semantic assimilation would once more be the fusion of verbs, adjectives, and nouns. Indeed, as semantic assimilation from the state-word category would have identical consequences, the outcome would not simply be fusion. It would also be redundancy.

Schlesinger is not the only researcher trying to refine the first assimilation model into a viable system. However, as he is the only one to produce explicit proposals, no other work needs to be considered. Let us turn instead to the researchers who have abandoned the model, remembering the point raised above that this was not typically in response to the problem of time-scale. It was rather in response to the feeling that the first assimilation model's forebears had been mistaken about grammar. It will be remembered that before the assimilation approach had even been dreamed of, several researchers were making claims about the form of children's grammars, assuming meaning-based categories. Because these claims were more or less in agreement, they were quickly (and mistakenly) treated as established facts, leading indirectly to the assimilation approach itself. By the mid-1970s the true status of the claims was more willingly acknowledged, resulting in their eventual rescrutiny. With rescrutiny came the view that even if grammars with meaning-based categories could be assumed, their form would differ from what had previously been proposed. In particular, they would employ categories that were considerably more specific. The prime mover of this viewpoint was Braine (1976), but hints of similar thinking appear in Gentner (1975, 1978) and Greenfield and Smith (1976).

It might be imagined that the revised position would terminate the assimilation approach in any form. How, it might be asked, could grammar arise by assimilation when its categories were no longer the ones defined as isomorphic with extralinguistic concepts? In answer, it will be recalled that the original ideas about extralinguistic concepts were derived from the notoriously imprecise text of Piaget (1955). With time this imprecision was recognised, and new ideas about extralinguistic categories also emerged. These ideas not only allowed, but in some cases produced a revised assimilation model, whereby grammar resulted from the mapping of sentences onto extralinguistic structures of a more specific kind. Was this revised model any better than its predecessor? At first sight, it might seem so in that the increased specificity often involved the subcategorisation of the action and state classes that caused the difficulties. However, the subcategorisation was only to the extent of six or so groupings. Every grouping would undoubtedly contain some members expressible by verbs and others expressible by nouns and/or adjectives meaning that overgeneralisation would be as much a problem with the revised model as it was with the original. Moreover, the problem is not going to be solved by further tinkering for, as we have seen, specific actions and states can sometimes be expressed by verbs, nouns, and adjectives. Hence, we should need subcategorisation on an enormous scale to have a significant impact on the overgeneralisation. The trouble is that such subcategorisation could never be contemplated within the assimilation framework, for, Piagetian vagueness notwithstanding, the idea of an extralinguistic basis would be rendered absurd.

However, this does not necessarily mean that extreme subcategorisation should be ignored. In the final analysis we are concerned not with the assimilation approach *per se* but with its approximation to the communicative process devoid of *a priori* knowledge. All we know about the latter is that children following it would specify sentences so that their meanings can be efficiently retrieved. Thinking about this in the light of assimilation, there can surely be no better way of achieving it than mapping lexical items onto their meanings. However, the meanings we are contemplating terminate in individual elements, and not in categories. Hence, it looks as if children following the communicative process without *a priori* knowledge would do precisely what has not hitherto been considered— map lexical items onto highly specific structures. Indeed, insofar as they would form structures ending in individual elements rather than categories, they could be regarded as taking the subcategorisation mooted in the previous paragraph to its logical conclusion. Is this, then, what following the communicative process in the absence of *a priori* knowledge would amount to? If it is, children might avoid a grammar that treats every action and state word as a verb, adjective, and noun. However, they would end up with a grammar with other shortcomings. Recall that on the assimilation approach the mapping stage is followed by the abstraction of lexical items with specific content and the expression of the remainder in rules. With the mappings currently being contemplated, there will obviously be no items whose content is more specific than what appears in the structure. Hence, if rules are induced, they will simply describe the mappings. They will be vast in number and finite in product. As natural languages permit an infinite set of strings these rules will not, therefore, be consistent with observational adequacy on any time-scale.

In response to the problem, the first question is whether children following the communicative process without *a priori* knowledge would really induce rules in such an automatic fashion. Insofar as the rules will simply describe the mappings that have already been formulated, they will add nothing to the interpretability of sentences and probably lose something. As children following the communicative process without *a priori* knowledge are motivated solely by interpretive efficiency this surely implies a negative answer. However, interpretive efficiency will not, I think, involve children in storing the mappings in an unordered set. On the contrary, it will surely involve them in integrating newly formed mappings with existing ones to achieve the most parsimonious system possible. In the absence of detailed information about what the mappings would be like, it will be fruitless to discuss the integration in any detail. However, there is one obvious consequence, which probably bears mentioning. Over time children are clearly going to experience sentences whose contextually completed meanings have elements in common. After all, as Chapter 2 pointed out, these meanings will be restricted to four function elements and two polarities, and will probably be restricted to three completions, minute in relation to the total experience. Surely, on formulating a mapping whose elements are partially or wholly known, the desire for parsimony will, in the absence of *a priori* constraints, lead children to fuse the commonalities into single elements, and organise their modes of expression in as economical a fashion as is feasible. The fusion would not constitute a direct attempt at rule induction and hence would avoid the specific and unhelpful rules pinpointed above. However, because it would create a system that goes beyond its input mapping, the induction of rules by an indirect route would not be precluded. As the need for rules of some kind has been assumed from Chapter 1, this has to be welcome. However, whether rules would be induced in practice and how helpful their properties would be remains to be seen.

ACCOMMODATION TO SENTENTIAL PROPERTIES

Looking to the literature for clarification, we should almost certainly hit on the work of Anderson (1975, 1977, 1981). After all, Anderson presents two acquisition processes, both of which take sentences and what are assumed to be their contextually-completed meanings and both of which are initially devoid of grammar-specific knowledge. Using a complex set of procedures, which essentially accommodates the putative meanings to the sentences' properties, the processes create structures where lexical items are mapped onto meaning elements. The structures are then fused with others that are similar in form, meaning that in Anderson's work we have both mapping and fusion, procedures now established as crucial to our communicative process. Thus the work is clearly relevant and in this section we shall discuss it further. In doing so, we shall be covering ground that is fairly unfamiliar for, unlike the assimilation approach, Anderson's work has still to strike a chord with students of language. Maratsos (1982; Maratsos & Chalkley, 1980) and Stemmer (1987) may have derived inspiration from some of its claims, and it certainly shows parallels with the thinking of Braine (1976). By and large, however, it is not well known outside mainstream cognitive science. Nevertheless, it has much to offer, in terms of both clarifying ideas and analytical rigour, and its occupancy of a complete section will be more than warranted.

The Formulation of LAS

In his initial work with the accommodation approach, Anderson (1975, 1977) formulated a model that he called LAS (for Language Acquisition System). Despite its name, LAS was actually a general language processing programme that happened to include an acquisition component. This component was activated by sentences containing open class words whose meanings were known. Faced with a sentence of this kind, LAS would construct its meaning from the context of usage and identify its "topic/s", "predicate/s" and "main proposition". To appreciate what Anderson meant by these terms, note that in a sentence like "The square is above the small thing which is also circular", "The square" would indicate the topic, "is above the small thing" the predicate, and "The square is above the small thing" the main proposition. Armed with topics, predicates, and main proposition, LAS would construct a "prototype" structure. This prototype structure was assumed to be an hierarchical, tree-like arrangement reflecting what Anderson took as the form of the meaning. Having constructed a prototype structure, LAS would use it to "bracket" the sentence, rearranging elements at various levels in the hierarchy to match the relative positions of the lexical items that express them. LAS was given considerable freedom over this rearrangement, but there was one constraint. Rearrangement was not allowed to lead to "branches" in the tree-like structures crossing over each other. Thus, a legitimate bracketing for "The square is above the triangle" would, given Anderson's conception of contextually completed meaning, be something like (3.10), where the non-terminal nodes represent prototype elements and the terminal nodes represent lexical items.

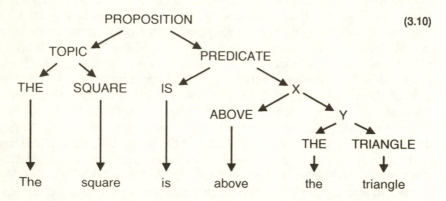

(3.10)

Given the bracketing, LAS would then check whether the sentence was compatible with its existing knowledge, making modifications in response to incompatibilities. To illustrate these modifications, suppose that at some early stage the model could cope only with "The triangle is red", perhaps using rules like in (3.11).[1]

MAIN PROPOSITION	- - - ➤	TOPIC + PREDICATE	(3.11)
TOPIC	- - - ➤	THE + TRIANGLE	
PREDICATE	- - - ➤	IS + RED	
THE	- - - ➤	the	
TRIANGLE	- - - ➤	triangle	
IS	- - - ➤	is	
RED	- - - ➤	red	

Encountering "The square is blue", it would recognise that "the square" like "the triangle" refers to the topic, and "is blue" like "is red" refers to the predicate. Hence it would make a simple modification along the lines of (3.12).

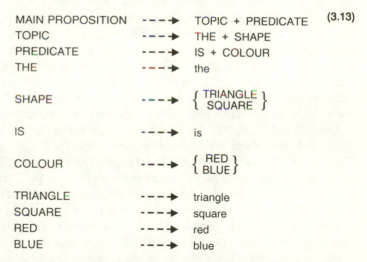

(3.12)

MAIN PROPOSITION - - - ➤ TOPIC + PREDICATE

TOPIC   - - - ➤ THE + { TRIANGLE }
                                        { SQUARE }

PREDICATE   - - - ➤ IS + { RED }
                                     { BLUE }

THE   - - - ➤ the
TRIANGLE   - - - ➤ triangle
SQUARE   - - - ➤ square
IS   - - - ➤ is
RED   - - - ➤ red
BLUE   - - - ➤ blue

However, the rules in (3.12) would only be temporary because LAS would assume that triangles and squares, on the one hand, and red and blue, on the other, share features of meaning. Hence, a more general solution would be found, perhaps like (3.13).

MAIN PROPOSITION - - - ➤ TOPIC + PREDICATE   (3.13)
TOPIC   - - - ➤ THE + SHAPE
PREDICATE   - - - ➤ IS + COLOUR
THE   - - - ➤ the

SHAPE   - - - ➤ { TRIANGLE }
                           { SQUARE   }

IS   - - - ➤ is

COLOUR   - - - ➤ { RED }
                           { BLUE }

TRIANGLE   - - - ➤ triangle
SQUARE   - - - ➤ square
RED   - - - ➤ red
BLUE   - - - ➤ blue

A sentence like "The triangle which is small is also red" would require more extensive modifications, but LAS was designed to cope. Essentially the bracketing underlying "The triangle + which is small" would be fused with the bracketing underlying "the triangle +∅" with extra rules being added to cope with the relative clause. Indeed, this is the principle behind LAS's response to any incompatibility. Two bracketings would be fused if their components are in one-to-one correspondence. Otherwise new rules would be added.

The Emergence of ALAS

What then would such mechanisms lead to? Anderson was himself quite optimistic when he (Anderson, 1975, 1977) asked the question. His reason was a series of computer simulations involving sentences from natural and not-so-natural languages. For one of these simulations he presented a string of English declaratives whose common function was to provide information about the properties and spatial relations of various shapes. Examples of these declaratives included "The square is red", "The circle is above the square", and "The blue circle is to the right of the red square". Confronted with them, LAS acquired a system that, to Anderson, implied the ability to converge on an "augmented transition network" grammar. Furthermore it did this in a relatively small number of trials and, at first sight, this is a very promising outcome. Augmented transition network grammars have been used extensively by researchers engaged in computer simulation. For present purposes, they can be regarded as a subclass of phrase structure grammars, though in both their terminology and their rule ordering, they are a far cry from the systems introduced in Chapter 1. They were pioneered by Woods (1970), and Winograd (1982) has compiled a useful summary of their subsequent development. As regards natural languages they are not observationally adequate grammars, being unable, amongst other things, to represent sentences like "Pinkie and Spicer purred and mewed respectively". However, augmented transition network grammars come close to observational adequacy and, should LAS be capable of achieving one in a restricted time period, it would be very impressive indeed.

Unfortunately, LAS's final resting place turns out to be something quite different from an augmented transition network grammar. As Pinker (1979) has pointed out, the suggestion of this kind of grammar was an illusion created by restrictions on the input sentences. The reality is nothing like so promising, for two basic reasons. The first stems from the constraint on crossing branches, for it leads to an unacceptable number of sentences being debarred from grammatical representation. The sentences include the likes of "Pinkie and Spicer purred and mewed respectively", which, as we have just seen, are also excluded from augmented transition network grammars. If it were only these sentences we might not have to worry, but it is not. As employed by LAS, the constraint on crossing branches precludes any sentence where non-adjacent items are related in meaning. In addition to examples like "The mother picked her baby up" and "The wolf blew the house down" where the particle is displaced from the verb, this would also prohibit any sentences involving auxiliaries before their subject noun phrases. Recalling Chapter 2, this would mean many of the interrogatives in the

English language. What is the solution? Subsequently Anderson (1981) showed that it would really be quite simple. Instead of excluding sentences whose bracketing would, on LAS, involve crossing, the trick is to derive a non-crossed representation and induce transformations to make constituent order recoverable. The outcome would no longer be an augmented transition network grammar. Nevertheless it would ensure that any sentence could be treated as input and it is adopted by Anderson in his 1981 work. In that work the process is now, hopefully not in desperation, renamed ALAS!

Returning, however, to LAS, there is a second problem relating to the manner in which bracketings are fused. To appreciate the problem, suppose we concentrate on the bracketing that on Anderson's conception of contextually completed meaning, LAS would produce for "The triangle is red". Recalling (3.11) it would obviously be something like (3.14).

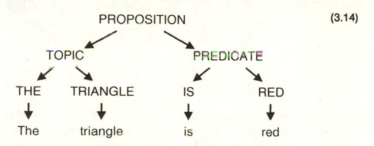

(3.14)

What other sentences would, on Anderson's conception, be bracketed in the same fashion? Undoubtedly "The square is blue", "That apple is round", "Our car is broken", "The dog is hungry", and "Their professor was brilliant", suggesting that under LAS's method of fusion, the eventual outcome might be (3.15).

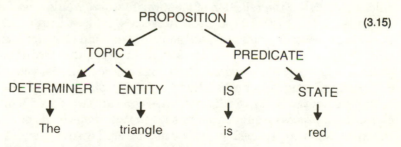

(3.15)

Certainly (3.15) looks like the eventual outcome if we restrict our attention to the sentences listed above. Unfortunately, however, "The guitarist was noisy", "The kitten was playful", and, ominously, "The baby was fretful" would, on Anderson's conception of contextually completed

meaning, also be given bracketings isomorphic with (3.14). Fusing
themwith (3.15) should lead not to a state category, but to something
more general. "Predicator" might be the best label consistent with
Anderson's terminology and yet expressing its all-embracing character.

Whatever we choose we must face the fact that it would not simply
appear at the rightmost extremity of (3.15). As we have already seen
verbs can also express both states and actions. Hence, the "predicator"-
designate category should also appear where indicated in (3.16).

(3.16)

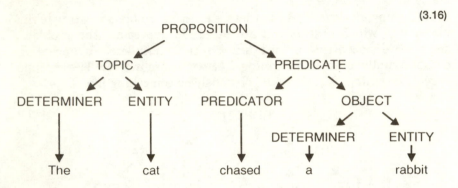

Hence, on LAS, every adjective and every verb should eventually be
characterised as a predicator, making them interchangable. The consequences of this should, from the previous section, be all too familiar:
horrendous overgeneralisation and little chance of easy recovery.

Coming to recognise this, Anderson made his later model, ALAS,
consolidate word-related rules rather than abstract meaning features.
To understand what this involves, let us return to "The triangle is red"
and "The square is blue". The revised process could still construct the
rules in (3.12) but the rejection of meaning features would eliminate the
progression to (3.13). Rather, the process would call up other rules
involving the words "triangle" and "square", and find of course that some
of the rules involved other words as well. In effect, this means that the
process would be confronted with two form classes: the class comprising
of "triangle" and "square", which we can call Σw_i and the class
comprising of the other words, which we can call Σw_j. Faced with these
classes, the process would check to see whether two-thirds of the rules
involving Σw_i also involve Σw_j. If they do, it would fuse Σw_i, and Σw_j into
a single class Σw_{i+j} and predict that the full set of rules applying to Σw_i
now apply to Σw_{i+j}. It would also predict that the rules that originally
applied only to Σw_j now apply to Σw_{i+j}. This clearly amounts to a very
different procedure and, as with LAS, Anderson subjected it to a series
of empirical tests. Once more, some of the tests involved computer

simulation, though this time the target "languages" included the auxiliary system of English together with fragments of Latin and French. The ensuing success seems far less sample-specific than with LAS, and yet should we cheer? It depends on whether children following the communicative process without *a priori* grammatical knowledge would operate like ALAS and so far we have not found out.

The Relevance of Accommodation

Taking an overall perspective it is clear that, *a priori* knowledge or not, our conception of the communicative process precludes ALAS for one very simple reason. Like LAS, ALAS forms bracketings and then checks their consistency with what it knows already. As emphasised from Chapter 1 onwards, learning on the communicative process is deemed to start with an attempt at interpreting meanings from sentence properties alone. Only when this fails will meanings be completed by contextual inference. Only when meanings are so completed will lexical items be mapped onto them, implying that following the communicative process involves checking sentences against what is known already before engaging in bracketing. Judged in terms of computational efficiency, this is a distinct plus for the communicative process. However, judged in terms of the consequences for grammar, it makes very little difference. Irrespective of whether a system brackets on every occasion or only in response to challenge, the overall form of its knowledge will remain the same. Much more significant are the procedures by which it forms knowledge and we need to consider whether in the case of ALAS these reflect the communicative process without *a priori* knowledge.

We already know that following the communicative process without *a priori* knowledge would involve mapping lexical items onto meaning elements and, certainly, as its bracketing procedures follow LAS in all but their transformation-inducing capacity, ALAS would claim to do this. However, can the claim be accepted? Glancing back at (3.10) and (3.14), it will be clear that Anderson's conception of contextually completed meaning departs from the present chapter's. Anderson is discounting function, polarity, and completion elements, but including determiner. The present chapter is doing the opposite with grounds that are surely reasonable. Thus, ALAS does not map lexical items onto the elements of contextually completed meanings because it probably mis-construes the latter. However, does it even map lexical items onto the elements of what it takes to be the contextually completed meanings? Surely only to the extent that the input meanings are treated as inviolable and superficially this seems not to be the case. True to its accommodative perspective, ALAS' primary concern is to reorder meaning elements so that they follow the lexical sequence. The only brake on this is the prohibition on the crossing of branches in bracketings. There, lexical items are reordered and transformations induced. On the face of it this seems to make meanings anything but inviolable and yet I should like to argue that here appearances are deceptive. The picture of contextually completed meanings that was painted in Chapter 2 and summarised early in the present chapter implies hierarchically ordered elements. However, as Chapter 2 pointed out on several occasions, serial order can in fact probably be denied. In which case treating meanings as inviolable is consistent with putting their elements in any order, as long as it avoids crossing branches in the hierarchical structure.

ALAS does not, however, put the elements in just any order. It selects the order that minimises the disruption to lexical positioning. As Slobin (1973) would put it, it "pays attention to the order of words". Would children following the communicative process without *a priori* knowledge minimise lexical disruption as well? Indeed, would they induce transformations when disruption is inevitable rather than the drop input along the lines of LAS? I think the answer to both questions must be affirmative. The basic goal of the communicative process, the ready retrieval of meanings from sentences, must demand maximal storage of whatever is meaningful and maximal recoverability of whatever is stored. This implies transformations rather than exclusion, and minimal disruption rather than more, and with this point comes an important consequence. As expressed by Anderson, the constraint on crossing branches and the transformation-inducing capacity seem like highly specific pieces of *a priori* knowledge. It is true that they need not be expressed as knowledge of grammar. However, they appear sufficiently specialised to create difficulties for the general learning theory that is our (and Anderson's [see Anderson, 1983]) ultimate goal. However, from points raised above, the specificity is more apparent than real. The constraint on crossing branches and the transformation-inducing capacity are logical consequences of an acquisition process that, on the one hand, treats the meanings we are imagining as inviolable and on the other, seeks to minimise both the disruption to lexical positioning and the exclusion of meaningful input.

Thus ALAS has some encouraging features, but is it really the process we are looking for? Continuing the assumption of ready retrievability beyond the input stage, children following our process would, as the previous section argued, fuse meaning elements that occur in several mappings. Considered from the perspective of ALAS this would seem to involve taking the prototype structures of input bracketings and calling up others that share meaning elements. Then an attempt would be made to align the identical elements remembering in the light of what has just been established to minimise the overall disruption to the lexical sequence while preserving the initial meaning. Finally, identical elements and, where possible, their modes of expression would be fused into a composite structure. Is this, then, what ALAS does? Clearly not. Both ALAS and LAS take their input bracketings as a whole and call up others that, regardless of elements, are equivalent in shape. Certainly they next integrate these bracketings into a composite structure. However, they make no attempt to guarantee that identical elements will be in equivalent positions. Given the shifting of elements during the formation of bracketings, it is almost certain that identical elements will not be in equivalent positions.

Because of this we cannot claim that ALAS reflects what children following the communicative process without *a priori* grammatical knowledge would do. However, does ALAS reflect what children following the process in these circumstances would do in all respects apart from fusion? Looking at the consolidation of word-related rules that follows fusion, it is hard to imagine that it does, and yet here again appearances are partially deceptive. To see why, suppose that the first sentence experienced by a child following the communicative process is "The dog is sleeping" and the second is "A dog is sleeping". Suppose for a moment that the child memorises the sentences exactly and knows precisely which items express each element. Post-mapping, we should have two structures with identical elements and nearly identical items. Thus, the structures would be fused along the lines described in the previous paragraph. Given our conception of contextually completed meaning, this would result in a composite structure that included (3.17).[2]

(3.17)

Suppose now that the third sentence to be experienced is "The cat is sleeping". Alignment and fusion of the identical elements would lead to a situation like (3.18).

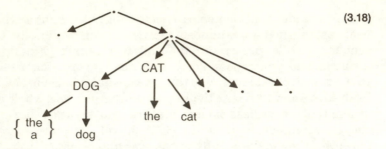

(3.18)

Is this what a child following our process in the absence of *a priori* knowledge would end up with? Surely not when, as intimated in the previous section, following the process implies integrating into the most parsimonious system possible. (3.19) presents an integrated structure that preserves the sentence-meaning relation of (3.18) but does so more elegantly.

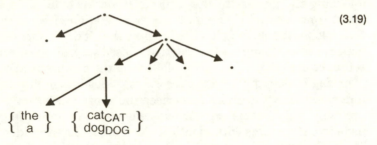

(3.19)

There is, in fact, no structure more elegant than (3.19) that would preserve the sentence-meaning relation. Hence, I think we can assume that a child following the communicative process in the absence of *a priori* knowledge would derive it. Funnily enough, in doing this the child would be engaging in a process of "context generalisation" similar to the one proposed by Braine (1963b). Its result, as Braine would of course recognise, would be a new expression for CAT, to wit "a cat" and in the present context this is what is relevant. After all, in allowing "cat" to appear in "a + —" from its substitutability for "dog" in "the + —" the child would, like ALAS, be consolidating on the basis of word relatedness.

Thus, there is similarity, but once more there is also difference. In the first place the consolidation envisaged in the previous paragraph would not follow ALAS in requiring substitutability in two-thirds of the possible contexts. Substitutability in one would be evidence enough. In the second the consolidation would only involve items dominated by equivalently positioned elements. Consolidations on ALAS would involve items dominated by non-equivalently positioned elements and this is surely necessary. Unless it takes place it is hard to see how the "cat" in "The cat is sleeping" would ever be placed in the same form class as the "cat" in "I've put the cat out". As ordinary speakers obviously do place them in the same form class this would be a major drawback. At least it would be a drawback if the communicative process is really debarred from consolidation across differently positioned elements. However, perhaps our piecemeal discussion has missed some crucial consequence that avoids this outcome. Perhaps it is a consequence that also avoids the objections that were raised about Braine's context generalisation (see Bever, Fodor, & Weskel, 1965). To find out, we shall have to consider the communicative process in total and I think we now know enough about it to make a serious attempt. This will be the subject of the section to follow.

THREE STAGES IN GRAMMAR LEARNING

To proceed, we need to take stock for, clearly, learning on the communicative process without *a priori* knowledge would involve children in a complex series of interlocking steps. Nevertheless, reviewing the previous sections, I think we can organise the steps into three broad "stages" by which the learning procedures can be characterised. The first would start when children take contextually completed meanings whose elements are hierarchically, but not serially, ordered. During this stage, children would try to identify the lexical items that express the elements, mapping the former onto the latter. Simultaneously, they would rearrange the meaning elements so that, without eclipsing the meaning, their order corresponds as closely as possible to the lexical sequence. During the second stage, children would call up their existing store of sentence-meaning mappings, scrutinising them for elements identical to those in the input. Within the constraints of preserving the meaning, they would align the input's elements with their equivalents in the store, fusing them into one. At the same time they would endeavour to minimise the disruption to the lexical sequence. During the third stage children would compare the lexical items associated with equivalently positioned elements, fusing the shared ones into single items. Accepting the stages, there is no need to see their sequence as immutably fixed. There is no need even to see them as sequential, though I fear for the intelligibility of discussing them in parallel! All that is being claimed is that given the communicative process without *a priori* knowledge of grammar, these stages would occur. Assuming that they would do, we can now proceed to our central question, whether children who followed them with the sentence-meaning input that Chapter 2 has led us to posit could achieve observational adequacy in a reasonable time period. As emphasised already, an affirmative answer would not only involve showing that the stages lead relatively quickly to a grammar that generates all the sentences of English, it would also require a demonstration that, to the extent the stages failed to generate all and only those sentences, the sole overgeneralisations would be sentences that treat mutually exclusive rules as alternatives. It is these conditions that will guide the section's discussion.

The Formation of Input Mappings

The meaning input that we have been led to posit consists of structures that are hierarchically but not serially ordered. This means that any given meaning can be conceptualised in several different ways. Thus, the diagrams in (3.20) present two of many possible conceptualisations of the meaning we should be assuming for "John offered Mary a drink" given that POS (for "Positive") represents the polarity element and PAST the completion.

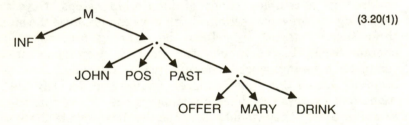

(3.20(1))

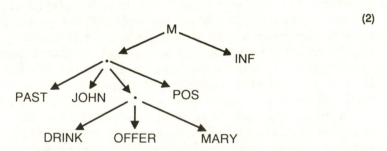

(2)

The indeterminacy in (3.20) is obviously going to be of consequence and we need to note it. Nevertheless, while doing so, we must not lose sight of the constancies for, far from being artifacts of the selected example, many represent what we have come to take as universal features of contextually completed meaning. The first constancy of this kind is the division of the topmost node into two branches. It reflects the fact that contextually completed meanings (M) are being assumed to comprise a function element (INF, ASK(F), ASK(C), or DIR) and a content. However, although the branching caused by the function element and the content is a constancy, it will not always occur in the straightforward fashion illustrated by (3.20). The existence of co-ordinated sentences like "John offered Mary a drink and she accepted/but she refused/because she was thirsty" would entail an optional level along the lines of (3.21).

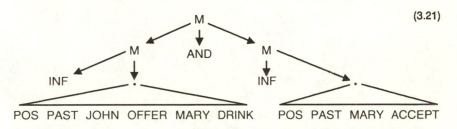

(3.21)

The second constancy that transcends (3.20) is the division of the content into four branches reflecting its constituents of topic/performer, polarity, completion, and predicate. There will be an enormous number of possible topic/performers and predicates. However, there will only be two possible polarities (POS plus NEG for "Negative") and three possible completions (PAST plus PROG for "In progress" and POSS for "Possible").

By way of contrast, we should note that certain features that appear in both halves of (3.20) would not be found in all meanings, and other features that do not appear in either half of (3.20) would be found in some meanings. With respect to the first point the predicates need not contain two associates. With sentences like "John offered Mary a drink during dinner" and "Mary carried the drink from the bar to her seat", they would contain more than two. With sentences like "John poured the drink" and "Mary accepted", they would contain less. It is noteworthy that sentences that lack predicate associates would have a two-tier structure rather than the three tiers of (3.20). With "Mary accepted" the lower tier would read MARY + POS + PAST + ACCEPT. With respect to the second of the two points noted above, consider the topic/performer and associate elements. They could be the unembellished items they appear in (3.20). However, noun phrases like "A friend of John's cousin", "My favourite aunt from Glasgow", and "John who owned a Porsche" would require more complex outcomes. The flexibility over serial order means once more that there are several ways of conceptualising these outcomes. However (3.22) presents some possibilities, taking the noun phrases as markers of topic/performers and remembering in the case of (3.22(3)) what Chapter 2 said about relative clauses:

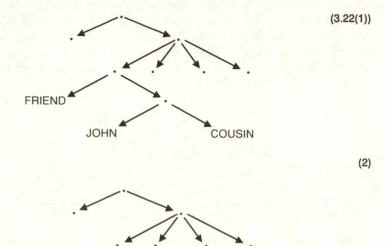

(3.22(1))

(2)

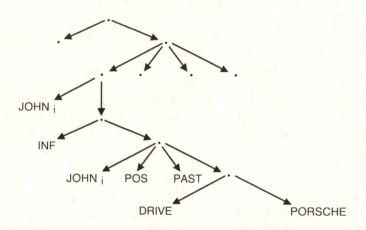

(3)

The expansions of the topic/performer and, by implication, associate elements exemplified by (3.22) are unfortunately not the only sources of complexity. Consider sentences like "Mary told John not to be sexist" and "John replied that his intentions were honourable" which involve verb phrase complements. Chapter Two also had something to say about their meanings. Its message was structures along the lines of (3.23).

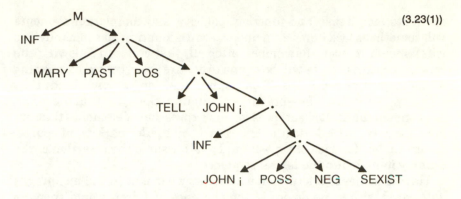

(3.23(1))

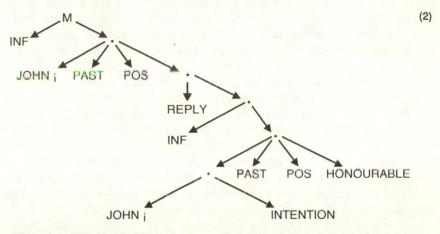

(2)

Faced with (3.23) we can begin to appreciate just how complex contextually completed meanings could be, even before the mapping into lexical items and examples of much greater intricacy could readily be produced. However, let us now take the point for granted and turn instead to the mapping procedure itself. As mentioned earlier, children following the communicative process would take each element and try to identify the lexical items that express it. In theory, they could select lexical items that turn out to be the wrong ones, but this seems unlikely in practice. The literature does contain examples of blatant element–item misassociations, as with Brown et al.'s (1969) Adam treating the copula in "it's" as a topicalising item. Nevertheless, such examples are rare, suggesting that lexical items are normally paired with appropriate elements. What does seem likely is that children fail to select lexical items when they are available for, as Chapter 1 pointed out, there is evidence of widespread discounting until as late as three years. When elements lack items (and function, polarity, and completion elements will sometimes lack items even under zero discounting), it seems obvious what should happen. Remember, after all, that children following the communicative process will be trying to ensure the retrieval of meaning as a function of sentences. This implies that, on the one hand, they should preserve the elements rather than drop them, and, on the other, they should mark the sentences for the expression of elements that are not associated with lexical items. How they would mark is, of course, uncertain but for ease of exposition, I shall assume the insertion of the dummy item $\emptyset$ into the lexical sequence.

Having achieved a situation where every element in the meaning is associated with some device in the sentence, children would then, as outlined earlier, try to align the elements with the items that express them. Remembering their policy of minimising the disruption to the lexical sequence, they would start, like ALAS, by attempting to shift the elements into the sequence (or one of the sequences) that corresponded most closely to the surface structure. However, they would not pursue this regardless. To preserve the meaning they would baulk at orders that violated the hierarchical structure. Their solutions would obviously depend on the accuracy with which they recall the actual input order, but here there are few grounds for anxiety. The work of Brown and Fraser (1964) that was cited in Chapter 1 suggests that children seldom distort the order of the items that they do remember. Follow-up work by Rodd and Braine (1971) and Slobin and Welsh (1973) largely confirms this. This means that as discounting itself diminishes, children will move to a situation where they would have to place the elements in an example like (3.20) in one of the six orders listed in (3.24).

INF + JOHN + POS + PAST + OFFER + MARY + DRINK   (3.24)
JOHN + POS + PAST + OFFER + MARY + DRINK + INF
INF + POS + JOHN + PAST + OFFER + MARY + DRINK
POS + JOHN + PAST + OFFER + MARY + DRINK + POS
INF + JOHN + PAST + OFFER + MARY + DRINK + POS
JOHN + PAST + OFFER + MARY + DRINK + POS + INF

Children following the communicative process would not put the elements in the order INF + JOHN + POS + OFFER + MARY + DRINK + PAST because this would move PAST two steps from its rightful expression instead of the possible one. They would not place them in the INF + JOHN + POS + OFFER + PAST + MARY + DRINK order because inserting an element between OFFER and MARY, which was not subordinate to the predicate, would violate the hierarchical structure. Of course, in avoiding the ... —OFFER + PAST + MARY— ... order, children would be avoiding the order that corresponds to the lexical sequence. Hence, they would be obliged to reposition the lexical items. However, to make the meaning recoverable as a function of the sentence, they would have to preserve the original sequence. To do this, they would have to introduce what can be construed as a dummy item in the initial position. They would, as intimated earlier, also have to formulate a primitive transformation that recorded the movement.

With the alignment of element–item pairings, children following the communicative process would probably feel ready to form their input mappings. To do this, they would obviously have to expand the elements so that there were branches for every relevant item. Then they could, quite simply, hang on the items. However, if they tried to do this they should periodically experience a number of difficulties. First, even assuming no errors in element–item pairings, they should sometimes find lexical items that lack meaning elements. From points raised in Chapter 2, these will include performative clauses. Faced with such items, it seems that children following the communicative process would be obliged to drop them. Second, children should sometimes find lexical items that express several elements. Instances of this are not hard to produce. Wh-phrases invariably mark both a function and either a topic/performer or an associate. Return to (3.23) and it will be clear that the "John" of "Mary told John not to be sexist" marks two meaning elements. Faced with such examples it is clear what children following the communicative process would not do. They would not drop one of the elements because that would preclude the meaning from being subsequently recovered. They would not duplicate the lexical items because that would create a different sentence and hence inhibit interpretation from the experienced sentence. What, then, would they do? In theory, there seem to be two further possibilities, represented with respect to "What did you say?" in (3.25).

(3.25(1))

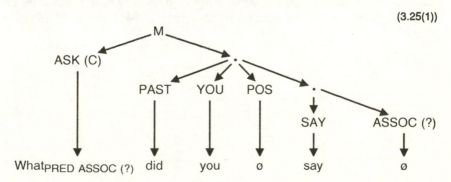

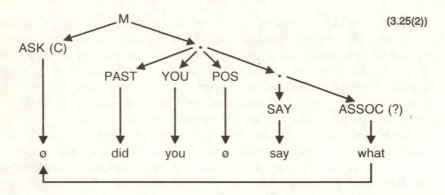

(3.25(1)) associates the problematic item with the element that reflects its sentence position and annotates it for the other one. The other element is marked with a dummy. (3.25(2)) associates the problematic item with the element that does not reflect its sentence position, and records the movement to ∅ with a primitive transformation. To decide which children following the communicative process would adopt, recall that their aim is to optimise the recovery of given meanings as a function of given sentences. It should be obvious that, with this in mind, they should plump for (3.25(1)).

Having dealt with items that are associated with more than one element, the section has probably said all that is necessary about the mechanics of mapping. Clearly what mapping would lead to at any point in time will depend on the proportion of sentential items that are remembered. However, because the items that are remembered seem seldom to be associated with erroneous elements or placed in erroneous orders, the mappings created by very young children will not be a distortion of what they subsequently produce. Rather, they will be a partial representation. As such, it seems reasonable to sum up the discussion by presenting (3.26) as mappings that would eventually be created given sentences related in meaning to "John offered Mary a drink".

(3.26(1))

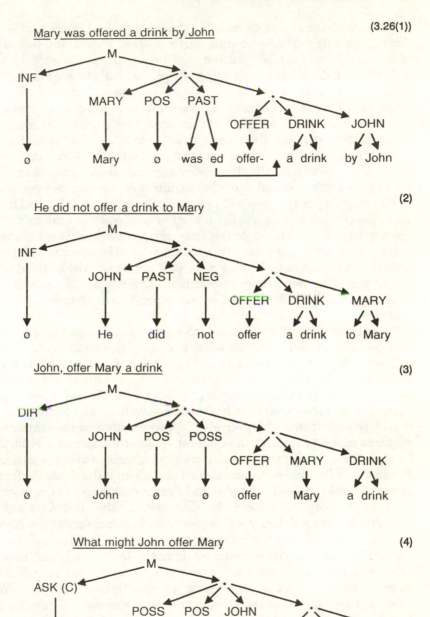

Mary was offered a drink by John

He did not offer a drink to Mary   (2)

John, offer Mary a drink   (3)

What might John offer Mary   (4)

Faced with the mappings in (3.26), the most obvious conclusion is that if children followed the communicative process they would formulate hierarchically and serially ordered structures that end in lexical items. This at least should be encouraging, given that our ultimate demand of the communicative process is consistency with observationally adequate grammar. Recalling Chapter 1, observational adequacy implies a grammar that produces phrase markers, and phrase markers are hierarchically and serially ordered structures that end in lexical items. Yet, while drawing some encouragement, we certainly need to be careful. First and foremost, all observationally adequate grammars will generate an infinite number of phrase markers. The number generated by the mapping procedures will always be finite, being delimited by the quantity of input sentences. In addition, the products of mapping will, despite their overall form, depart from phrase markers in a number of ways. Although usually serially ordered when the meaning elements map into lexical items, the mappings will not be serially ordered when the meaning elements map into dummies. Moreover, even when the order is fixed, it will not always correspond to conventional phrase markers.

To the linguistically untrained, the point about conventional order will be hard to verify. Perhaps the best way to appreciate it is with reference to the phrase markers presented for exemplification in Chapter 1. As Chapter 1 pointed out, those phrase markers are oversimplified by contemporary standards. Nevertheless, they contain many features that would still be deemed conventional. Looking at them it will be clear that, whatever else, approximation to conventionality requires concurrence with the Content → Topic/Performer + Polarity + Completion + Predicate order and, when predicate associates occur, the Predicate → Predicate + Associate order. Although the Topic/Performer element would be fixed in front of the Predicate, thanks to the vagaries of subject usage discussed in Chapter 2, the full Content → Topic/Performer + Polarity + Completion + Predicate order would only be obligatory with those literally used declaratives that lexicalise every element. As the Polarity element would not be lexicalised in affirmative sentences and the Completion would not be lexicalised in infinitival complements, this is by no means every literal declarative. With interrogatives and imperatives conventionality about the Polarity and Completion elements could never be guaranteed. Finally, with declaratives that, like "The wolf blew the house down" and "The mother picked her baby up", have particles separated from their verbs, Predicate → Associate + Predicate would be as likely as Predicate → Predicate + Associate. No doubt other examples could be given, but these should suffice to make the main point: the procedures by which input mappings are formed would not only permit departures from conventional phrase markers; in some cases, they would actually require them.

Because the mappings would be unfixed or unconventional, the transformational "postscripts" would also be far removed from mainstream linguistics. Indeed, they would also be far removed in being item specific for, as mentioned in Chapter 1, the practice has been to write transformations for lexical categories and not for individual examples. Nevertheless, when judged by the standards of mainstream linguistics, the transformations would have some promising features. As a consequence of their purpose, the transformations would apply after lexical insertion rather than before. An analogous claim appeared in such early sources as Chomsky (1957, 1965) but it was challenged by the "generative semanticists" of the late 1960s. For many generative semanticists, most notably the followers of McCawley (1968), lexical insertion was partly or wholly post-transformational. However, this was quickly found to create insuperable problems. Hence, although the generative semanticists highlighted many important facts about language, the grammars they produced proved short-lived (for details, see Newmeyer, 1986) and the original position on transformations is now generally accepted.

Where opinions have changed is over the contribution that transformations will make. Twenty years ago, transformations were all important. The grammars that inspired discussion were invariably of the transformational type. Moreover, within those grammars, transformations played an extremely significant role. Nowadays things have changed. The grammars of Kaplan and Bresnan (1982) and Gazdar et al. (1985) have been widely acclaimed and yet they avoid transformations altogether. Even grammars that, like Chomsky (1981), preserve transformations to some extent, now invoke them in a much diluted form. Thus it is gratifying to find that the mappings derived on the communicative process would also make modest demands of the transformational facility. As the linguistically expert may care to verify, the contexts in which transformations are derived mean they would be restricted to what Emonds (1976) has called the "local" variety, which, put crudely, means they are restricted to adjacent parts of the lexical string. Should the communicative process opt for transformations in situations where given items express several elements, the restriction to local transformations could not be claimed. However, I think the non-transformational, annotative solution has to be predicted and this is interesting on several counts. Not only does it warrant the notion of local transformations only, it also has much in common with the devices employed by Kaplan and Bresnan and Gazdar et al. to avoid transformations altogether. As we shall see, this is by no means the only similarity between the communicative process and the work of those authors.

The Integration of Meaning Elements

Thus, we clearly have some grounds for optimism. The question is whether we can sustain them during the second stage of the learning procedures, and yet deal with the undeniable problems. This stage would, as intimated earlier, start by calling up the existing stock of sentence-meaning mappings. The stock would then be scrutinised for elements identical to those in the input. Assuming identical elements were found, the next step would be an attempt at aligning the elements in the new mappings with their equivalents in the old. Returning to (3.26(1)) this would mean trying to align the INF element with the existing INFs and the MARY-as-TOPIC element with the existing MARY'S-as-TOPIC. Thinking of the meanings already discussed, it should be clear that alignment would pose no threat either to the meaning structure or to the lexical mappings so long as both the new and the old mappings were restricted to, at most, one function element, one topic/performer, one polarity, one completion, one predicate, one associate or attribute of the topic/performer, and one associate or attribute of the predicate. Hence, we can assume that in these circumstances alignment would proceed, allowing the final step in the second stage, the fusion of identical elements.

One important consequence of these integrative procedures is that even when restricted to mappings containing one of the various types of element, the logical conclusion would be structures in which all topic/performers and all predicates have a two-tier structure. Glancing back over the section, this will seem counterintuitive. Few of the input mappings had a two-tier topic/performer structure, and the two-tier predicate structure looks decidedly optional. Nevertheless, I think the claim is valid and, to see why, imagine the mappings in (3.27) being integrated according to the procedures outlined earlier.

(3.27(1))

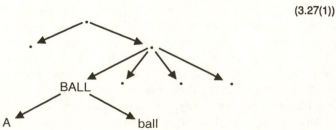

(3.27(2))

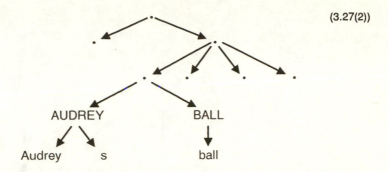

AUDREY   BALL

Audrey   s   ball

Taking (3.27(1)) as the existing knowledge and (3.27(2)) as the input we would, of course, find that they had an element in common, namely BALL-as-TOPIC. To integrate the shared elements we should, however, be forced to add a node above the BALL in (3.27(1)) meaning that as an eventual consequence of integration, no noun phrase should be dominated by a single topic/performer. At the input stage, the topic/performers expressed by "A ball", "The girl", "Those dolls", "The girl", "John Smith", and "Cups of tea" would involve a single tier. However, it would only require integration with mappings involving one associate or attribute to dispense with this.

Moreover, given the consequences with the topic/performer element we can see an analogous situation for the predicate. Even though a predicate without associates such as "— opened" would lead to a mapping including (3.28(1)) at the input stage, integration with a predicate with associates such as "— opened the door" would produce a structure like (3.28(2)) implying the introduction of a further level into the eventual structure.

(3.28(1))

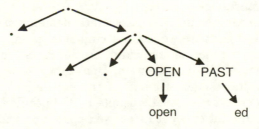

OPEN   PAST

open   ed

(3.28(2))

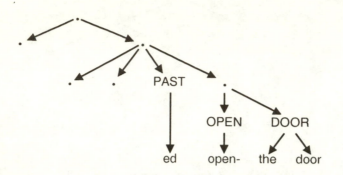

Thus, extrapolating more generally, we can claim that every English sentence should, through integration, move to being mapped onto a structure like (3.29).

(3.29)

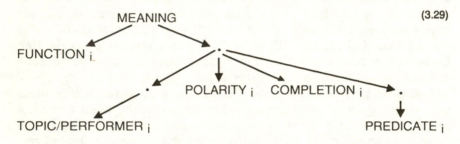

With some sentences the postintegration mappings would not simply include (3.29); they would be (3.29). With other sentences, particularly those whose meanings include associates or attributes, there would be additional nodes. Indeed, we should perhaps note that because noun phrases like "The dog in the basket's dinner" imply associates of associates, the logical conclusion of integration should also be two-tier associate structures.

Mention of meanings involving associate elements should, however, signal a problem. Suppose we had a string of mappings containing an ever-increasing number of associate elements, all of which were identical. This would be the case with "Democracy is government of the people", "Democracy is government of the people by the people" and "Democracy is government of the people by the people for the people". Following the integration procedures, we might expect the associates to be compressed onto a single node. Certainly, we might expect this until we remember that our communicative process is constrained to preserve input meanings. There is no way in which this could be achieved if elements attached to the same superordinate node were superimposed.

As attachment to the same superordinate would always be the case given multiple associates and single functions, topic/performers, polarities, completions, and predicates, we can assume that children following the process would balk at associate compression in these circumstances.

However, suppose we relax the single function, etc. requirement and, by dint of this, permit the meanings expressed by sentences with subordinate clauses. Return briefly to (3.22(3)) or (3.23) and it will be clear that here we could have identical elements attached to different superordinates. So long as the superordinate of one element is subordinate to the superordinate of the other/s it would be possible to compress them onto a single node and ensure the recoverability of the input meaning. The trick? To move from a figurative representation to a rule-bound one. An example will make matters clearer, so imagine (3.22(3)) ordered as required by "John who owned a Porsche offered Mary a drink". In these circumstances rules like (3.30) would constitute a representation that both integrated identical elements and yet preserved input meanings.

(3.30)

M $- - - \rightarrow$ INF + CONTENT

CONTENT $- - - \rightarrow$ TOPIC/PERFORMER + POS + PAST + PREDICATE

TOPIC/PERFORMER $- - - \rightarrow$ JOHN + (M)

PREDICATE $- - - \rightarrow$ $\left\{ \begin{array}{l} \text{OFFER + MARY + DRINK} \\ \text{OWN + PORSCHE} \end{array} \right\}$

The rules in (3.30) are not the only possible solution. However, the alternatives would still imply rules, just rules of a different kind. Moreover, the rules would, of necessity, preserve an important feature of (3.30), to wit their recursiveness. Within linguistics, recursion is said to occur when one rule produces a node to which another rule can apply, and the second rule leads to a node to which the first can be reapplied. As the third rule in (3.30) produces the M node to which the first rule applies, and the first rule indirectly generates the third, we are clearly confronted with a recursive set-up, and this is quite important. Recursive rules can apply indefinitely, producing sentences that are indefinitely long and hence infinite in number. Thus, although the input mappings would be finite in number, the result of fusing their elements would be an open-ended system.

Recognising that one of the problems identified in our discussion of mapping would thereby be overcome, let us turn to the others. Let us consider in particular whether element integration would impose a more conventional ordering on individual mappings. To see that it would, we must recall that the integration procedures would be constrained not only by meaning recoverability but also by the lexical items whose sequence children following the communicative process would strive to preserve. This would have a number of consequences, all of which would contribute to a positive outcome. To appreciate the first we should note that given identical but differently positioned elements, some of which dominate lexical items and some of which dominate dummies, a process striving to minimise lexical disruption should move the latter during alignment rather than the former. Look closely at the function elements that appear in (3.26). They illustrate a point that actually applies generally, namely that whenever the function elements of input mappings dominate lexical items as opposed to dummies, they will be fixed in the clause-initial position. What this means is that the demands of preserving the lexical sequence during element integration must lead to all function elements being shifted into the clause-initial position. Thus, by virtue of the "minimal disruption principle", there should be gradual convergence on the Meaning → Function + Content order.

In addition, we should note that it is not just dummy items which would produce optionality over ordering. When lexical items governed by single elements are separated by other items (as, remember, with "The wolf blew the house down"), there could also be several permissible orders. Now, suppose we have a set of mappings, some of whose elements are, by our criteria, optionally ordered and others of whose elements are obligatorily ordered. Following the minimal disruption principle, it would be the former and not the latter which should be re-ordered (and, of course, appended with recovery transformations) allowing us to solve one or two of the specific problems identified earlier. In particular, the Content → Completion + Topic/Performer + — ordering should disappear where it is optional for interrogatives, as for example with "Why have you opened the window?". The Predicate → Associate + Predicate + — ordering should disappear with particled verbs, meaning that a "particle movement" transformation that created "Pick Jeremy up" from "Pick up Jeremy" would no longer be optional but required.

So far so good, but what would allow us to dispense with unconventional orderings when they are obligatory in individual structures? To ensure the universality of the Content → Topic/Performer + Completion + Predicate order, we need only note that English grammar would permit the three completion elements to dominate up to four auxiliaries (AUX) and inflections (INFL), and that these auxiliaries and inflections can lie in the sequences indicated in (3.31).

AUX	NP	V				e.g. Shall we dance?
NP	AUX	V				e.g. We shall dance
NP	V	INFL				e.g. We danced
AUX	NP	V	INFL			e.g. Have we danced?
NP	AUX	V	INFL			e.g. We are dancing
AUX	NP	AUX	V	INFL		e.g. Shall we have danced?
NP	AUX	AUX	V	INFL		e.g. We have been dancing
AUX	NP	AUX	AUX	V	INFL	e.g. Could we have been dancing
NP	AUX	AUX	AUX	V	INFL	e.g. We may have been dancing

Take the sequences separately and work out the ordering of the completion, topic/performer, and predicate elements that each would be mapped onto. Then think of the mappings being aligned one by one in a fashion that concurred with the minimal disruption principle. It should be clear that the outcome will be Topic/Performer + Completion + Predicate, with the consequence of an obligatory AUX-movement transformation to make the ordering of yes/no-interrogatives recoverable.

Indeed, as Topic/Performer + Completion + Predicate would be the logical conclusion when Completion is marked lexically, it would also be the logical conclusion when, as with imperatives and infinitival complements, it is not. This solves another of the problems. Indeed, once completion is fixed relative to topic/performer and predicate, polarity must be slotted between topic/performer and completion. To see why, just supplement the sequences of (3.31) with the negative items that realise polarity. Thus, we seem to have dealt with each of the difficulties mentioned earlier. In principle there could, I suppose, be difficulties not mentioned earlier, which are not so satisfactorily resolved. However, at the time of writing, I cannot imagine what they might be, allowing, perhaps, for one positive conclusion. Stated baldly, it would be that integrating meaning elements while ensuring the efficient recovery of input mappings should lead eventually to rules that were not simply recursive. They would also order lexical items in the style of conventional phrase markers.

However, while the order might be conventional for phrase markers it would not correspond to standard English, and recovery transformations would still be needed. During integration these transformations could undergo two changes, the first relating to their form. After all, given a shift to rules, the transformations could no longer be specified as appendages to mappings. Nevertheless, like the appendages, they would still be restricted to specific lexical movements, suggesting that after rule formulation they would be specified along the lines of ed + offer $\rightarrow$ + offer + ed. The second change would relate to content for, as hinted earlier, the effect of integration would be to make obligatory transformations that were previously optional. Thus, postintegration, there would be a shift towards obligatory AUX and particle movement transformations instead of the optional ones achievable during mapping. On the other hand, the growing obligatoriness would be the only content change to result from integration, meaning that the point raised earlier about the restriction to "local" transformations would still hold good. As the logical conclusion of meaning element integration would, on the communicative process, determine the eventual pretransformational lexical sequence, this restriction to "local" transformations can, even now, be stated as a final result. We can wait until Chapter 4 to discuss whether the restriction is a better result than one that, on the one hand, had non-local transformations and, on the other, avoided transformations altogether. For now, we can simply be encouraged by the potential derivation of something contemporary linguists would recognise.

Overall then, the second stage of learning should, given the communicative process without *a priori* knowledge, have several welcome results. It would not have the results immediately. Indeed, the time it would take would be lengthened by the fact that input mappings would gradually converge on the likes of (3.26) rather than resemble them from the start. Nevertheless, its results would be real, and this must be encouraging. However, the encouragement should not be taken too far because the second stage of learning would also have a very worrying consequence, which needs to be noted. The recursive rules that the stage would lead to would never, no matter how many sentences were experienced, be accurately described as "phrase structure". To see why not, note that the rules resulting from the integration of meaning elements must gradually come to include (3.32).

As defined in Chapter 1, phrase structure rules translate categories either into further categories or into lexical items. From (3.32) it should be clear that the rules attainable during our second stage would translate categories into elements as well as further categories. Moreover, they would never translate categories into lexical items, this being the prerogative of elements alone. Thus, on two counts, the rules in (3.32) depart from phrase structuredness and since, as Chapter 1 emphasised, phrase structure rules are a prerequisite for observationally adequate grammar, this is a serious problem. However, it is not necessarily decisive because the second stage of our learning procedures would, as intimated earlier, be followed by a third, and judgement must be reserved until this has been considered.

(3.32)

$$\text{MEANING} \dashrightarrow \left\{ \begin{array}{c} \text{DIR} \\ \text{ASK (C)} \\ \text{ASK (F)} \\ \text{INF} \end{array} \right\} + \text{CONTENT}$$

$$\text{CONTENT} \dashrightarrow \text{TOPIC/PERFORMER} + \left\{ \begin{array}{c} \text{POS} \\ \text{NEG} \end{array} \right\} + \left\{ \begin{array}{c} \text{POSS} \\ \text{PROG} \\ \text{PAST} \end{array} \right\} + \text{PREDICATE}$$

$$\text{TOPIC/PERFORMER} \dashrightarrow (\text{-----}) + \left\{ \begin{array}{c} \text{AARDVARK} \\ \cdot \\ \cdot \\ \cdot \\ \text{ZOOLOGY} \end{array} \right\} + (\text{-----})$$

$$\text{AARDVARK} \dashrightarrow \left\{ \begin{array}{c} \text{the aardvark} \\ \text{an aardvark} \\ \text{aardvarks} \\ \cdot \end{array} \right\}$$

The Fusion of Lexical Items

The third stage would begin with children looking at the lexical items associated with, on the one hand the identical elements they fused in the second stage, and on the other the equivalently positioned but non-identical elements they did not fuse. To the extent that the lexical items have something in common they too would be fused, and to see where this would lead let us start with the items associated with identical (and now fused) elements. Let us take a concrete example, say, SPICER used as a topic. In this guise SPICER might, in theory, be expressed by "the cat", "our cat", "Spicer", "old puss", "Pinkie's twin", "he", and "that animal". Focusing on the first three expressions, integrating their commonalities should lead to a tightening of the rules along the lines of (3.33).

(3.33)

$$\text{SPICER} \dashrightarrow \left\{ \begin{array}{c} \left\{ \begin{array}{c} \text{the} \\ \text{our} \end{array} \right\} + \text{cat} \\ \text{Spicer} \end{array} \right\}$$

It is not hard to see how the expansion of SPICER could soon become exceedingly complex, yet over time there should be one favourable consequence. This is the eventual sorting of the items into the noun phrase form classes. This is no mean feat for, as Jackendoff (1977) has most tellingly illustrated, noun phrases are extremely heterogeneous entities. To appreciate this, note that although "the cat", "that cat", "my cat", and "murderous cat" suggest a simple "— + noun" format, the possibility of "that brute of a cat" and "the dimmest cat in the world" means that we actually require something much less straightforward. Nevertheless, an adequate solution is attainable given the operations of our process.

Moreover, if the operations mean this for SPICER, they must obviously mean it for any other topic/performer. Indeed, they must also mean something equivalent for the form classes dominated by the other types of element, the auxiliaries, and inflections dominated by the completions, the verbs and dummies dominated by the predicates and the vagaries of prepositional and possessive phrase dominated by the associates. Note, however, that all this sorting, welcome though it would be, is element specific. Thus, SPICER would eventually have his proper form classes, as would PINKIE, and as would every other topic/performer. However, there would be no integration across elements involving the continuation of both element-specific rules and, as a corollary, rules that translate categories into either categories or elements. Thus, returning to the initial problem, integrating the lexical items associated with identical elements would not lead to the phrase structure rules that, for approximation to observational adequacy, we must eventually derive.

How about integrating lexical items associated with equivalently positioned but non-identical elements? As mentioned above, children following the communicative process would be expected to attempt this, so would it allow for more acceptable results? It is difficult to be hopeful when, at the early stages of learning, the equivalently positioned but non-identical elements would not necessarily be of the same type. After all, a topic could be cast by alignment into the same position as a completion. A predicate could be cast into the same position as an associate. If this happens, there would be no overlap in modes of expression and hence no opportunities for lexical integration. This may protect children from bizarre lexical classes but it would take us no nearer a phrase structure system. Fortunately over time (and as a consequence of the shift to conventionally ordered mappings) the tendency would be for equivalently positioned elements to be of the same type. Here, there could be overlap in modes of expression, and hence integration could ensue. Our discussion of ALAS has already considered what such integration would lead to. The conclusion of that discussion amounted to the claim that if the mapping underpinning "The dog is outside" was integrated with the mappings underpinning "The/a/this/that ball is outside", the outcome would, on the communicative process, be (3.34(2)) and not (3.34(1)).

The most obvious point about (3.34(2)), which was commented on while discussing ALAS, is that integrating "the dog" with "the ball" would result in "a + —", "this + —" and "that + —" previously only associated with "ball" being extended to "dog". This result shows that even if it was unfettered by *a priori* knowledge, the communicative process would lead to the noun phrase form classes being integrated across all topic/performer elements, the auxiliary and inflection form classes being integrated across all completion elements and so on for the other classes. This, clearly, is excellent, but it is not the only conclusion to be drawn from (3.34(2)). There is a further point that was not brought out earlier but that in the present context is arguably more significant. This is the abstraction of the specific elements. Repeated over the function, completion, predicate, and associate nodes, it would mean the gradual removal of all non-categorial features from the mappings and by implication the rules that generate them. With rules that translate categories into categories or lexical items, we should have achieved phrase structuredness.

What, then, would the rules be like? Looking at (3.34(2)) it might seem as if they should include (3.35).

(3.34(1))

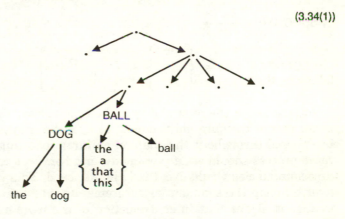

(2)

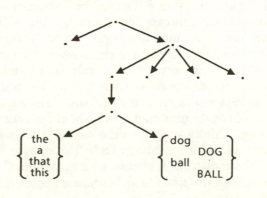

MEANING ---→ FUNCTION + CONTENT (3.35)

CONTENT ---→ + TOPIC/PERFORMER' + ...

TOPIC/PERFORMER' ---→ .... + TOPIC/PERFORMER + ...

$$\text{TOPIC/PERFORMER} \ \text{---→} \ \left\{\begin{array}{c} \text{the} \\ \text{a} \\ \text{that} \\ \text{this} \end{array}\right\} + \left\{\begin{array}{c} \text{dog} \\ \text{ball} \end{array} \ \begin{array}{c} \text{DOG} \\ \\ \text{BALL} \end{array}\right\}$$

If rules including (3.35) are implied by (3.34(2)), rules including (3.36) must be implied by "I kicked the ball/the dog".

MEANING ---→ FUNCTION + CONTENT (3.36)

CONTENT ---→ .... + PREDICATE'

PREDICATE' ---→ PREDICATE + ASSOCIATE'$_1$ + ...

ASSOCIATE'$_1$ ---→ .... + ASSOCIATE$_1$ + ...

$$\text{ASSOCIATE}_1 \ \text{---→} \ \left\{\begin{array}{c} \text{the} \\ \text{a} \end{array}\right\} + \left\{\begin{array}{c} \text{dog} \\ \text{ball} \end{array} \ \begin{array}{c} \text{DOG} \\ \\ \text{BALL} \end{array}\right\}$$

Note, however, the redundancy in the final rules of (3.35) and (3.36), meaning that they are not the most parsimonious system achievable. As stressed throughout the chapter, children following the communicative process should want parsimony, and hence we can assume that the redundancies would eventually be removed. This would obviously involve fusing the common lexical items, an interesting development because it means that in contradiction of the fears expressed in the previous section, children following the communicative process would integrate in all the contexts considered by ALAS. However, the fusion should not result in one rule beginning with TOPIC/PERFORMER/ ASSOCIATE → for insofar as associates sometimes involve prepositional phrases, the commonalities would only be partial. Rather, it should result in two separate rules with the lexical items abstracted and replaced by representative symbols. These, given the tendency towards nouns, verbs, etc. documented above, should eventually be deemable N, V and so on. Thinking of this schematically, it would mean eventual convergence on rules including (3.37). The rules in (3.37), like those in (3.35), fulfil our criteria of phrase structuredness. They also guarantee that the transformations will become categorial rather than item-specific.

Finally, unlike LAS and the assimilation models, they derive syntactic categories like N and V. Nevertheless, the rules seem a far cry from the phrase structure examples given in Chapter 1 and this has to be worrying. Of the rules presented in Chapter 1, the ones that were derived from Chomsky (1957) could move from the "start" node to the lexical items in as few as three steps. The subject noun phrase could, for example, be generated by S → NP + VP, NP → Det + N and Det → the etc., N → dog, etc. Looking at (3.37) it is clear that the communicative process could never escape with only three steps. Of the rules that

MEANING   - - - ➤ FUNCTION + CONTENT   (3.37)

CONTENT   - - - ➤ TOPIC/PERFORMER′ + ... + PREDICATE′

TOPIC/PERFORMER′ - - - ➤ ..... + TOPIC/PERFORMER + ...

PREDICATE′   - - - ➤ PREDICATE + ASSOCIATE′ $_1$ + ...

ASSOCIATE′ $_1$ - - - ➤ .... + ASSOCIATE $_1$ + ...

TOPIC/PERFORMER - - - ➤ T + ... + N

ASSOCIATE $_1$ - - - ➤ T + ... + N

T   - - - ➤ $\left\{ \begin{array}{c} \text{the} \\ \text{a} \\ \text{this} \\ \text{that} \end{array} \right\}$

N   - - - ➤ $\left\{ \begin{array}{c} \text{dog}_{\text{DOG}} \\ \text{ball}_{\text{BALL}} \end{array} \right\}$

Chapter 1 mentioned as successors of Chomsky the majority use the X-bar convention, meaning terms like N″, N′, and N instead of CONTENT, TOPIC, and ASSOCIATE. Indeed, thanks ultimately to Bresnan (1970), many contemporary systems begin with S′ → COMP + S before they use N′. At first sight, such conventions are hard to relate to (3.37). However, on closer inspection, parallels emerge. Noting the lexical items they govern, TOPIC′ and ASSOCIATE′ have much in common with N′ and TOPIC and ASSOCIATE with N. Likewise, once it is realised that the COMP in S′→ COMP + S stands for "complementiser" and that it governs both wh-phrases and "to" plus "that", parallels with MEANING → FUNCTION + CONTENT will be apparent to all.

The Convergence on Observational Adequacy

Without wanting to stretch the point too far, I think, therefore, that parallels can be claimed between the rules attainable through storing as the communicative process without *a priori* knowledge would require and recent developments in linguistic theory. This has to be encouraging when the desire is for rules consistent with observational adequacy in a reasonable time period. Yet is this what can be concluded about the rules under scrutiny? The rules must, I think, be capable of generating *all* the sentences of English. They can produce sentences with any number of clauses, and they must also be able to produce all permissible numbers and orderings of noun, verb, auxiliary, and prepositional phrases. They must additionally be capable of all permissible form class orderings. In achieving this the rules are superior to anything LAS could manage but they are not necessarily good enough. The assimilation models could probably derive rules capable of all the sentences of English but, as we have already seen, these rules would overshoot *all and only* those sentences by an impossibly wide margin. However, the main problem with the rules was the inevitable conflation of the noun, verb, and adjective categories. As we have just seen, the rules attainable on the communicative process differentiate nouns, verbs, and adjectives, and hence would sidestep the problem completely.

Thus, the rules come closer to generating all and only the sentences of English than anything the assimilation models could manage, but do they come close enough? For contemporary linguists, they would at the very least have to pass two further tests, the first being to account for wh-word placement. The problem with wh-word placement was first discussed in the mid 1960s by, for example, Chomsky (1964) and Ross (1967). It can be explained succinctly. In English it is permissible to say "John offered to buy what?" and "What did John offer to buy?". It is also permissible to say "John who did what bought a drink?". However, "What John who did bought a drink?" is unmistakably out. The linguistic literature contains numerous "principles", "constraints", "conditions", "conventions", and "metavariables", which have been proposed to solve the problem. Rather than discuss the proposals in detail, suffice it to say that the rules we are considering solve the problem as well. To see why, note first that the non-function element conveyed by the "What" in "What did John offer to buy?" is a predicate associate. Hence to produce it, children would have to have appended a "what" annotated with PRED ASSOC to the function element. This implies previous experience with some "what-fronted" interrogative that was used to refer to a predicate associate. Experience with an interrogative that, as with "John offered to buy what?" was not "what-fronted" would not be sufficient, because this would produce a dummy item appended to the function element. This recognised, now note that the "What" in "What John who did bought a drink" does not refer to a predicate associate; it is a predicate-associate-of-a-topic/performer-associate.   Hence   to   produce   this, children would have to have annotated "What" accordingly. However, to do this they would, in this case, have experienced some "what-fronted" interrogative that was used to refer to a predicate-associate-of-a-topic/producer-associate. Experience with a non-"what-fronted" equivalent like "John who did what bought a drink" would not be adequate. As "what-fronted" interrogatives referring to predicate-associates-of-topic/performer-associates never occur in English, children could never have the relevant experience and hence could never make the error.

The second test that contemporary linguists would undoubtedly pose would be to account for the restrictions on verb "argumentation". Verb argumentation refers to the combinations of noun and prepositional phrases that can follow any given verb. Its problematic nature was first noted by Baker (1979) when he identified certain difficulties with dativisation. To appreciate the difficulties, note that while "John offered a drink to Mary" and "John offered Mary a drink" are both grammatical, "John reported his misfortunes to Mary" is grammatical but "John reported Mary his misfortunes" is not. As Baker pointed out, analogous difficulties occur with "to be" deletion and subject raising. To see them, compare "The baby seems/happens to be awake" with "The baby seems/happens awake" and "It is likely/probable that John will win" with "John is likely/probable to win". Indeed, subsequent writers have added to Baker's list and summarising their claims, Pinker (1989) notes passivisation, causativisation, and locativisation as particularly interesting. As examples, compare "John understands/resembles Mary" with "Mary is understood/resembled by John", "The door opened/fell" with "John opened/fell the door" and "Mary splashed/poured disinfectant into the bath" with "Mary splashed/poured the bath with disinfectant".

As we shall see in Chapter 4, the learning of verb argumentation has been widely discussed, but no-one doubts that the method Baker himself advocated would guarantee success. This is, quite simply, the learning of argumentation on a verb-by-verb basis, and it is precisely this method that the communicative process would come to deploy. To see why, remember that the integration of partially overlapping expressions of topic/performer and associate elements would mean the gradual abstraction of these elements from preterminal positions in the rules. However, abstraction would remove what, from the perspective of children following the communicative process, would be a simple method of preserving the post-verb lexical sequence, namely associate element ordering. That the method would in practice lead to massive overgeneralisation is neither here nor there. Its imagined efficacy is the point at issue. Obliged to find a different method, children following the communicative process would be forced by the very fact of abstraction to learn the "associate phrases" that individual verbs can take.

What is interesting about the tests (and what amongst other things would lead linguists to set them) is that failure would amount to allowing the overgeneralisation of rules that do not have mutually exclusive counterparts. As we established as early as Chapter 1, children following the communicative process could only correct overgeneralisations when mutually exclusive counterparts are also available. In this context, the avoidance of failure over wh-placement and verb argumentation is a major plus, and is perhaps the first sign that the rules derivable by storing on the communicative process without *a priori* knowledge would be consistent with observational adequacy in a reasonable time period.

However, allowing a system that avoids incorrigible over-generalisation is only one step in the right direction. To demonstrate fulfilment of the conditions laid down early in the chapter, it would be necessary to show that the rules would be finalised sufficiently quickly to allow the ready elimination of those overgeneralisations that could be corrected. Certainly such overgeneralisations would occur, for under the rules we are envisaging, the noun, prepositional, and auxiliary phrase form classes would be entirely "context free". In other words, members of given form classes would be allowed to combine freely with members of neighbouring form classes within the same phrase. This would mean "a balls" as well as "the balls", "go a tree" as well as "go up a tree", and "will has" as well as "will have". Recognising this, the question is whether the rules under consideration could be finalised to a timetable consistent with efficient correction. I think that an affirmative answer can be given when it is recognised that the overgeneralisations would have to be removed and the learning of the rules would have to take place even if the communicative process was embellished with *a priori* knowledge of the richest possible hue.

The need to remove the overgeneralisations would arise because the combinations under discussion would be permitted by any context-free rules that deployed syntactic form classes. In view of what has preceded, we can assume that given the communicative process in any guise syntactic form classes would be essential in the avoidance of irredeemable error. Thus, the optimal *a priori* knowledge would contain them. *A priori* syntactic categories must, however, also be context-free because being lexical item-specific (and hence language-specific) their contextual constraints must be learned. Thus, the communicative process with *a priori* knowledge would also entail context-free rules that deploy syntactic categories, and hence that it would also entail the combinations currently being discussed.

To see that the learning that the rules would entail would also be required under *a priori* knowledge is somewhat harder. Nevertheless, it should become clear if we attempt, quite simply, to quantify the mappings that children would need to finalise the rules. To do this, we need only consider the meaning elements and lexical sequences that children would need. After all, as was mentioned earlier, children seem rarely to misconstrue the lexical items associated with particular elements nor to mistake their order. Hence in quantifying the requisite elements and sequences we should, in effect, be quantifying the requisite mappings. Taking this for granted, let us look first at the function, polarity, and completion elements and note that children following the communicative process in the circumstances we are envisaging would probably need all the possible elements plus a sizable proportion of their modes of expression. The former should scarcely cause problems. There are, we are assuming, only four possible functions, two possible polarities, and three possible completions. With the functions and polarities, the latter should also be self-evidently manageable but with the completions clarification may not come amiss. After all, "a sizable sample of their modes of expression" would not simply refer to the auxiliaries and relevant inflections taken in isolation; it would also refer to their legitimate sequences. Yet despite all this, and despite the need for multiple presentations to compensate for inattentiveness and discounting, the sample would be as necessary in the presence of *a priori* knowledge as it would be in its absence. There is nothing universal about the auxiliary form classes and hence knowledge of them cannot be innate. As it cannot be innate, it must be acquired and, no matter how learning proceeds, it is hard to see it proceeding with a smaller sample than the one we are considering.

So far so good, but experiences that fulfilled the function/ polarity/completion requirement are manifestly not all that would be needed. To acquire the structure and sequence of noun and prepositional phrases, children following the communicative process without *a priori* knowledge would need all possible patterings of topic/performer and predicate elements. That is, they would need these elements in their unembellished form as well as qualified by all conceivable associate arrangements. However, this is not a huge undertaking. To acquire rules, the child would also need instances where topic/performers and predicates were expanded into a subordinated M. However, there would be no need for instances with more than one subordinate, meaning that overall the number of necessary topic/performer and predicate patterings would be relatively small.

Thus, on the level of patterning, there would not be any problem, but how about the actual elements? Their number is potentially enormous, and there are at least as many nouns, verbs, and adjectives as conceivable topic/performers, predicates and associates. Should children have to experience everything their task would be even worse than the one posed by LAS. Fortunately, they would not have to do this. They would only need those topic/performer plus noun, predicate plus verb or adjective, and associate plus noun combination that allowed the fulfilment of three criteria. These are (i) that the possible arrangements of determiners, inflections, and prepositions around nouns, verbs, and adjectives be adequately displayed; (ii) that the arrangements mapped onto each topic/performer, predicate, or associate show partial overlap with the arrangements mapped onto at least one other topic/performer, predicate, or associate; and (iii) that at least one of the elements repeat itself at all the possible topic/performer and associate nodes.

The third criterion is, of course, straightforward, but the first two are not. The most efficient way to help children fulfil them would be to present the minimum number of elements consistent with both the range of possible patternings and the third criterion, and associate these elements with the full set of expressions. Perhaps adults addressing children tend to do this. The motherese literature discussed in Chapter 1, and the work of Broen (1972) in particular, is not discouraging. However, even if adults are not very helpful, the task cannot be too onerous. Being language-specific, the noun and prepositional phrase form classes would have to be learned even if the noun and prepositional phrase concepts were themselves innate. Moreover, as with the auxiliaries, it is hard to imagine the noun and prepositional phrase form classes being learned from data less extensive than those required by the communicative process. The data might be used differently but they would still be needed.

Thus, no matter what component of the rules is considered, the message seems to be the same. When children following the communicative process without *a priori* knowledge would have to achieve something not demanded if *a priori* knowledge was available, their task turns out to be trivial. When the task is non-trivial it would be as difficult in the presence of *a priori* knowledge as it is in its absence. Assuming that the argumentation has proceeded correctly, the message is extremely strong. It means that without having to engage in mathematical formalism or to compensate for the imperfect sentence analysis that children seem to conduct, the communicative process could, even in the absence of *a priori* knowledge, be deemed consistent with the learning timetable.

Yet, though strong, the message is not above question. It depends not just on the mechanics of the communicative process being as the chapter has described, but also on the conception of contextually completed meaning being largely correct. To see why, note first that the meanings presupposed in the chapter contain fewer types of element than the conventional ones. This was important because it led, in some cases, to lexical strings, not single items, being mapped onto elements, a prerequisite as it turned out for the formation of form classes and the abstraction of elements. Note, second, that the meanings presupposed in the chapter contain fewer elements of each type. This was particularly true of the function and completion elements, and it ensured the overlap in mode of expression essential once more for the abstraction of elements. Note, third, that the meanings, thanks especially to the orthogonality of polarity and completion and the absence of behavioural roles, were hierarchical arrangements with a particular shape. Without that shape there would have been problems not just with form class formation, but also with form class ordering. The conventional sequence of (3.37) would not have occurred, with adverse implications for the transformations. The local transformations would have been decidedly unorthodox, and there would have been some non-local ones as well. Taking these points together, there can be no doubt that the chapter's concluding message does depend on its conception of contextually completed meaning being largely correct. However, if the conclusions drawn in Chapter 2 seem warranted given the current state of research, the present argumentation is leading to one major point. Resting as it does on the time-scale of learning, the original case for innateness must be deemed non-proven as regards the English language.

NOTES

1. For ease of exposition, I have simplified Anderson's rules to the minimum necessary to convey his ideas. As a result, the rules presented in this section are not to be found in Anderson's writings.
2. For simplicity, the diagrams from now on will not label preterminal nodes in meanings. In other words, the most that the diagrams will contain is the terminal nodes in the meaning plus any associated lexical items. The nature of preterminal nodes can be established from Chapter 2. On some occasions, the labelling of terminal nodes will, as in (3.17), also be simplified.

CHAPTER FOUR

The Approximation to Psychological Reality

The focus of Chapter 3 was the time it would take children to acquire an observationally adequate grammar of English given that they were following the communicative process but lacked *a priori* knowledge of grammar itself. It was assumed that children following the process would engage in two major exercises. The first would be storing whatever they could remember of experienced sentences to optimise the retrieval of their contextually completed meanings. The second would be delimiting expressions that, as far as the store was concerned, were identical in meaning. It was recognised that by virtue of the second exercise, the important question was whether storage would lead in an acceptable time period to a grammar of English that, if not observationally adequate in its own right, would overshoot in a specified fashion. Chapter 3 discussed the question at length and concluded that given the conception of contextually completed meaning established in Chapter 2, an affirmative answer is probably warranted. Of course, the conception of contextually completed meaning is open to debate. However, given that it cannot at present be rejected and given that the notion of the communicative process cannot be shown to be unreasonable (and remember that many diehard nativists implicitly accept it), it follows that innate knowledge is not yet necessitated by the time that English grammar takes to learn. This is despite the fact that thirty years have elapsed since timing became the bedrock of the innateness hypothesis.

Thirty years is, however, a very long time and grammatical development has been a focus throughout its length. Yet the emphasis has not only been the issues that Chapter 3 discussed but also the accumulation of evidence about underlying knowledge. This raises a worrying possibility. Suppose the evidence is inconsistent with following the communicative process in the absence of *a priori* knowledge. If the process remains above question, we should be obliged, for reasons apart from timing, to take innateness for granted. Thus, we should be no nearer establishing an alternative to innateness than we were in Chapter 1. However, is the evidence inconsistent? The aim of the present chapter is to appraise the evidence from English with this question in mind. To proceed, it will be necessary to spell out how, given the communicative process without *a priori* constraints, knowledge would be expected to develop and at present we are not in a position to say much. We certainly know that following the communicative process in the circumstances of interest would, with English, mean deriving a particular kind of transformational grammar. However, we do not know when the grammar would be acquired nor what would precede it. Thus, to take things further, we shall have to do more theorising, and this is how the present chapter will begin. Having made its theoretical statement, the chapter will turn to the relevant research.

Clearly, the main constraints on development will be the contextually completed meanings and the approximations to English sentences available at given points in time. Thus, it is now highly relevant that developmental changes in both domains have already been implied. As regards contextually completed meanings, it was suggested in Chapter 2 that although most of the distinctive features will be available by 21 months, one will come later. This is subordination, for the evidence discussed in Chapter 2 suggests that it does not emerge until about two-and-a-half. As regards approximations to English sentences, it was suggested in Chapter 1 that children discount certain lexical items. Here also, two-and-a-half is an approximate cut-off for, prior to then, virtually all unstressed and/or mid-placed items appear to be discounted. For English (though not, as we have seen, for every other language), the treatment of unstressed items implies the discounting of determiners, auxiliaries, inflections, prepositions, and copulas. Taken together, the changes imply that it might be useful to consider development during two distinct periods—before and after two-and-a-half. This strategy will be adopted in the present chapter, although it is recognised that in practice the changes in contextually completed meanings are unlikely to coincide precisely with the changes in sentence form. Moreover, neither are likely to happen at exactly two-and-a-half in more than a small sample of children.

Proceeding nevertheless with the distinction, the chapter will move to the consequences for the growth of knowledge. It will argue that, with English, children following the communicative process without *a priori* knowledge should, during the period up to two-and-a-half years, make steady progress towards an integrated structure that is not only hierarchically ordered but in part also serially ordered. They should also attach an ever-increasing set of elements to the preterminal nodes of the structures, and the elements should gradually be mapped into single lexical items. The crucial point about these developments is that they are changes in the content of knowledge and not in its form. As the chapter will explain, knowledge up to about two-and-a-half should never be more than a composite mapping, non-categorial in nature and limited in its transformational subscripts. All the restructuring detailed in Chapter 3 should wait until after two-and-a-half, when it will proceed in a piecemeal fashion. However, although piecemeal, the restructuring should, once it gets underway, lead relatively straightforwardly to the final grammar. Moreover, it should do this via a particular path, meaning that, right up to the end, specific predictions can be made about the course of development. Are these predictions confounded by the mass of available data? The chapter will discuss the question drawing some generally positive conclusions.

A THEORETICAL ACCOUNT OF THE BASIC STEPS

The basic question is, then, whether the evidence currently available on evolving English grammar is consistent with following the communicative process without preformed knowledge. As mentioned earlier, answering the question would involve spelling out the expected pattern of development given the communicative process in these circumstances, and this is the motivation for the present section, which will proceed in a fashion that parallels the final part of Chapter 3. Thus, it will imagine an ever-increasing set of sentence-meaning pairs being available for processing. It will consider the consequences of both storing the pairs in accordance with the communicative process devoid of *a priori* knowledge and differentiating the apparently synonymous expressions that the store will create. The only difference from Chapter 3 is that the present section will acknowledge the fact that, prior to two-and-a-half, contextually completed meanings will lack subordinated Ms and associated sentences will lack unstressed and mid-placed items. It will, in other words, recognise the two periods of development identified above. To refer to the earlier period, the section will respect a point, frequently made in the literature, that sequences that lack the unstressed items of English resemble telegraphs, and use the term "telegraphic period". Thus, it will talk also of "telegraphic strings", "telegraphic mappings", and so forth. To refer to the later period, the section will acknowledge the fact that "expansions", as discussed in Chapter 1, must typically add unstressed items. Hence, it will use the term "expanded period", together correspondingly with "expanded strings", "expanded mappings", and so on. As intimated already, the section will argue that during the telegraphic period, knowledge should never be more than a composite mapping, whose transformational subscripts are few in number and non-categorial in nature. However, the mapping should, over time, be increasingly serialised, categorised, and lexicalised, making for an output at two-and-a-half that is considerably more conventionalised than it could have been before. By contrast, the result of communicative processing during the expanded period should be a rule system in flux. More specifically, it should be a rule system which moves steadily from element-specific proscriptions to the full-fledged grammar that was described in Chapter 3.

The Nature of Telegraphic Mappings

Let us focus initially on the telegraphic period. Let us imagine once more the communicative process without *a priori* knowledge and ask what kind of mappings would be formed with English input and what kind of system would evolve. Taking the former question, it must first be noted that the absence of subordinated meanings throughout the period implies that contextually completed meanings will be limited to one M element, one function, one content, one topic/performer, one polarity, one completion, and one predicate. However, the single topic/performer and predicate elements will be accompanied by any of the possible number of associates or attributes. Thus, until the middle of the third year, we can imagine meanings that range from (4.1(1)) through (4.1(2)) to (4.1(3)), these being the meanings that contextual completion would associate with "It's broken", "Put the cup on the table now" and "Jeremy's broken Mummy's cup":

(4.1(1))

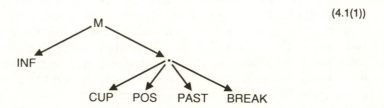

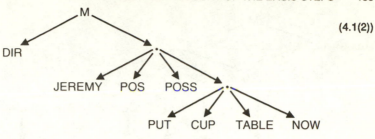

(4.1(2))

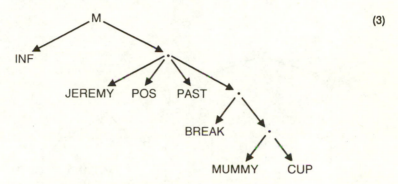

(3)

There are three points to note about the representations in (4.1). First, given the absence of serial order in contextually completed meanings, they are not the only representations that could have been chosen. Second, they have between three and five tiers and, given the restriction to only one M, all other contextually completed meanings will, during the telegraphic period, fall within this range. Third, the elements are obviously more numerous than the items they would, given the communicative process, map into. The principles of discounting that we are assuming during the telegraphic period, mean that (4.1(1)) would probably map into "broke", (4.1(2)) into "put" and "now", and (4.1(3)) into "Jeremy" and "cup" or given heavy stress on the verb, "Jeremy", "broke", and "cup". The consequences of this would be mappings that, like the ones in (4.2), contain a large number of dummy items.

(4.2(1))

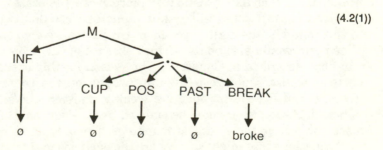

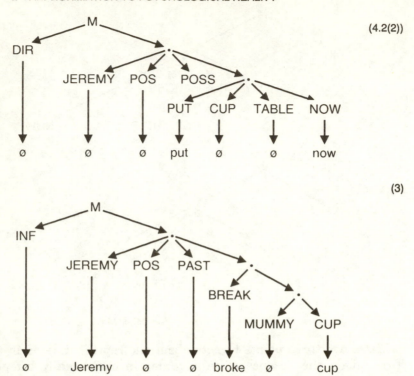

(4.2(2))

(3)

Because there would be a large number of dummy items in telegraphic mappings there could not, even in principle, be much in the way of serial order. After all, meaning elements that map into dummies could be no more serially ordered after mapping than they were before. For example, as only one element in (4.2(1)) does not map into a dummy, it could be no more ordered than (4.1(1)). (4.2(2)) and (4.2(3)) could do somewhat better with, in principle, PUT fixed before NOW in (4.2(2)) and BROKE fixed before CUP and after JEREMY in (4.2(3)). Remembering that children in the present age group appear to preserve the sequence of those lexical items that they do recall, we can be reasonably optimistic that such fixing would take place. Nevertheless, even if it did, (4.2(2)) and (4.2(3)) would still contain numerous free-floating elements and this would be the norm throughout the period we are considering.

The norm would also be the virtual absence of the primitive transformations described in Chapter 3. The reason for this is that most of the items whose sentence positioning would, on the communicative process, entail transformations are weakly stressed and/or centrally positioned. Hence, they would be omitted from telegraphic strings and consequently from the emergent mappings. The only items relevant to transformations that might survive are the particles in strings like "Put it down" and "Pick it up". However, here "it" should disappear and hence the rationale for particle movement outlined in Chapter 3 would no longer be fulfilled. Thus, during the telegraphic period, there would be no transformations at the mapping stage, and only partial serial order. On the other hand, there would, from the beginning, be hierarchical structures that end in lexical items, a significant step in view of the eventual grammar.

The Creation of Composite Mappings

As time passes, children following the communicative process without *a priori* knowledge should form numerous mappings comparable to (4.2). However, they should not store them as autonomous structures. Remembering Chapter 3, they should align and fuse the elements in the new mappings with their equivalents in the old, striving always to reduce the disruption to the lexical sequence. To see what this should result in, apply it first to the elements in (4.2(1)), (4.2(2)), and (4.2(3)). The solution should be something along the lines of (4.3) given that the elements in curved brackets are alternatives, the elements headed by slashed lines are optional, and the elements in boxes are ordered in the sequence 1 before 2 and 2 before 3.

(4.3)

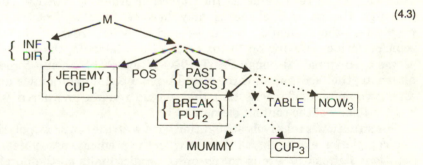

Looked at as an illustration of element integration up to two-and-a-half, (4.3) possesses three important features. First, it shows that integration should maintain the hierarchical structure of the input mappings but increase the number of elements at the various nodes. The number of elements at the function node would, of course, be limited to four, the number at the completion to three and the number at the polarity to two. However, the number at the other nodes would be potentially enormous. Second, (4.3) shows that integration should lead gradually to the two-tier topic/performer, predicate, and associate structures discussed in Chapter 3 and essential to the X-bar flavour of the process' final rules. Thus, there should be a steady elimination of mappings whose overall meaning component is only three tiers. Third (4.3) shows that integration should, in its own right, lead to free-floating elements being placed in a serial order. For example, none of the mappings in (4.2) fix JEREMY as topic/performer before NOW as predicate associate. Yet that would be one consequence of integrating their elements.

What (4.3) does not show is that in the period under consideration there should be definite limits on the level of serial ordering. To appreciate where they lie, consider the elements that are not fixed in (4.3), the functions, the polarities, the completions, and the predicate associates. Thinking what telegraphic strings are like, it is not hard to see how the function elements could be fixed in front of the content. One wh-word would do the trick, and as wh-words are endplaced and heavily stressed they ought to be preserved. But how about the polarity and completion elements? Over time, POS should come to alternate with NEG, and NEG, unlike POS, should sometimes be lexicalised in telegraphic mappings. This is not because "not" would be preserved. It would not be. Rather, it is because the "No's" in "No, give it to me" and "No, don't drop it" would be endplaced, heavily stressed and thus preserved. However, thinking of the consequences of mapping such "No's" onto meaning, it will be clear that the Polarity + Topic/Performer order is just as reasonable as the Topic/Performer + Polarity. Thus, although the polarity elements may become fixed in front of the predicate, they should be free-floating with respect to the topic/performer. Moving on to the completion elements, the situation seems even worse. Although PAST, PROG, and POSS should come to alternate, the fact that all three would be mapped into dummies until after two-and-a-half means that they would remain unordered with respect to any of the content elements.

The situation is relatively straightforward with the function, polarity, and completion elements. It is less so with the predicate associates. As mentioned already, there is no reason to predict limits on the number of predicate associates that children would impute. However, regardless of number, the principle of discounting means that only one associate would probably be lexicalised in any input string. The consequence would be free-floating predicate associates in individual mappings, and hence in the integrated structure that would subsequently be produced. Thus, the fact that in (4.3) CUP is unordered with respect to NOW should not be seen as an accidental by-product of the constituent mappings. Rather, it should be seen as a necessary consequence of integration during the telegraphic period. Indeed, it should probably be seen as an enduring feature of telegraphic knowledge. It is true that free-floating predicate associates would result in optionality over expressive devices. "Put cup now" and "Put now cup" would, after all, both be permissible given (4.3). It is also true that optionality is being assumed to lead children following the communicative process to scrutinise adult usage for clues as to preference. However, to make sense of data relevant to the problem at hand, they would have to preserve from adult speech the very items that telegraphic processing leads them to discount. It looks like a vicious circle, suggesting that predicate associates would remain unordered throughout the early period. It is simply the number of elements at each associate node that should change.

Summing up then, during the telegraphic period the polarity, completion, and predicate associate elements should not become fixed. The other elements, on the other hand, should probably achieve a fixed serial order. Moreover, in becoming fixed, the function, topic/performer, predicate, and topic/performer associate elements should also impose an ordering on their accompanying lexical items. The ordering should, in effect, be Function Items + (Topic/Performer Associate Item) + Topic/ Performer Item + (Topic/Performer Associate Item) + Predicate Item + (Predicate Associate Item) + (Predicate Associate Item) + (Predicate Associate Item) + (Predicate Associate Item). Interestingly, *en route* to the ordering, it is not impossible that children following the communicative process would be led to a different sequence. This is despite being assumed to preserve the adult lexical sequence in input mappings.

To comprehend the apparent paradox, imagine that it was "Jeremy cup" that was mapped onto (4.2(3)) and not "Jeremy broke cup". In integrating this new (4.2(3)) with (4.2(1)) and (4.2(2)), placing the predicate element after its associates would be just as legitimate as placing it before. Noting which elements are lexicalised, this could lead to a system that allowed "Jeremy cup broke" and "Jeremy cup put". Obviously such a system would be short-lived, and would not necessarily occur in every child. Nevertheless, it could happen, highlighting two further points. First, despite the poverty of their input mappings during the period of interest, children following the communicative process should still evolve a capacity for novel strings. Second, the novelty would not simply be in the arrangement of lexical items but also in their number. "Jeremy cup broke" and "Jeremy cup put" were created from input mappings that never contained more than two items, and it would be possible to do much better. As far as I can see, children following the communicative process during the telegraphic period could come to create strings of up to ten items without needing an input lengthier than two.

All in all then, the integration of meaning elements should, given the communicative process without *a priori* knowledge, have interesting implications for lexical strings. Is the reverse also true? As we saw in

Chapter 3, it was when the lexical strings amounted to full-fledged sentences, but how about now? The impact must, I think, be more modest. After all, although lexical integration was seen to imply the abstraction of meaning elements, it was only when differing but equivalently positioned elements were expressed by partially identical items. The telegraphic system should have plenty of differing but equivalently positioned elements, but seeing that each one would be associated with at most one item, partial identity is just not possible. On the other hand, the differing but equivalently positioned elements should sometimes be associated with items that are completely identical. Thinking of the numerous different teddies, dolls, drinks, and cars that "teddy", "dolly", "drink", and "car" would be associated with, there should also be identity across the topic/performer elements, the associate and, by analogous reasoning with behaviour, the predicate. Given the mechanics of the communicative process without *a priori* knowledge, identical items that express different elements should be fused, with the elements being represented in the most parsimonious fashion that concurred with their subsequent retrieval. Whatever the representation, and there is little point in going into details (although Barrett (1982a) provides a useful summary of a lively debate), it should lead to lexically-defined groupings replacing the elements at the preterminal nodes in the hierarchy.

Summarising the points raised in the discussion so far, children following the communicative process without *a priori* knowledge should, during the period up to two-and-a-half years, elaborate a system that allows an increasing number of elements to realise the major components of meaning. These elements should be increasingly ordered by the components they realise. The function elements should precede the topic/performer, the topic/performer should be flanked by its associates and/or attributes and should precede the predicate, and the predicate should precede its associates and/or attributes. The elements should also be increasingly associated with single lexical items ordered equivalently and organised into lexically defined groupings. These changes should mean a system of growing communicative power, a system, in other words, that is increasingly able to interpret speech directly and to produce speech for direct interpretation by others.

This said, it is easy to see that the system should not constitute a grammar in the sense of possessing rules and form classes. There can be no doubt, after all, that the features identified in Chapter 3 as essential for the formation of grammar in that sense would be systematically omitted from telegraphic mappings. The absence of subordinated meanings implies that there would be no mappings with the multiple Ms deemed crucial for the derivation of rules. The absence of elements associated with strings of lexical items means that there will be no mappings with the partial overlap deemed crucial for classes. As a result, we have to accept that although the system derived by children following the communicative process without *a priori* knowledge may not be the figurative representation adopted (for expositional purposes) in this essay, it should nevertheless be little more than a composite mapping. It may be a communicative system of considerable power but it will be no different in form from its input mappings.

The Metamorphosis into Adult Grammar

On the other hand, we should not have to imagine that children's knowledge would be resistant to change once, after two-and-a-half, they could extend their input mappings. As mentioned earlier, input mappings should, given the communicative process, evolve in two ways after two-and-a-half. First, they should involve increasingly "expanded" strings, that is strings including determiners, auxiliaries, prepositions, and inflections as well as mid-placed items. This is what warranted the term "expanded period" for the period after two-and-a-half. Second, the mappings should, on occasion, involve meanings with more than one M. Taken together these evolutions mean that input mappings should come to approximate the structures that appear in (4.4), these being the mappings that children during the expanded period should come to form for "Put the cup on the table now", "Jeremy has broken Mummy's cup", and "Who's the boy that has broken my cup?"

(4.4(1))

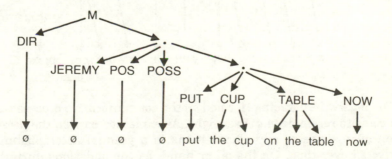

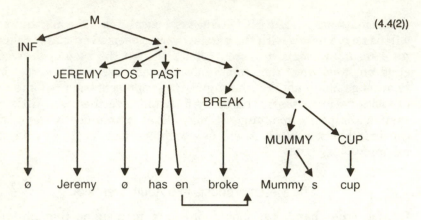

(4.4(2))

(3)

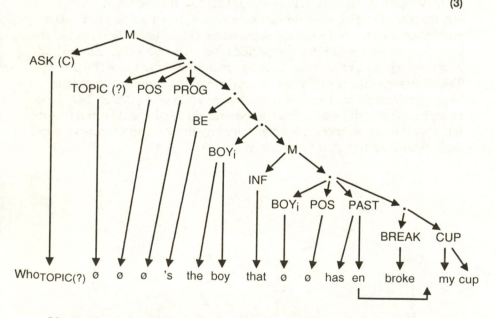

Obviously the mappings formed on the communicative process would
not come to resemble (4.4) overnight. As explained earlier, the preserv-
ation of unstressed, mid-placed items is a gradual accomplishment,
perfected over time. On the other hand, as the omissions during the
expanded period are seemingly random, we can imagine mappings like
(4.4) as a synthesis of what would be created over several trials. Doing
so, we have the foundations for a composite mapping, which is a

considerable improvement on the telegraphic system. In particular the lexicalisation of the completion elements would allow for three significant advances. The first would be the fixing of the completion elements after the topic/performer and polarity and before the predicate. This, remembering (3.31) in Chapter 3, would follow from the alignment and integration of the completion elements themselves. The second advance would be the refining of the semantics of completion. This would follow because element integration would align a range of apparently synonymous items, whose expressive values would then be studiously computed. The final advance would be the appearance of transformational subscripts that show the movements of inflections and auxiliaries from the completion "positions" to elsewhere in the sentence, these subscripts being a first step towards the local transformations on which the grammar depends. Of course, here, there would be a cost. "Has+ed" should become integrated with "Has+en" as partially overlapping expressions of PAST. This in turn should lead to overgeneralisations like "broked" and "menden" as complements to "broken" and "mended". Here again, the computation of expressive values would be triggered to deal with the problem.

However, in addition to permitting these advances, the appearance of mappings like (4.4) would also provide the basis for rapid structural change. After all, once the mappings contained multiple Ms, there would be the possibility of a more or less instantaneous switch to a rule-based system. Even allowing for less than perfect insight the switch should not take long. Once it occurs it should lead to rules like (4.5)—rules very similar to the ones in (3.32).

(4.5)

$$\text{MEANING} \dashrightarrow \left\{ \begin{array}{l} \text{DIR} \\ \text{ASK (C)} \\ \text{ASK (F)} \\ \text{INF} \end{array} \right\} + \text{CONTENT}$$

$$\text{CONTENT} \dashrightarrow \text{TOPIC/PERFORMER} + \left\{ \begin{array}{l} \text{POS} \\ \text{NEG} \end{array} \right\} + \left\{ \begin{array}{l} \text{POSS} \\ \text{PROG} \\ \text{PAST} \end{array} \right\} + \text{PREDICATE}$$

$$\text{TOPIC/PERFORMER} \dashrightarrow (\text{------}) + \left\{ \begin{array}{c} \text{APPLE} \\ \vdots \\ \text{ZEBRA} \end{array} \right\} + (\text{---------})$$

$$\text{APPLE} \dashrightarrow \text{apple}$$

However, the switch should also lead to rules like (4.6(1)) and (4.6(2)).

TOPIC/PERFORMER $- - \rightarrow$ (TOPIC/PERFORMER ASSOCIATE$_1$)   (4.6(1))

$+$ ---- $+$ (TOPIC/PERFORMER ASSOCIATE$_2$)

TOPIC ASSOCIATE$_1$ $- - \rightarrow$ $\left\{ \begin{array}{c} \text{APPLE} \\ \vdots \\ \text{ZEBRA} \end{array} \right\}$

APPLE $- - - \rightarrow$ apple

PREDICATE $- - - \rightarrow$ PREDICATE $+$ (PREDICATE ASSOCIATE$_1$)   (2)

PREDICATE ASSOCIATE$_1$ $- - - \rightarrow$ $\left\{ \begin{array}{c} \text{APPLE} \\ \vdots \\ \text{ZEBRA} \end{array} \right\}$

APPLE $- - - \rightarrow$ apple

The point about (4.5) and (4.6) is that so long as there is overlap between the topic/performer and associate elements and their modes of expression, there will be redundancy in the rules, in this case APPLE → apple. Given redundancy, children following the communicative process without *a priori* knowledge would be expected to eliminate it. Would there be redundancy in practice? I think so, once we remember that by the onset of the expanded period children following the communicative process would have had many months to accumulate elements at the appropriate nodes. Moreover, the kinds of element that would operate as topic/performers would, in the vast majority of cases, also operate as topic/performer associates and/or predicate associates. In the light of this, I think that we can confidently anticipate a rapid reduction in rules like APPLE → apple.

The reduction is straightforward in its own right. Yet, note once more that it would be taking place when expanded strings were being mapped onto contextually completed meanings. This should mean that when elements in the mappings are fused with identical elements (or, more accurately, element groupings) in the existing knowledge, their expressions would, on occasion, show partial rather than full overlap. This, extrapolating from Chapter 3, should provide an opportunity to derive the determiner, preposition, inflection, and auxiliary form classes for each element grouping separately. However, because of the rapid reduction in redundancy outlined in the previous paragraph, the form classes should not discriminate between given groupings as topic/performers rather than associates, or as topic/performer associates rather than predicate. Thus, as an indirect consequence of element accumulation prior to rules, the components of meaning that given nouns realise should make little difference to the determiners and inflections they are deemed to take.

However, while this should be true for each noun separately, it would not necessarily be true for nouns as a group. As Chapter 3 pointed out, when lexical items are attached to equivalently positioned but different elements they should not invariably benefit from each other's development. Rather benefit should be contingent on lexical overlap. Thus, the only circumstances in which "the + —" for APPLE-as-TOPIC would be extended to "— + orange" for ORANGE-as-TOPIC are those where APPLE-as-TOPIC and ORANGE-as-TOPIC already have partially overlapping expressions. For instance, given prior experience with "That apple is rotten" and "That orange is fresh" and hence with overlap in "That + —", extension of "the + —" should take place. Because of the need for partially overlapping expressions, the finalisation of the noun and prepositional phrase form classes would be piecemeal and time-consuming. However, it would both inform and be informed by the developments outlined in the previous paragraph.

What does the integration of partially overlapping expressions of topic/performer and associate elements mean for the evolution of knowledge? It means most obviously that when determiners, prepositions, and inflections are first used, they would lead to a system that incorporates them in the context of particular nouns. The system would soon start generalising the items further and should, indeed, quickly begin to overextend. It would, after all, only take experience with "the cake", "the cakes", and "a cake" to generate "a cakes". However, context-specificity and, in other words, undergeneralisation would also be the norm in the early stages. Over time, both overgeneralisation and undergeneralisation should begin to decrease. In the case of the latter, it would be by virtue of an ever-increasing supply of partially overlapping expressions. In the case of the former, it would be because children following the communicative process are believed to concern themselves with the expressive value of apparent synonyms.

This much is straightforward. However, it will be remembered from Chapter 3 that the integration of partially overlapping expressions of topic/performer and associate elements must, in the interests of efficient representation, mean the gradual abstraction of these elements from preterminal positions in the rules. As a corollary, it must also mean that topic/performer and associate elements are steadily replaced in the rules by the equivalents of noun and prepositional phrases. The abstraction of these elements would, however, as Chapter 3 explained, mean changes elsewhere in the system. For one thing, it would create new problems for the representation of predicate associate orderings. In particular, it would create problems during the integration stage when, as we have seen, the problems during the telegraphic period would (as far as the child is concerned) be purely at the stage of selecting expressions.

To appreciate the problems, note that at the mapping stage, the response to predicate associate ordering would be as shown in (4.4), to swing the predicate associate elements into the sequence of items that express them. If, at the integration stage, the predicate associate elements were represented as shown in (4.6), the solution would be deemed preserved in the rules. However, as the abstraction of associate elements means that they will not be so represented, the child would be faced with a dilemma, and the alternative solution outlined in Chapter 3 would gradually be demanded. This, it will be recalled, would be to learn the "associate phrases" that individual verbs can take, amounting in other words to a verb-by-verb learning of argument structure. It was clear in Chapter 3 that such learning would take considerable time, requiring both that every verb be experienced with every permissible associate ordering and that the concepts of noun and prepositional phrases be fully specified. What the present chapter can add is, first, that learning should start after two-and-a-half and, second, that advancing against a backcloth of telegraphic knowledge, there should be considerable overgeneralisation of the passive, causative, dative, and locative constructions until learning is complete. As we shall see, this will help us make sense of a substantial body of recent research.

What all these developments mean is that after two-and-a-half a considerable amount of learning has to take place. This is not because the acquisition of rules is rendered problematic. On the contrary, once contextually completed meanings contain multiple Ms, rules should quickly emerge. Indeed, the developments during the telegraphic period, particularly the adoption of the appropriate number of tiers, mean that these rules should soon take the "shape", in terms of tiers and branches, of the final phrase structure system. Furthermore, they should also be accompanied by transformations that, again thanks to developments during the telegraphic period (this time the serial ordering of meaning elements), should mirror the eventual grammar. The problem is not, then, with the form of the rules. It is rather with their content, for the message of the last few paragraphs is that the real difficulties lie with the lexical and phrasal categories. It is their emergence that would take the time. Moreover, until they emerge, knowledge would be an untidy mixture of categorial and element-specific rules, with the precise distribution varying from child to child, and age to age. Indeed, this would not only be the case for the precursors to the phrase structure and transformational rules. It would, as a necessary consequence, apply to the lexical rules that emerge to deal with predicate associate ordering. Could this be what happens, or can the whole picture be falsified by the mass of available data? It is to these questions that we shall now turn.

A COMMUNICATIVE SYSTEM OF GROWING POWER

Let us look first at the period when no rules should be present, the period before about two-and-a-half. Although there should be no progress during this period towards rules as such, there should be changes in the system that will, as we have seen, have consequences for the rules once they appear. Three changes seem particularly noteworthy. They relate to the anticipated increases in the elements, which are: first, associated with each component of meaning, second, lexicalisable in any given expression, and third, organised in a fixed serial order. Should the changes take place, the result would be a system that, although rule-free, would be of considerable communicative power, but do the changes take place? The aim of the present section is to ascertain whether current data demonstrate that they do not. This is, of course, a more modest aim than seeking to ascertain whether current data demonstrate that the changes actually occur, but it is nevertheless the relevant one for purposes of this chapter. To pursue it, the section will take the anticipated changes one by one, and survey the relevant data. It will look particularly for indications that the changes are precluded because the anticipated end-states are present from the start. It will do this in recognition that the data will be drawn from the behaviour of very young children, as it will turn out both their spontaneous speech and their experimental responses. With such children, behaviour indicating the absence of the end-states at two-and-a-half could be attributed to poor sampling, inattentive subjects and a myriad of other methodological problems. Behaviour indicating the presence of the end-states before two-and-a-half would be hard to dismiss. Accepting this point, the section will conclude on a reasonably positive note.

The Multiplication of Meaning Elements

The multiplication of meaning elements is such a central point that the rationale for it needs only the briefest of mentions. It follows from the fact that input mappings will vary in the elements at each node in the meaning. As children following the communicative process without *a priori* knowledge are deemed to organise each input mapping into an integrated store, the elements at the nodes will gradually mount up. The notion sounds so straightforward that a serious challenge is hard to imagine. Nevertheless, it would be challenged by, amongst others, the theorists who still subscribe to the assimilation approach discussed in Chapter 3. It will be remembered that, for such theorists, lexical items are mapped onto categorial structures derived from extralinguistic experiences. As the structures will thereby be transformed into meaning representations, it follows that the nodes will contain generalised categories not individual elements. Hence, they will start and finish with the same degree of breadth. Could this be what happens? Do we, in other words, have to deny the steady increment in elements that our model would predict?

By way of an answer, it might seem sufficient to reiterate the problems with generalised meaning categories that were raised in Chapter 3. This, however, will not do. The problems related to generalised categories in the absence of innate knowledge, not generalised categories in total. It is still possible, for example, that children utilise generalised meaning categories in the early stages and then discover by maturation that syntactic categories are what grammar deploys. Gleitman (1981) is explicit in her acceptance of such a position, and it is hard to see how Berman (1988) and Maratsos (1982; Maratsos & Chalkley, 1980) could avoid it. It certainly means that the issue of generalised categories cannot be pre-empted, and hence we need here to consider it carefully. To do this, it would be useful to consult studies that have taken representative samples of children's communicative expressions, analysed their meanings from the perspective of this essay, and quantified the elements as a function of age. Needless to say, such studies do not exist. Far from analysing meanings from the perspective of the essay, research into early communicative expressions has been almost proselytising in its adultomorphism, arguing particularly strongly for awareness of behavioural roles. How, then, about studies that could be transformed by reanalysis into what we require? Even they are rare. Virtually all seemingly usable studies have been limited to the portion of overall meaning expressed in words. Ideally, we should want the overall meaning regardless of its expression. In addition, most of the studies have presented the types of element associated with each component, and not their number. For both reasons it is hard to find anything that bears incisively on our question, and this has to be recognised.

There are, however, a few studies that could, via some judicious reading between the lines, be deemed to be relevant. There is, for example, the work of Bloom et al. (1975) and Greenfield and Smith (1976). This work was based on lengthy, home-based observations of children aged between one and two. In the case of Bloom et al., three children were observed every six weeks and one every three; in the case of Greenfield and Smith two children were observed every month. The work could be relevant because although it is restricted to elements expressed in words, it selects those elements that, according to McShane (1980), are never expressed non-lexically in the period we are considering. Moreover, although it emphasises element groupings, it also presents the raw frequencies for specific exemplars. It does not use concepts like "predicate" or "associate" but it is, in fact, unambiguously reanalysable in these terms. It shows a steady increase in instances from 21 months onwards.

The research of Barrett (1983), Edwards (1978), and Edwards and Goodwin (1980) might be regarded as another source of evidence. This research also involved intensive observations of small numbers of children during their second year of life. The focus was on the referential properties of verbs as a function of age, with the data being presented verb by verb. The data were supplemented with notes on the non-verbal context. These notes reveal the associates and/or topic/performers of whatever the verbs referred to. We could look to them for evidence of a steadily increasing number. Fortunately evidence seems to be forthcoming. For instance, at first Barrett's subject Tina used "catch" only when she herself was the topic/performer. Gradually, she brought in other people and, somewhat later, toys. A similar pattern was observed in the use of "off" by Barrett's subject Emily and "dropped it" by Edwards and Goodwin's subject Alice. Indeed, something analogous could also be inferred from research by Bowerman (1976), Braine (1976) and Ewing (1982). In this research, which involved children learning Finnish, Hebrew, Samoan, and Swedish as well as English, the focus was on the verbal contexts in which words are used, and not the non-verbal. The finding was that in most cases the contexts increased. Thus, initially, Bowerman's daughter Eva used no verb but "want" in the "— + (noun)" frame. Braine's son Jonathan used no adjectives but "big" and "little". Later, a wide range of other words began to appear.

Of course the findings of Bowerman, Braine, and Ewing could result from the growing lexicalisation of elements that were always known. They could also result, as Bowerman in particular hints, from elements that were expressible in single word utterances (and hence self-evidently known) being gradually brought into the combinatorial system. However, the work of McShane (1980), which was mentioned above, could be used to argue against the former. The work of Brown and Leonard (1986), which shows no close relation between the familiarity of lexical items and the scope of their frames, could be used to argue against the latter. In any event, the work of Bowerman and her compatriots is certainly no problem for the model we are considering. At best, it is positive evidence that meaning elements multiply. At worst, it does not deny this, and that seems the pattern more generally. Thus we can safely conclude that, as far as the multiplication of the meaning elements is concerned, the predictions of the communicative process without *a priori* knowledge are not confounded by available facts.

The Lexicalisation of Communicative Expressions

How, then, about the second prediction, that following the communicative process without *a priori* knowledge implies an increasing lexicalisation of meaning elements? This follows from the fact that although only two or three elements will be lexicalised in input mappings, they will not necessarily be elements that realise the same components of meaning. Hence the integrative procedures should produce a situation where more than two or three elements will be lexicalised, and the question is whether the available data show this not to happen. To provide a clear-cut answer, we should need studies that have obtained representative samples of children's communicative expressions and that have either identified the meaning elements or provided data that would allow us to do this. Then we could compute an index of lexicalised elements in total elements and plot it against age. As it happens, the tendency, discussed earlier, to focus on the lexicalised portions of communicative expressions and not the whole thing, means that the studies are just not available. Should we conclude then that our prediction is untestable on the basis of current research, or is there an alternative approach that we could still adopt?

Contemplating the latter, there is the seductive possibility of mean length of utterance or "MLU". As research presented in Chapter 1 made clear, MLU has been a popular index of grammatical development. Hence there are probably thousands of studies that plot it with age. Research by Rondal, Ghiotto, Bredart, and Bachelet (1987) indicates that the plots will be reliable with the age group of interest, so there are no statistical reasons for avoiding them. Are there conceptual reasons? I think not. MLU would not bear on the issue at stake if the number of lexical items associated with given meaning elements changed with age. After all if this happened, changes in MLU could result from changes in the lengths of strings associated with a constant number of lexicalisable elements, and not with changes in the number of elements being lexicalised. However, as mentioned in the previous section, the discounting of non-stressed items means that, in the vast majority of cases, only one lexical item will be associated with each meaning element throughout the period of interest.

Likewise MLU could not be used if the number of elements associated with given communicative expressions changed with age. This is because in these circumstances changing lexicalisation could not be differentiated from proportionately equivalent lexicalisation of changing numbers of elements. Once more, however, reassurances can be given on the basis of points raised earlier. After all, one of the fundamental assumptions is that children's meanings lack subordinated Ms up to two-and-a-half. In which case, age-related changes in the number of elements are contingent only on age-related changes in topic/performer and/or predicate associates (and associates of those associates), and this has been deemed unlikely. Indeed, the work on verbs by Barrett (1983), Edwards (1978), Edwards and Goodwin (1980) and, for that matter, Antinucci and Parisi (1973) helps confirm the point. It indicates that as early as 21 months children are expressing meanings that entail at least two associates, and work by Bloom (1970), Bowerman (1973), Braine (1976), Brown (1973), Edwards (1973), Kernan (1970), Schlesinger (1971), Slobin (1971), and Wells (1974) suggests little change over the succeeding months. Through its analysis of two-word combinations, this work also endorses the availability throughout the period of topic/performer plus associate pairings and associate plus associate of associate.

Overall then, there seems no reason to avoid MLU for the purposes we have in mind.[1] Is there any reason to deny that it increases with age? Most child language researchers have an indelible image of a graph presented by Brown (1973 and elsewhere) showing the MLUs of his subjects Adam, Eve, and Sarah between 18 and 44 months. The slope of the curve as age increases is indisputably upwards. Without being so instantly memorable, most of the other studies cited in this section present data that show exactly the same thing. Like Brown's these studies were, by and large, longitudinal and hence their results are particularly revealing about the issue at hand. They can, however, be supplemented with data from cross-sectional studies. Of such studies, only Klee and Fitzgerald (1985—but see also Conant, 1987) obtained disappointing results, finding a correlation of only +0.26 between age and MLU. With larger samples, Miller and Chapman (1981) obtained a correlation of +0.88, and Rondal et al. a correlation of +0.75. In view of these findings, the findings of the longitudinal studies and the fact that Klee and Fitzgerald's correlation, though low, was still positive, I think we can end on an optimistic note. If MLU can be treated as a relevant index, there is certainly no need to deny the increasing lexicalisation of elements as a function of age.

The Sequencing of Lexical Items

As meaning elements become increasingly lexicalised, they should, however, also be increasingly serially ordered. Furthermore, they should not take on just any serial order. Rather they should move towards the particular sequence that follows from the minimalisation of lexical disruption. The sequence for English was outlined earlier but it can be summarised as in (4.7).

(1)   The function element will be first   (4.7)
(2)   The topic/performer element immediately preceded and/or followed by an
       associate will precede the predicate
(3)   The predicate element will precede any associates that it may have

With some children the sequence should be achieved quite rapidly. With others it may take time, for apart from anything else, progress will depend on a lucky sequence of input mappings. Across samples of children, however, the sequence should be steadily approximated, and as it is, it should come to impose a corresponding ordering on lexical items. Is there any reason to deny that this is what happens? Not surely if the ordering, on the one hand, gradually appears in children's own speech and, on the other, steadily comes to dictate their interpretation of the decontextualised speech of others.

Looking first at children's own speech, it seems initially that we are spoiled for choice. The question of lexical sequencing by the age group of interest has generated an enormous amount of research, and not just with children learning English. At the time of writing, I have located work on Finnish, French, German, Hebrew, Hungarian, Italian, Japanese, Kaluli (from New Guinea), Korean, Luo (from Kenya), Polish, Russian, Samoan, and Swedish! Yet once we delve into the research, we must begin to wonder. The question it typically addresses is whether children place the subject noun phrase, the verb, and the object noun phrase in the order that is normal for their language. Thus, the research is about word order as a function of grammatical category and not of meaning. However, when we look at how grammatical category is assigned, things become more relevant. With a string like "Pinkie hates babies", it would be clear from the "number" of the verb that the normal subject–verb–object order of English was being preserved. With "Babies hates Pinkie" it would be equally clear that the normal order was being violated, but how about "Pinkie hate baby" and "Baby hate Pinkie"? It will be these kinds of strings that will be produced by children under two-and-a-half, and they lack the linguistic features by which subject and object could be differentiated. So how were subject and object identified in the research we are considering? As far as I can see, it was with reference to behavioural roles. Items referring to entities in the agent role were deemed to be subjects. Items referring to entities in the patient role were deemed to be objects. This being the case, we hardly need refer back to Chapter 2 to recognise that, so long as the studies can claim gradual convergence on the subject–verb–object order, their evidence will be equally consistent with our present proposals about topic/performers, predicates, and predicate associates.

Unfortunately, commenting on the studies of children learning English which were then available, Brown (1973) wrote that from about 18 months onwards "violations of normal order are triflingly few". If subsequent studies also found this, we should be faced with a problem. We should have to conclude that children's knowledge does not just lead them to the topic/performer–predicate–predicate associate ordering. In all cases, it allows them to use it from the start. As it turns out, however, there is a major methodological problem with the studies that provided the basis for Brown's review. The behavioural roles from which subject and object were identified were themselves partly determined by the lexical sequence, introducing circularity into the argumentation (see Howe (1976) for a more detailed discussion). Thus, for compelling evidence, we have to turn to a group of more recent studies, which have attempted to redress the problem.

The message from the studies is somewhat different. Reanalysing data reported by Bowerman (1973) and Kernan (1970) and adding new observations of his own, Braine (1976) demonstrated that for some children early word combinations are not conventionally ordered. Far from it, they are not even unconventionally ordered, for all possible sequences can sometimes be observed. Thus, during the course of a single recording, a child might say "Here baby" and "Baby here", "Wheels lorry" and "Lorry wheels", and "Horsie down" and "Down horsie", behaviour which Braine terms "groping". Importantly, children who groped at one recording would, with the same lexical items, produce sequences consistent with the topic/performer–predicate–predicate associate ordering at a later recording. Similar results have been obtained by Brown and Leonard (1986) in a study that, like Braine's, involved data derived from spontaneous speech. Here two girls were recorded every two or three weeks from the middle of their second year. There were individual differences as the communicative process without a priori knowledge would predict, but both girls gave evidence of groping prior to convergence on our predicted sequence. Finally, note must be taken of a cross-sectional study by Angiolillo and Goldin-Meadow (1982) where descriptions were elicited from children aged 28 to 35 months. Here the analysis was in terms of agent–action–patient rather than subject–verb–object, but this, of course, makes the data even more readily translatable into the terms we are using. Not surprisingly, given their relatively advanced ages, all but one of the subjects produced sequences that were consistent with the topic/performer–predicate–predicate associate ordering already being established. However, the one exception, who showed no strong preferences, was in terms of MLU by far the least advanced.

Thus, studies of spontaneous speech give no grounds for anxiety, but then the interpretable examples involved only a handful of children. For decent samples we have to turn to the second source of data. This is studies concerned with the interpretations that children place on the speech of others when supportive contextual cues have been studiously removed. We have already encountered the studies in the course of Chapter 2, and as Chapter 2 made clear, their modal approach, exemplified by the work of Bates et al. (1984), Bever (1970), Chapman and Kohn (1977), de Villiers and de Villiers (1973), Lempert and Kinsbourne (1980), Roberts (1983), Slobin and Bever (1982) and Strohner and Nelson (1974), has been to ask children to act out subject–verb–object sequences. However, although this has been the modal approach, it cannot be said to have been the only approach. In addition to acting out, Bridges (1980) asked children to complete scenes that had already been started, to choose scenes that matched simple descriptions and to use scenes to verify sentences. Golinkoff, Hirsh-Pasek, Cauley, and Gordon (1987) used video monitors side-by-side to present such scenes as the Cookie Monster tickling Big Bird and Big Bird tickling the Cookie Monster. Their task involved audio-presented instructions like "Show me Big Bird tickling the Cookie Monster" and their measures were response latency and fixation time. Finally Wetstone and Friedlander (1973) observed the degree of compliance to three kinds of directive imperative: (i) normal, for example "Show the clown to Mummy"; (ii) misplaced, for example "Show to clown the Mummy"; and (iii) scrambled, for example "Mummy clown to the show".

Paralleling the studies of spontaneous speech, the primary concern was whether children make the referents of the first nouns operate as agents and the referents of the second nouns operate as patients. Once more, however, evidence on this issue would be evidence on the topic/performer–predicate–predicate associate issue that concerns us here. From what was said in Chapter 2, there is clearly a time when first nouns are not routinely taken as agents nor second nouns as patients. However, Chapter 2 was far from explicit about when this time occurs and returning to the studies for clarification is not entirely rewarding. Typically, their youngest subjects were well past their second birthday. Thus, while it is gratifying to find them reporting good but still imperfect performances up to two-and-a-half, it would be preferable to find data from a younger age group. For this reason, the studies of Roberts (1983) and Wetstone and Friedlander (1973) are probably the most relevant, and both provide evidence that is reassuring to us. In the Roberts study, the older and, in terms of MLU, more advanced children were about twice as likely to give first-noun-as-agent responses as their younger counterparts. In the Wetstone and Friedlander study, the children were classified as fluent and non-fluent (using criteria that correspond to our expanded and telegraphic, respectively). It turned out that only the fluent responded differentially to the normal, misplaced and scrambled speech.

Relating the studies of Roberts and Wetstone and Friedlander to the research on spontaneous speech, I feel reasonably confident that nothing in the literature as it currently stands counters the claim that children come gradually to order lexical items as our model predicts. As a result, nothing counters the claim that the items are appended to meaning elements that come gradually to be ordered as outlined in (4.7). Thus the whole section can end encouragingly. Given the communicative process without *a priori* knowledge, a number of changes should take place during what we have termed the "telegraphic period". There is research relevant to each of the changes, though certainly not as much as one would like. Nevertheless, the research is sufficient to allow a non-trivial appraisal, and after an attempt to do this, I see no reason to deny that the changes take place.

A RULE-BOUND SYSTEM IN FLUX

The crucial point about the changes during the telegraphic period is that they should alter the content of the knowledge possessed by children learning English and increase its communicative power but they should not affect its form. Thus, during the period, the system should, given the communicative process without *a priori* knowledge, be isomorphic with the input mappings. During the expanded period by contrast, which starts around two-and-a-half, children learning English should begin to restructure. Thus, the changes during this period can be viewed as metamorphosing the input mappings into the final system. As we have seen, the changes should, thanks partly to the nature of the telegraphic system, proceed by a particular path. Specifically, they should involve the speedy generation of a rule-bound system that is equivalent in shape to the final grammar. By "equivalence in shape" is meant the production of hierarchical structures with the requisite number of tiers and branches, and the possession of transformations that move the requisite lexical items. The changes should also involve the slow and piecemeal generation of a system that has abstracted meaning elements from its preterminal nodes. Thus, there should, during the expanded period, be a system that moves gradually towards syntactic form classes at its preterminal nodes. Correspondingly, there should be a system that moves gradually towards lexical adjuncts that resolve the dilemmas that element abstraction is seen to create. Recognising these as the predicted changes during the expanded period, let us consider whether there is any reason to deny them.

The Switch to a Rule-bound System

Let us start with the rule-bound system. As outlined earlier, children following the communicative process without *a priori* knowledge should switch to a rule-bound system that has the shape of the final one once they integrate mappings with subordinated Ms. In ideal circumstances one such mapping would do the trick but, even allowing for less than perfect insight, the switch should not take long. As the literature suggests subordinated Ms at around two-and-a-half, this is the age at which the system would be predicted. This recognised, we should probably be advised, given the literature as it stands, to separate our analysis into two separate parts, the first concerned with the location of rule emergence at about two-and-a-half, and the second with the identification of adult shape in the posited terms. Hence, this will be the strategy in the section to follow.

Beginning with the first issue, few researchers would deny a system containing rules after two-and-a-half, for it is around this time that children start to show signs of an infinite capacity. This is not to say that children explicitly acknowledge that sentences can be indefinitely long, and hence provide the evidence for infinity used in Chapter 1. Rather, it is that children produce sentences that make recognition of indefinite length hard to deny. The sentences frequently involve co-ordination, a phenomenon whose development has been charted by Bloom, Lahey, Hood, Lifter, and Fiess (1980a), Lust and Mervis (1980) and Tager-Flusberg et al. (1982). A beautiful example was generated by my son Jeremy who, when cuddling into a bath-towel, announced "I love Mummy and Daddy and Miriam and Fiona and Pinkie and Keith and Julia and Uncle Derek … and Uncle Derek … and Uncle Derek". At the time he was 32 months and three days, and it was clearly not his sentence-making capacity that made him stop!

However, if rules are implausibly denied after two-and-a-half, should they be denied before? It will come as no surprise to hear that most child language experts would feel they should not be. After all, Chapter 3 began with a string of studies all concerned with the "rules" used by children who were considerably younger than two-and-a-half. The possibility that the children might not be using any rules was not seriously contemplated and, considering the issue more generally, the received wisdom in child language research seems to be that once combinatorial speech appears (and this is typically well before two), there must be rules. Indeed, this has been so much taken for granted that the main debate has been over whether rules should be postulated before combinatorial speech, not whether they should be postulated at its onset (see, for example, the contrasting positions of McNeill (1970) and Barrett (1982b)).

Yet, reviewing the literature, I find it hard to establish why rules from the beginnings of word combination have been so universally assumed. Perhaps it is the creativity of children at this stage when, as Chapter 1 documented, they juxtapose items that they could never have experienced in adjacent positions. However, Chapter 1 never used creativity of this kind as an argument for rules, and whatever else the first section of the present chapter demonstrated how creativity would be possible if rules were absent. As it turns out, the literature contains several other demonstrations of precisely the point. For instance, MacWhinney (1975) showed how "generalisation-by-analogy" could account for the creativity in a classic experiment by Berko (1958). In that experiment, children extended the plural inflection to nonsense syllables to produce, for example, "wugs". The fact that MacWhinney performed a subsequent experiment that ruled out generalisation-by-analogy in children who were over two-and-a-half is, of course, neither here nor there.

Such work allows us to say that the creativity of young children in juxtaposing novel items is no argument for grammatical rules before two-and-a-half. However, is this why grammatical rules were postulated? Is there anything else that could make the case? As we have seen, children certainly do not order items randomly, but does this mean anything? Randomness would be avoided by MacWhinney's generalisation-by-analogy and it must now be axiomatic that the communicative process without *a priori* knowledge would avoid it as well. All in all, then, I cannot think of anything that would entail a rule-bound system before two-and-a-half. Hence I should like to leave the issue with conclusions favourable to our model and turn to the second problem—the shape, in terms of tiers, branches, and transformations, of the adult system.

In turning, we should note from the outset the presentation of relevant information during the course of Chapter 3. This is because Chapter 3 pinpointed features of the shape predicted given our process that would find parallels in current linguistic thinking. The point in Chapter 3 was to obtain indications that observational adequacy in a reasonable time period was not untenable. However, as we saw in Chapter 1, observational adequacy has not been the only concern of modern linguistics. Since about 1960, there has also been an interest in the psychologically real grammar, making the parallels documented in Chapter 3 of relevance here.

This said, it should not be imagined that contemporary linguistics has reached a consensus about the psychologically real grammar. On the contrary, virtually all issues relevant to shape are still being debated. For example, although work in Chomsky's (1981) "government-binding" theory uses the S' → Comp + S rule that was highlighted in Chapter 3, there is nothing equivalent in Gazdar et al. (1985) nor Kaplan and Bresnan (1982). Although Chomsky (1970) used an equivalent number of X-bar levels to the ones implied by Chapter 3, Jackendoff (1977) notes that elsewhere as many as four levels have been proposed for nouns and as many as six for verbs. Although Chomsky (1981) favours local transformations, both he and, in their "relational grammar", Perlmutter and Postal (1977) add non-local supplements. Moreover, as we have seen, Gazdar et al. and Kaplan and Bresnan avoid transformations altogether.

What is interesting about the debate is that, when stripped of its detail it is conducted very largely about the capacity to deal with wh-placement and verb argumentation. One example is recent discussions of passivisation, a concept that, it will be remembered, was introduced in Chapter 3. It turns out that underlying Perlmutter and Postal's advocacy of a passivisation transformation is the belief that it follows naturally from the mechanisms that are needed to constrain wh-placement. Underlying Kaplan and Bresnan's denial is Bresnan's (1978) claim that a passivisation transformation would render verb argumentation non-tractable as a learning proposition. A further example is past inflection movement. For instance, underlying the advocacy of local transformations in the government-binding tradition is work like Anderson (1982), which defends past inflection movement as a corollary of wh-placement constraining. Underlying the denial elsewhere is work like Jensen and Stong-Jensen (1984), which suggests that past inflection movement creates problems for subject raising. In view of this, it is easy to understand why, as Chapter 3 pointed out, wh-placement and verb argumentation are the tests linguists would set for the communicative process! It is also easy to understand why, as the process passed the tests without inbuilt knowledge, the debate in linguistics has not precluded our rules from the psychologically valid shape.

Accepting this, it might seem as if more incisive evidence should be obtainable from psychological research. The pinpointing of grammar as part of human knowledge motivated many psychologists to join linguists in the quest for specification. Hence, during the 1960s, there was an explosion of purportedly relevant studies, many of them concerned with transformational rules. The studies, which have been reviewed in detail by Fodor, Bever, and Garrett (1974), involved the formulation of predictions about which sentences would be easy to process and which would be hard given contrasting claims about their transformational base. Ease of processing was then computed against, for example, the time to convert one sentence into another and the accuracy of recalling one sentence given another. The results were usually taken as consistent with whatever transformational grammar was contemporaneously fashionable! This aside, the studies have also turned out to be virtually uninterpretable. As Carlson and Tanenhaus (1989) and Garnham (1985) point out, they have invariably confounded ease of grammatical processing with ease of interpretation. Given that the results usually amounted to differences in processing, this is a major problem.

The problem might have been circumvented had the studies used a more qualitative approach to analysis, but qualitative analysis seems to have been the prerogative of developmental research. Yet developmental research is not irrelevant, for the pattern of children's errors is, as we have seen, indicative of what they could be evolving. Thus, it is of interest that work on interrogative formation has generated two findings that appear problematic for the model we are considering. The first stems from the research of Bellugi (1971, see also Klima and Bellugi, 1966), and is the apparent tendency to invert the auxiliary in yes/no-interrogatives before doing so in wh-interrogatives. This means sentences like "Did you go home?" at the same time as sentences like "Where you did go?". The tendency was interpreted by Bellugi as evidence that yes/no-interrogatives involve one transformation—auxiliary inversion—but wh-interrogatives involve two—auxiliary inversion and wh-movement. Since, as we have seen in Chapter 3, the communicative process without *a priori* knowledge denies wh-movement, the finding definitely seems to challenge. Nevertheless, it has to be noted that it emerged from a study of only three children, the ubiquitous Adam, Eve, and Sarah. Moreover although it was replicated by Kuczaj and Maratsos (1975a) in their longitudinal study of a boy named Abe, it failed to appear in the data of Erreich (1984), Ingram and Tyack (1979), and Richards (1990). As Erreich, Ingram, and Tyack, and Richards studied a total of forty-six children and contrasted spontaneous speech with elicited, their data has surely to be given the greater weight.

The second developmental finding that is potentially problematic was first reported by Hurford (1975). According to Hurford, his daughter frequently duplicated auxiliaries in interrogatives, producing, for example, "What's that is?" and "What did you did?". As Hurford pointed out, a plausible interpretation is that the child was moving towards a two component transformation: copy the first auxiliary and then delete it. However, at the stage she was observed, she had only mastered the copying. If this were the case, it would be problematic, because the communicative process without *a priori* knowledge posits single component AUX-movement, not two component copying and deletion. Certainly, there is no denying the validity of Hurford's observation, for it has been endorsed by Kuczaj (1976, see also Maratsos and Kuczaj, 1978) and Nakayama (1987). However, it is not clear that the copying without deletion needs to be accepted. As Kuczaj points out, utterances like "What's this is?" could result from treating "What's" as a single word. Moreover, the errors that cannot be explained in these terms look too specific to constitute a faulty rule. They depend, first, on the type of auxiliary and, second, on the complexity of the subject noun phrase. According to Nakayama, the appearance of a relative clause as in "Is the boy who is watching Mickey Mouse is happy?" is particularly problematic. This being the case, it is conceivable that the duplications result from memory limitations, leaving the possibility of simple AUX-movement still intact.

The Emergence of Grammatical Categories

The point about the shape of the rules was that, given the communicative process without *a priori* knowledge, it ought to be a constant from about two-and-a-half. However, the shape is only one of the properties of current concern, and as regards the others changes have been predicted. For instance, in the absence of *a priori* knowledge, children following the communicative process should start with three kinds of translational rules. There should be rules that translate components of meaning into other components, rules that translate components of meaning into specific elements, and rules that translate specific elements into single lexical items. With the integration of mappings containing expanded strings, the latter should soon be supplemented with rules that translate elements into lexical strings. However, these new translations would be inherently unstable because they would produce partial overlap of expression across equivalently positioned elements. This should trigger the fusion of identical items and the abstraction of meaning elements, leading in a piecemeal fashion to rules that translate meaning components into syntactic form classes.

Is there any reason to deny that this happens? With syntactic form classes, few researchers reject their eventual emergence as components of adult knowledge. However, there is a group—heirs of Bloom (1970) and McNeill (1966), discussed in Chapter 3—who are convinced that those syntactic form classes that are also open (that is, nouns, verbs, adjectives, etc.) are present from the earliest combinatorial speech. There is also a group—heirs of the meaning-based grammarians also discussed into Chapter 3—who are convinced that although open form classes emerge during learning, they do so by an alternative route. Does either group have a compelling argument? The aim here is to try and find out.

It will be remembered that Bloom and McNeill's work was succeeded by the work of the meaning-based grammarians. In fact, it was not simply succeeded but also largely replaced, because meaning-based grammars became the ruling orthodoxy until around 1980. Then, a counter-reformation occurred and new versions of the Bloom/McNeill "syntactic" hypothesis started to emerge, also postulating early knowledge of the open classes. These were invariably versions of the innateness hypothesis, because open classes from the early stages constitute the kind of highly specific knowledge that, as we have recognised already, must be innate. Thus, the assertion of the open classes has frequently been couched in an innateness framework, and a good example of this is the work of Erreich, Valian, and Winzemer (1980). These authors view children as innately constrained to formulate hypotheses that could be true of a Chomskyan transformational grammar. As they recognise, this would include innate knowledge of "the stock of elements and operations for constructing syntactic rules", which include, self-evidently, the open classes. A similar position is taken by Wexler and Culicover (1980) and also by Berwick and Weinberg (1984) and Hyams (1986). However, while Erreich et al. and Wexler and Culicover take the constraints to be towards some Chomskyan grammar, Berwick and Weinberg and Hyams assume that they are towards one of the versions that involve X-bar rules. Indeed, Hyams assumes the constraints are towards the precise version outlined in Chomsky (1981). Diverging from Hyams and Berwick and Weinberg but still committed to X-bar constraints (and hence to *a priori* knowledge of the open classes) is Pinker (1984). For Pinker, the constraints arise because "the child is equipped to learn a rule system conforming to Kaplan and Bresnan's (1982) theory of lexical functional grammar". Thus, Pinker is the only theorist in the group to posit predispositions that are inherently non-transformational.

Given their partially overlapping perspectives, it is not surprising to find both common threads and differences in the evidence that the theorists present. For example, both Erreich et al. and Pinker cite what they see as a repeated failure in the literature to explain how the open classes could gradually emerge. More indirectly but along the same lines, Berwick and Weinberg, Hyams, and Wexler and Culicover cite other properties of adult grammar that by, in their view, having defied gradualist explanation intimate *a priori* knowledge that includes the open classes. One property that is discussed by all of them is the constraining necessary to ensure, amongst other things, accurate wh-placement. It is seen to require *a priori* knowledge of noun phrases, meaning that *a priori* knowledge of the noun form class can be taken as read. This kind of evidence requires little comment. We should not have embarked on the chapter had the communicative process without *a priori* knowledge not yielded an account, necessarily gradualist, of the open classes and the constraints on wh-placement.

Thus, some of the evidence presented by the theorists has implicitly been dealt with. Is this true of the remainder? The remaining evidence was derived largely from children's speech around two years of age, and was used in a fashion that, by and large, parallels the above. Thus, Pinker and, elaborating on Erreich et al., Valian (1986) identify speech that, for them, provides direct evidence for the open classes. Hyams identifies speech which by, for her, strongly suggesting parameterised templates in the sense of Chomsky (1981) provides indirect evidence for inbuilt knowledge involving the open classes. Taking Hyams first, it turns out that the template of central concern is the so-called AG/PRO, which deals with the agreement in person, number, and/or gender between verbs and their subjects. The template, so the theory goes, has two possible values, AG = PRO and AG ≠ PRO. When AG = PRO, agreement is lexicalised and subjects (being partially redundant) can be omitted. When AG ≠ PRO, agreement is not lexicalised and subjects cannot be omitted. The point Hyams would like to make is that children learning English produce speech consistent with their having chosen AG = PRO initially and AG ≠ PRO subsequently. Should the point be warranted, inbuilt knowledge of the open classes would, to reiterate, follow from the theory in which the template is embedded.

Of course, to make her point, Hyams has not only to show that children learning English do switch from AG = PRO to AG ≠ PRO. She has also to provide an account of why the shift occurs. As she seems partially to have recognised (see Radford, 1990), her 1986 work was not particularly convincing on either score. Although young children learning English are more likely than older ones to omit sentence subjects, they are not, according to Valian (1989), as likely to do this as children learning Italian, a true AG = PRO language. In addition Valian (and recently also Ingham, 1992) point out that subject usage in children learning English is statistically uncorrelated with further features, which, on a shift to AG ≠ PRO, they should be. As regards explaining the putative shift, Hyams implicates the "it" and "there" expletives that appear in sentences like "It seems cold" and "There's a wind outside". She argues that once children start using them they must realise the impossibility of subjectless sentences. However, she can only pursue this line if she believes that expletive usage is motivated by extragrammatical factors. If she does, though, how can she in the absence of other evidence use intragrammatical factors, namely new values to the AG/PRO template to explain the changes in subject usage? How, in particular when there is a plausible extragrammatical factor, namely the discounting of unstressed items in the early stages of learning. Indeed, this would not only predict the spasmodic deployment of subjects. It would also mesh with O'Grady, Peters, and Masterson's (1989) observation that the movement from spasmodic to obligatory subjects is not instantaneous.

Having considered Hyam's indirect evidence, let us return to the supposedly direct evidence of Pinker (1984) and Valian (1986). Rather, it is to Valian we should return because her analysis of children's speech subsumes Pinker's and extends it. It is based on the speech of six children recorded in one or two sessions. Amongst other things, the children's speech was analysed for lexical items that in adult usage would be adjectives and nouns. The question was whether in child usage the items fulfilled the criteria in (4.8).

Criteria for Category Assignment		No of Children Correct	(4.8)
Adjective			
A1	Must appear, post-Det and pre-Noun in NP	3 (but only one error in each of remaining children)	
A2	Can form acceptable but not grammatical utterance as sole content of utterance or phrase	4	
A3	Can be sequenced: repetitions of same Adj, or different Adjs	4	
A4	Can appear as predicate Adj	4	
Noun			
N1	Single/plural distinction (via restriction of Det to subclass)	6	
N2	Count/mass distinction	2	
N3	N/ProN distinction	6	
N4	Single Det used with all N subclasses	5	

Inspecting (4.8), it should be noted that A2, A3 and A4 are options for adjective usage. Hence, unlike the other criteria, failure to fulfil them does not preclude knowledge of the category. It should also be noted that when Valian considers N1 and N2 she asks whether the distinctions are applied to appropriate nouns, not whether they are applied to nouns rather than adjectives, etc. In fact, the latter would, given Valian's concerns, have been the proper question and if it had been asked, all children would have passed. Bearing these points in mind, the results show an impressive success rate. Moreover, it is a success rate that has subsequently been replicated by Ihns and Leonard (1988). However, does it signify that, from the beginnings of combinatorial speech, the categories were known? Of course not. In the first place, the children were well over two and from both their reported MLUs and their ability to use determiners and inflections (implied even by 4.8) way beyond their first combinations. In the second, it should be clear that if we revise N1 and N2, as we undoubtedly should, children following the communicative process without *a priori* knowledge should be able to fulfil every criterion in (4.8) before they have even started to formulate the categories. Thus, again we have a situation where the evidence for the open classes is answerable with reference to the model we are considering.

I would not be alone in being unconvinced by the case for open classes at the start of language. The backlash of the 1980s touched only a proportion, perhaps even a minority, of child language researchers for many still believe that early knowledge is meaning-based. However, amongst those who subscribe to meaning-based grammar, few would accept the version outlined here for children as old as two-and-half. Some, as intimated already, still subscribe to some version of the assimilation approach. Others, influenced particularly by Braine (1976), posit the induction of ever-broadening meaning features along the lines we observed with LAS. Either way, the prediction would be items dominated by generalised meaning categories by two-and-a-half, and not individual elements. As we have noted already, generalised categories would entail a discontinuous process of development whereby syntactic categories are "discovered" perhaps maturationally, at a later stage. However, this is by no means impossible. If it is what happens, children should at some point after two-and-a-half begin to subdivide meaning-based categories for their distributional properties. By this means, the open classes would *de facto* emerge, but their emergence would not be the piecemeal procedure that we are predicting. Because the verbs, say, in each meaning-based category would be treated autonomously, the pattern of emergence should be meaning correlated.

The empirical evidence on the issue is extremely confusing. On the one hand, Gordon (1985, 1988) finds no evidence that the object–substance distinction underpins children's use of the indefinite article "a" and the plural inflection "-s". Indefinite articles and plural inflections were applied to count nouns regardless of whether they were object (e.g. "loaf") or substance (e.g. "drink"). They were omitted with mass nouns regardless once more of being object (e.g. "bread") or substance (e.g. "water"). Likewise, summarising work with languages that, unlike English, categorise nouns by gender, Levy (1983) finds no evidence for referent sex being developmentally relevant. However, the force of Gordon and Levy's points depends on objectivity and sex being the kinds of distinction that meaning-based grammars would make, and I have yet to see this proposed. Moreover, in apparent contradiction of Gordon and Levy, there is not simply the counter-evidence on the count/mass distinction reported by McPherson (1991). There is also work by Maratsos, Kuczaj, Fox, and Chalkley (1979) and Maratsos, Fox, Becker, and Chalkley (1985) suggesting that passivisation is initially restricted to verbs of action, and a study by Bloom, Lifter, and Hafitz (1980b) showing that with children in the age range 1.10 to 2.4, the present progressive "-ing" was supplied most often with action verbs of lasting duration (e.g. singing), the third person singular "-s" with action and state verbs of placement (e.g. fits), and the regular past "-ed" with action verbs of immediate result (e.g. closed). Corroborating earlier results by Brown (1973) and Kuczaj (1978), they also found no evidence of "-ing" being overgeneralised to verbs of state (e.g. needing). Cziko (1989) is in no doubt that findings such as these, supplemented by numerous cross-linguistic parallels, indicate the differentiation of verbs as a function of meaning.

However, as with the work of Gordon and Levy, the true situation is much less clear. Although Sudhalter and Braine (1985) manage a partial replication of Maratsos et al., they find so much variability in the passivisation of non-action verbs that homogeneous categories are hard to posit. Likewise, close inspection of Bloom et al.'s results yields no straightforwardly predictive feature. Indeed, the results are also explicable in terms of "-ing" being aligned with PROG, "-s" with POSS, and "-ed" with PAST of the three completion elements introduced in Chapter 2. In addition, Bloom et al. do not report "-ing", "-s", and "-ed" being extended to action adjectives of duration, placement, and result. Although this would be expected if meaning-based distinctions were important, it seems from further work reported by Maratsos et al. that it is hardly surprising. The work, which was based on recordings lasting six hours apiece of children aged 2.6 to 5.6, found no evidence of verb inflections being extended to adjectives. In contrast to Bloom et al., it found few restrictions on the usage of "-ed", observing extension not just to all varieties of actions but also to states. For instance, their data contain overgeneralisations like "knowed", "feeled", "thinked", and "haved".

Thus, the evidence is undeniably confusing. Yet there is nothing in it, surely, to entail a developmental pattern dictated by generalised meaning categories and this, for the present, is all that is needed. Indeed, this is particularly the case when there is additional evidence that, if anything, is easier to reconcile with the piecemeal approach that our process is positing. For instance, in their follow up to Valian (1986), Ihns and Leonard (1988) show that although there was a steady increase in the number of nouns that Adam used with articles, there were never any signs of articles being restricted to a semantically homogeneous set. More generally, the piecemeal approach predicts exponential growth in the assignment of closed class items to open class contexts, and the data of Maratsos et al. (1979) are certainly consistent. There is an accelerating increase with age in the proportion of verbs marked with past inflections. However, these data are cross-sectional, meaning perhaps that the most compelling evidence comes from Brown's (1973) analysis of Adam, Eve, and Sarah. Other graphs, almost as memorable as Brown's MLU curves, map Sarah's use of inflections as a function of age and Eve's use of prepositions. They are as close to exponential growth as anything conceivable from empirical research.

Perhaps, then, there is a little evidence as regards the open form classes that is easier to reconcile with our process than with its obvious alternatives. Be that as it may, our process certainly does not come off badly when discussed in the context of open form classes. One set of alternative processes has postulated the open classes from the start of combinational speech. However, there are no data presented in support of those processes that our model cannot accommodate. Another set has accepted the open classes as an emergent phenomenon, but predicted a meaning-correlated development rather than a piecemeal. However, the evidence for meaning correlations is highly ambiguous, and the exponential developments in some domains seem evidence against.

The Introduction of Context Specificity

Of course in emphasising exponentiality in the insertion of closed class items, we are focusing on the expanded period as a time when children following the communicative process without *a priori* knowledge would create rules that allow the closed and open classes to combine freely within a phrase. Such rules should definitely become part of the system, and indeed they should not be the only source of context freedom. As the associate elements are abstracted from the predicate, the product should be rules that, as with the telegraphic system, allow all verbs to combine with all possible combinations of noun and prepositional phrases, meaning context freedom between phrases as well as within. Faced with this situation, it is tempting to predict massive overgeneralisation in the later half of the preschool years, yet this would undoubtedly be wrong. In the first place, the introduction and subsequent integration of expanded mappings that permit context freedom within phrases should also produce considerable choice over forms of expression. As children following the communicative process are thought to look to adult usage to constrain such choice, they should be taking steps that will lead overgeneralisation to be eliminated at the same time as they are constructing the rules that bring it into being. In the second place, the abstraction of associate elements, which allows context freedom across phrases should, as we have seen, lead children following the communicative process to perceive problems in retrieving elements as a function of lexical strings. These problems should force the learning of verb argumentation from adult usage on an item-by-item basis. Thus, once more, children following the communicative process should begin taking steps that lead to overgeneralisation being eliminated at the same time as embarking on the restructuring that brings it into being.

Accepting what amount to two opposing forces, the extent of overgeneralisation will depend on the time that adult usage takes to predict relative to the time that the context-free rules take to emerge. This, alas, creates a situation of the greatest complexity as regards the testing of our model. It can certainly be assumed that prediction will be easiest when adult usage correlates with features that are both general and accessible to children, but investigating whether this is associated with limited overgeneralisation is well nigh impossible. The problem is not with identifying areas where adult usage correlates with features that are general. The noun, auxiliary, and prepositional form classes all provide examples. Rather, the difficulty is with demonstrating the accessibility of the features to grammar-learning children. To avoid circularity in the study of overgeneralisation, evidence that was independent of language would have to be used. However, evidence that was derived from non-linguistic sources might (unless one was a diehard assimilationist) say nothing about what is salient for language!

In view of this, I do not wish to devote much space to overgeneralisation in the domain of noun, auxiliary, and prepositional phrases. However, I will make a few general points. The first is that with the noun phrase form classes, there is work on overgeneralisation, but its message conflicts. For instance, Gordon (1988) has studied the use of the plural inflection "-s" by children aged 21 months to three-and-a-half. Menyuk (1964) has done the same via what she calls "substitution" errors in the speech of children aged 34 months to over seven. Gordon denies overgeneralisation; Menyuk affirms it. Emslie and Stevenson (1981), Karmiloff-Smith (1979), Power and Dal Martello (1986), and Warden (1976) have all studied the use of the indefinite article "a" by children aged three and over. Emslie and Stevenson and Power and Dal Martello think that problems of generalisation are sorted out in the preschool years; Karmiloff-Smith and Warden think that even nine year olds can be found to make errors.

With the auxiliary phrase form classes, a somewhat different point can be made, namely that relevant research probably does not even exist. After all, it seems unlikely that children produce the combinations of auxiliaries and/or inflections that would allow overgeneralisation to be studied through spontaneous speech. Thus, we should be left with judging children's reactions to strings like "I will has finished soon" and "You did be silly", given once more independent criteria for predicting which overgeneralisations should be tractable and which should pose problems. Unfortunately, reviews like Richards (1990), Stephany (1986), Weist (1986), and Wells (1979) attest to an unremitting emphasis in research on auxiliaries and inflections as isolated phenomena.

With the noun and auxiliary phrase form classes, the conclusion must be that overgeneralisation cannot be estimated from the literature as it stands. With the prepositional, the message is somewhat clearer. Amongst the prepositions themselves, there seems to be less overgeneralisation when the items encode "topological" relations than when they encode "Euclidean". Topological relations are relations that are not defined by the observer's perspective, prime examples being "in", "on", and "under". Inspired by Clark (1973) there have been numerous studies of children's usage of the prepositions "in", "on", and "under". The results depend partly on the methods used, with responses to "on" showing greater conformity to adult usage when the task involves pointing to scenes than when it involves acting out (compare for example the results of Clark (1973) and Wilcox and Palermo (1974/75) with those of Bernstein (1984) and Grieve, Hoogenraad, and Murray (1977)). This notwithstanding, the overall picture is rapid convergence on adult usage, with some studies, Brown (1973) for example, finding no over-generalisation at all. Euclidean relations are by contrast only defined from the observer's perspective, paradigm examples being in front of and behind. Here, Cohen Levine and Carey (1982), Durkin (1980), Johnston and Slobin (1979), Kuczaj and Maratsos (1975b), and Sinha and Walkerdine (1974) have all documented considerable overgeneral-isation of the corresponding lexical items during the preschool years.

It would be gratifying for our process to argue that topological relations are more tractable for children than Euclidean, and certainly this would be the position of Piaget and Inhelder (1956). However, I want to resist this, for my basic contention remains the same: tractability can probably never be established in a non-circular fashion. Suppose, however, that we accept the point, and abandon our hypothesis of limited overgeneralisation when adult usage correlates with general and accessible features. It does not follow that our process cannot be tested. It may be possible to turn matters around and look for extensive overgeneralisation when adult usage is idiosyncratic and, as a corollary, challenging to children. In which case, verb argumentation might be worth considering, for a case can be made that the verbs that are restricted for dativisation, "to be" deletion, subject raising, passivisation, causativisation, and/or locativisation fail to form a definable set.

Admittedly, some writers would demur. Mazurkewich and White (1984), for instance, believe that the verbs that are unrestricted as regards dativisation can be defined as having non-Latin stems and marking the recipient as the possessor. Thus "offered" is non-Latin and "Mary" is the potential possessor in "John offered Mary a drink". Hence, it is as well-formed as "John offered a drink to Mary". "Reported" is Latin and "Mary" is not the possessor in "John reported Mary his misfortunes". Hence, this is not as well-formed as "John reported his misfortunes to Mary". Pinker (1989) also appeals to features like "plus or minus possessor", but "plus or minus Latin" is dispensed with in favour of highly specific properties of meaning. For example, it is deemed relevant to dativisation whether the causes of verbs of motion are instantaneous (supposedly as in "throw" and "toss") or non-instantaneous (supposedly as in "propel" and "lob"). However, against Mazurkewich and White and Pinker (and indeed against all theorists who attempt to constrain the set) is the way in which the restrictions on, say, dativisation fluctuate as a function of dialect. For example, most American discussions of dativisation pinpoint "give" and "donate" as a contrasting pair, yet I have found many speakers of British (perhaps Scottish) English who regard "John donated the museum a painting" as entirely uncontentious.

Accepting the absence of general and accessible features, the prediction has to be that children following the communicative process without *a priori* knowledge should overgeneralise verb argumentation throughout the expanded period. Indeed, the posited inability to fix predicate associate elements before two-and-a-half means that children following the communicative process without *a priori* knowledge should also overgeneralise during the telegraphic period. Is this then what happens? The answer is undoubtedly "Yes", and paradoxically Mazurkewich and White and Pinker are amongst those who warrant it (others include Braine et al., 1990). Mazurkewich and White have found nine- to fifteen-year-olds judging strings like "Nancy drove Ted the car" and "David suggested Ruth the trip" to be acceptable. In a follow-up study, White (1987) found that six of a sample of twenty-two three- to five-year-olds were consistently willing to act out sentences like "The doll is opening the monkey the door" and to imitate them. Pinker participated in analyses of Adam, Eve, and Sarah that yielded evidence of illegitimacy in dativisation (see also Gropen et al., 1989) and passivisation (see also Pinker, Lebeaux, & Frost, 1987). Moreover, he fills eight pages of printed text with overgeneralisations culled from the reports of others. Thus, there are passivisation errors like "Until I'm four, I don't have to be gone", dativisation errors like "Button me the rest", causativisation errors like "Kendall fall that toy" and locativisation errors like "Look Mom, I'm going to pour it with water". It is good news for the model we are considering that the over-generalisations were from children of all ages from two to nine.[2]

Of course, in saying that the news is good, we are not saying that the model has been shown to be correct. The point of the preceding discussion, as with the remainder of the chapter, has not been to establish the model's veracity but rather to find out whether it can be shown to be wrong. Yet while this is true, there is a sense in which, as regards the overgeneralisation of verb argumentation, something fresh is on offer. This is because the model under consideration is, as far as I can see, the only one that makes both overgeneralisation and its elimination consequences of general processes. By this token, the model avoids the *ad hoc*ery of Pinker (1989) where overgeneralisation is posited to occur because "broad conflation classes" like "plus or minus possessor" are learned before "narrow conflation classes" like "plus or minus instantaneous cause of motion". It also avoids the specificity of Randall (1985) when she explains how overgeneralisation should occur in dativisation and how it should be removed if children are innately constrained to represent arguments as modern transformational grammar would tend to suppose. Most importantly, in making the learning of argumentation a general consequence, the process we are considering neatly answers a question that Bowerman (1988) has recently posed—why should children take so much trouble to eliminate verb argumentation overgeneralisation when elimination does nothing to enhance the comprehension of adult speech? It is perhaps the ultimate strength, if not the ultimate paradox, of the communicative process without *a priori* knowledge that elimination is predicted despite comprehension of adult speech being a driving goal.

NOTES

1. This is not, of course, to endorse MLU for all the purposes that it has been used. On the contrary, recent criticisms of the measure are fully appreciated.
2. It might seem less good news that Pinker and his associates (see Gropen et al., 1989; Gropen, Pinker, Hollander, & Goldberg, 1991; Pinker, 1989) have argued that the overgeneralisations were constrained by features of meaning. However, I find their evidence unconvincing, with an account based on referent saliency seeming (to me at least) equally plausible.

CHAPTER FIVE

The Establishment of an Alternative Theory

Chapter 4 proceeded on the assumption that although children following the communicative process without *a priori* knowledge might acquire an observationally adequate grammar of English in a reasonable time period, it would be inappropriate to herald an alternative to the innateness hypothesis unless they would move to the grammar by an empirically plausible route. Thus, Chapter 4 spelled out the steps by which the grammar should be constructed given the communicative process without *a priori* knowledge, and checked their consistency with the data as they stand. It is, of course, a strength of the process (a strength not true of the innateness hypothesis in all its forms) that precise steps could be predicted, and hence that checking their consistency was a non-vacuous task. However, it is an even greater strength that despite the presentation of data that bore on a range of distinct and sometimes counterintuitive hypotheses, nothing discussed in Chapter 4 was seriously troubling for the predictions at stake. Taking this with the points about timing advanced in Chapter 3, it may begin to look as if the communicative process without *a priori* knowledge does concur with the known facts about English. In which case, the question posed early in Chapter 1 could receive a partially affirmative answer. As regards English, there is an alternative to the innateness hypothesis for the explanation of learning.

Having said that the question could receive a partially affirmative answer, it has to be recognised that the answer will not be accepted by every interested party. Some scholars will disagree with the conception of contextually completed meaning that has played a crucial role. Others will feel that the mechanics of the process have been portrayed inaccurately. Still others will dislike the argumentation that was directed at timing. Finally, some will balk at Chapter 4's conclusions about the emergence of knowledge. To such critics, there is little more to be said, except perhaps for one general point. This is that whatever faults are to be found with the details, the approach taken by the essay is surely correct. In other words, to ascertain whether an acquisition model consistent with what Chapter 1 sketched as the communicative process is truly an alternative to the innateness hypothesis, the painstaking analysis attempted by the essay cannot be avoided. This means the empirically driven depiction of contextually completed meaning, and the detailed specification of its processing by the model. It also means a laying out of the predictions for the development of knowledge and their testing against empirical evidence. As a corollary, it amounts to an exercise in which psychological research, and developmental work in particular, plays a central part. This is important because it is sometimes implied that the innateness issue can be resolved through theoretical (perhaps even linguistic) analysis alone. Whatever else, the essay should have shown that this is an illusion.

It is to be hoped, however, that the essay will be deemed to have shown more than this. Hence, there will be more than casual interest in the present chapter's topic. This is the place of the communicative process without *a priori* knowledge in psychological theory, for not even the most sympathetic reading of the preceding chapters would guarantee it a welcome. In the first place, there is the obvious problem that the putative success with English might not be repeated with other natural languages. It is possible that one or both of the contextually completed meanings and the integrative procedures were especially well-tailored to English strings. In the second place, there is the possibility that the communicative process is no more consistent with a general learning theory than the innateness hypothesis. It may be viable without inbuilt knowledge of grammar. However, there might be something about its learning procedures that is equally language specific. Both possibilities need discussion, and this chapter will make a start. As mentioned already, it stands no chance of comprehensiveness over cross-language analysis. Certainly, it can pinpoint, amongst the myriad of differences between English and other languages, the ones that are likely to be consequential for the course of development. This, it will do. However, it can only speculate in general terms about the form that the consequences will take. Thus, the discussion that the chapter will attempt of the likely concurrence with the timing and known path of development will necessarily be sketchy. More manageable is an analysis of the implications for a general theory of learning, and this will be the substance of the chapter's second section. Its conclusion will be that the major mechanisms used by the communicative process without *a priori* knowledge have all been implicated by developments in non-linguistic domains.

PROLEGOMENA TO A CROSS-LINGUISTIC ANALYSIS

A relatively straightforward answer can be given to the question of which differences between English and other languages are potentially important. It is these differences that change the structure of the input mappings. Differences that change the content, like for instance the specific lexical items, will be irrelevant. This recognised, there are three sources of potentially significant difference: (i) the contextually completed meanings onto which items are appended, for these determine the mappings' hierarchical structure; (ii) the sequence in which items are placed, for this determines the mappings' serial ordering and their transformational adjuncts; and (iii) the frequency with which elements are realised by item strings, for this determines the opportunities for meaning abstraction. Thus, the present section will take each source in turn, and consider the extent to which differences actually occur. In doing so, it will be fulfilling a commitment made in Chapter 1, for it will, in effect, be defining the sample of further languages to study. To aid such investigation, the section will offer general thoughts about the implications of the differences for the time-scale of grammar learning and the path it is known to take.

The Universality of Contextually Completed Meaning

Let us start with the contextually completed meanings and ask whether children learning languages other than English are likely to differ in what they attribute. By way of introduction, let us remind ourselves that the meanings attributed by children learning English have been deemed to depart from adult intention, and moreover that they have been deemed to do so for two major reasons. They have been deemed to omit non-literal supplements and performative clauses as necessary consequences of contextual inference. They have been deemed to treat behavioural roles as non-specific associations, to fuse temporality and modality into a "completion" dimension, and to treat the dimension orthogonally to polarity as empirically contingent results. By virtue of the two reasons, we can talk about two kinds of departure, and on a worldwide scale this is very interesting. Brown and Levinson (1978) and Leech (1983) make a strong case for the cross-language universality of non-literal supplements and performative clauses, seeing them as opportunities for politeness, which are essential for societal cohesion. For example, they would see all societies as having to use equivalents of "What time is it?" as hints to leave. This is because occasions will occur where anything more direct would create intolerable social tension. By contrast, anthropologically-inclined linguists of a much earlier age make a strong case against the universality of behavioural roles, differentiated temporality and modality, and interacting polarity. Amongst the most famous are Sapir (1921) and Whorf (1956), who claim respectively that amongst North American Indian languages, Nootka excludes behavioural roles (while recognising Chapter 2's concept of performer) and Hopi fuses temporality and modality.

It looks then as if non-literal supplements and performative clauses are both cross-linguistically present and necessarily intractable to language learning children. In which case, it follows that they must be universally absent from contextually completed meanings. It also looks as if behavioural roles, differentiated temporality and modality, and interacting polarity are both cross-linguistically variable and contingently intractable to children learning English. In which case it follows here that the notions could be either universally absent or variably present in contextually completed meanings. In fact, if the evidence presented in Chapter 2 is taken seriously, there must be a strong presumption in favour of the former. It is after all hard to see how culturally specific experiences could lead children learning English to omit features that are marked in their language. Thus, if the omissions really occur, they must reflect aspects of cognition that are relatively culture general. Being so, they ought to operate universally, leading to the universal absence of the features we are considering. In addition, it would be strange to find the features being used by children where the language does not demand them, when they are presumed omitted by children learning English where the language makes them compulsory. In view of these points, the major claims must surely be granted. Accepting the evidence presented in Chapter 2, there must be a strong presumption that behavioural roles, differentiated temporality and modality, and interacting polarity are universally omitted. Thus, returning to the central point, there must be a strong presumption that the contextually completed meanings that, given the communicative process, appear in input mappings, do not differ between the natural languages.

Of course, presumption is not proof, and it would be reassuring to find supportive empirical data. However, anyone looking for it would be sorely disappointed. It will be remembered that two types of study were adduced in Chapter 2 to exclude behavioural roles for children learning English. The first was studies that presented entities whose roles relative to each other were not strongly indicated, and asked children who were too young to make sense of the linguistic cues to carry some action out. The issue was whether the entities were used in a role-differentiating fashion. The second was studies that presented entities in a clear role relation, trained a conventional expression to children who were too young to know the linguistic cues, and presented the expression in a context where entity role relations were not so clear. The issue was whether the expression was used with an appropriate role relation. Only two instances of this type of study were found for Chapter 2. Thus it should not be surprising that if the remit was extended to languages other than English, a complete blank would be drawn. With the first type of study, the situation ought not to be so bad. While Nootka and Hopi have so far escaped attention, there is work in the general paradigm with children learning French, Italian, Japanese, Polish, Serbo-Croatian, and Turkish. Unfortunately, as with the work reported in Chapter 2, the focus has been the age at which the linguistic cues are dealt with. Thus, the results are presented in terms of percentages of children responding correctly. Little is said about whether children are differentiating regardless of correctness. For this reason, there would probably be little to add to the work on French by Sinclair and Bronckart (1972) that was mentioned in Chapter 2, apart perhaps from the Italian, Serbo-Croatian, and Turkish data that Bates et al. (1984) and/or Ammon and Slobin (1979) and Slobin and Bever (1982) use to complement their English. It would probably be concluded that nothing in those data countermands the conclusion drawn in Chapter 2 for Sinclair and Bronckart, that non-differentiating responses seem to be the norm. However, it is likely that most researchers would find the data inadequate for the issue at stake.

With temporality, modality, and polarity, the picture would probably be more or less the same. It is true that Chapter 2 used data from French and Italian to introduce the notion that temporality and modality are fused into a single dimension. However, the evidence used to support the notion, the difficulty children have with ongoing actions that begin in the past and the strong potentiality element in their references to the future, was taken exclusively from English. If the literature was scrutinised for cross-language research, the outcome would probably be disappointing. Erbaugh (1982) has reported on the use of the Mandarin -le particle, which codes current states that begin in the past. Toivainen

(1980) has considered the equivalent structures in Finnish. They both find usage that is late relative to other aspects of the temporal/modal system but early relative to the chronological ages reported for American children in Chapter 2. Unfortunately, Toivainen's data seem partially inconsistent with some recent results for Finnish reported by Weist, Wysocka, and Lyytinen (1991). Moreover, neither Erbaugh nor Toivainen considered the precise contexts in which the linguistic forms were used. It will be remembered that discrepancies over age between the American data and equivalent data from Britain were reconciled in Chapter 2 with reference to cultural differences over contextual constraints.

Thus, the issue of ongoing actions that begin in the past seems to be one that requires further research, and the same probably applies if we shift from past references to future. Certainly, the only relevant work that I have been able to find is Stephany's study of five Greek children (reported in Stephany, 1986) and Weist et al.'s (1984) study of six Polish children. It is reassuring that Stephany sees her analysis of future and subjunctive usage as "completely agreeing" with the work on English summarised in Chapter 2 that indicated the potentiality element. It is also reassuring that Weist et al. emphasise the use of future for predicted completions and anticipated situations. However, additional studies would undoubtedly be useful.

The Variable Sequencing of Lexical Items

An exhaustive review is essential. However, it seems likely that the only conclusions currently to be drawn are that data from English would be hard to reconcile with cross-language variability over contextually completed meaning, and that data from other languages are inadequate but not unduly troubling. This accepted, it would follow that there is no reason at present to anticipate cross-language variability over the hierarchical structure of the mappings that the communicative process would form, though admittedly no strong reason to anticipate the reverse. But how about the serial structure and the movement transformations that serial structure dictates? The present section began with a reminder that, given the communicative process, the serial order of mappings would depend to some considerable extent on the serial order of the input strings, and languages clearly differ in their typical lexical sequences. However, before we conclude widespread variation over serial structure, we need to remember a further point. As Chapter 3 must have made clear, the sequence of items within meaning elements has no bearing on structure. What is important is the sequence of items between meaning elements. Thus, it is of no consequence whether there are languages (as indeed there are) that differ from

English in having postpositions rather than prepositions, prefix inflections rather than suffix inflections, and post-noun adjectives rather than pre-noun adjectives. The important issue is whether there are languages that differ from English in the ordering of their major phrases.

Taking this as the issue, it is clear that critically different languages do exist. Chapter 4 had occasion to highlight the subject noun phrase, verb, object noun phrase (or SVO) order that is dominant in English, and intimated in passing that other languages differ. Cross-language surveys like Greenberg (1963) and Steele (1978) have amply confirmed this, even if we restrict ourselves to the dominant orders that virtually all languages appear to possess. Although SVO is the most popular dominant order, accounting for 60 per cent of the natural languages according to Osgood (1980), SOV and VSO are not insignificant. Osgood claims that they are the dominant order in, respectively, 30 and 10 per cent of the possible cases. Osgood's figures imply no other dominant orders, but this may be inaccurate. A preference for VOS has occasionally been reported, with only OSV and OVS most likely non-existent. However, even OSV and OVS are not excluded once we acknowledge that many (perhaps most) languages have permissible orders in addition to their dominant. An extreme example is Warlpiri (an Australian aboriginal language) where, according to Bavin and Shopen (1990), all six combinations of S, V, and O are perfectly acceptable.

Both the distinction between dominant and permissible orders and the potential breadth of the latter are relevant to us. To see why, recall first, that the communicative process strives to minimise the disruption to the lexical sequence both within and between input mappings. This means that no matter how variable the permissible orders, the outcome will be mappings that are as close as possible to what the dominant order alone would require. To see what this would mean, consider (5.1), which shows schematically the mappings that, given the communicative process, would result from individual strings in the SVO, SOV, VSO, and VOS orders.[1]

SVO

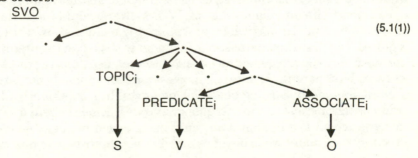

(5.1(1))

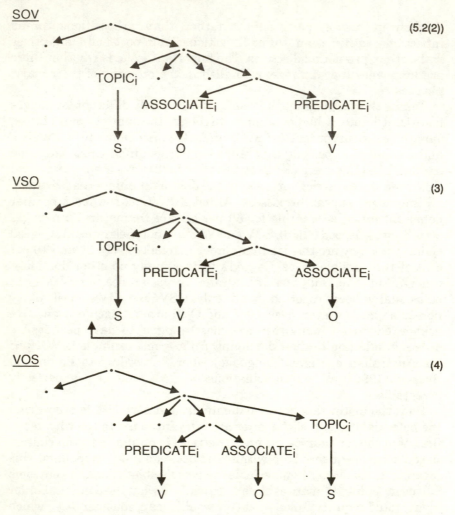

SOV

(5.2(2))

TOPICᵢ   ASSOCIATEᵢ   PREDICATEᵢ

S   O   V

VSO

(3)

TOPICᵢ   PREDICATEᵢ   ASSOCIATEᵢ

S   V   O

VOS

(4)

TOPICᵢ

PREDICATEᵢ   ASSOCIATEᵢ

V   O   S

With languages that have no permissible orders apart from their dominant ones, integration of input mappings would in no way disrupt what appears in (5.1). However, consider a language that allowed SOV in addition to its dominant order of SVO. Matters would immediately become different. In particular, an optional transformation would be required, which shifted the associate element to the left of the predicate. Consider also Warlpiri, and the extent of the requisite transformations will soon be apparent. Despite this, however, we are probably not talking about a mammoth learning task. So long as children experience all the orders with roughly the adult frequency and with some element overlap, convergence on the final system could be achieved in very few trials. Precisely how many trials depends on whether children learning other languages "grope" in the sense outlined in Chapter 4. It will be remembered that groping was predicted for English on the assumption that very young children discount mid-placed lexical items but do not distort the sequence of what they conserve. It is unclear whether the assumption would apply with other languages. The cross-language research on discounting that was alluded to in Chapter 1 is, for example, concerned with the open/closed class distinction, not the mid-placed/ end-placed item. If the assumption could be taken for granted, groping would surely be predicted, with a time-scale to elimination more or less equivalent to English.

With pure SVO, SOV, and VOS languages, groping is probably the only developmentally relevant prediction. With other languages, however, there might be more to consider. To see what, imagine first a pure VSO language. Certainly the ordering should appear to the time-scale of English, but because of the additional processing implied by the transformation, slips in the direction of SVO should sometimes occur. Moreover, this should happen even after VSO is well-established. Imagine also a SVO/SOV language whose dominant order was SVO. A situation identical to VSO would surely be predicted. With other combinations, the slippage would not necessarily always be towards SVO. However, given what has already been established about the frequency of the dominant orders across the world's languages, SVO predominance should probably be predicted.

Is the prediction likely to be supported empirically? It would certainly square with the conclusions drawn by early reviewers like Brown (1973). These are that although conformity with SVO is not universal in children's speech, it sometimes occurs where the adult language would avoid it. The prediction would also concur Slobin's (1977) hypothesis that orders that, like VSO, interrupt the predicate are cognitively distasteful. However, is the prediction correct? At first sight, it seems as if anyone trying to find out would have all the data they need. As Chapter 4 remarked, there is a mass of cross-language research concerned with the sequencing of lexical items. Moreover, although the research is predominantly addressed to spontaneous speech, it includes studies of children's responses to the speech of others. Yet despite its bulk, the research would probably prove disappointing because the languages it focuses on are usually SVO dominant. Furthermore, when the languages are not SVO dominant they are usually SOV and hence, as (5.1) makes clear, closely related to SVO from the communicative process' perspective.

It is true that one of the languages analysed in Slobin's (1985) encyclopaedic review—Samoan—is treatable (controversially) as VSO dominant, and that the developmental data are consistent with the prediction outlined above. Of five children aged between two and three years at the start of a longitudinal study, only the oldest conformed with VSO. Three of the others conformed with SVO. However, Samoan is only one language, five is a very limited sample, and the number of utterances per child was surprisingly small. Moreover, a quest for information elsewhere would prove equally disappointing. Hickey (1990) has studied the acquisition of Irish, which is also VSO dominant, during the second and third year, but again with a limited sample. Interestingly though, two of her three subjects were as likely to conform with SVO as with VSO. Thus, as with contextually completed meanings, the data on lexical sequencing are probably not at this moment inconsistent. They are just incomplete.

A Possible Explanation of Grammatical Structure

Summing up what has been said so far, it appears that even if the mappings on which the communicative process would operate have a universal hierarchical structure, their serial structure would vary between languages. This would have implications for the shape of the final rules including the transformational adjuncts. In this context, it may be worth noting that no grammar incorporating (5.1(3)) would be restricted to the "local" transformations highlighted in Chapter 3. Despite the differences, there may, however, be no reason to anticipate adverse consequences for the time-scale of learning. What should be anticipated as regards other aspects of development is far from clear. However, there is a chance, given the literature as it stands, of no glaring inconsistencies with the path learning takes.

These points must be reassuring but they are not enough. In Chapter 3, the crucial step as regards timing was not really the serial structure but rather the abstraction of meaning elements. It is not clear that this could be achieved for all the natural languages. Yet, it is not clear that there would be problems. As became apparent in Chapter 3, the abstraction of meaning elements would be forced on the communicative process when dealing with English because the lexical items attached to equivalently positioned elements would show partial but incomplete identity. This followed because the contextually completed meanings were deemed to contain fewer elements than their adult equivalents. However, as we have already seen, there is a chance that the contextually completed meanings may be universally restricted in their number of elements. This being the case, there should always be partially identical items at given nodes in the structure. Indeed, it should not matter whether the language is a richly inflected system along the lines of Russian or, to use the traditional term, as "isolating" as Chinese.

Of course in predicting abstraction, it is not necessarily being suggested that it would proceed by the route outlined in Chapter 4. That route was a step-by-step procedure beginning around the age of two-and-a-half. It was hypothesised for children learning English on the grounds that due to the discounting of unstressed items, there would never be more than one lexical item associated with each meaning element prior to two-and-a-half. Moreover, within noun phrases, the item would be a noun rather than a determiner or an inflection. As a consequence, there would be a massive build-up of equivalently positioned elements but, because of the impossibility of partially identical items, no abstraction. Hence when, around two-and-a-half, unstressed items begin to be preserved, partial identity across all the elements will take some time to achieve.

This said, it should be apparent that even if contextually completed meanings are constant across languages, there could be variability over the path to abstraction if there are differences over which items are stressed. That such differences exist will already by clear, because Chapter 1 mentioned work showing that the unstressed form classes in Mayan are virtually orthogonal to the ones in English. Another relevant case is Turkish for here, as Slobin (1982, 1985) has remarked, it is not just that different form classes are stressed. It is also that more are. It is particularly interesting that heavy stress falls on both nouns and their rich array of inflectional suffixes. Thus, "el (= hand)" is stressed, but so are all the syllables of "eller (= hands)", "ellerim (= my hands)" and "ellerinde (= in my hands)". This being the case, the abstraction of meaning elements (and the attendant derivation of syntactic categories) should be both quicker than for English and less fragmentary. This seems to be what happens. Summarising longitudinal research and his own (Slobin & Bever, 1982) cross-sectional investigation with acting out, Slobin (1985) concludes that "most of the agglutinative morphology (i.e. the suffixes)—nominal and verbal—is used productively in the two-word period, before the age of two".

Data from one language is not, however, enough, and it is not clear that a thorough review of the literature would yield anything more. Thus, further research will probably be required. In view of the preceding paragraphs, the principled way to proceed would be to lay out a taxonomy of stress patterns, and select languages accordingly. Indeed, the languages selected by this criterion should be crossed with languages selected for their dominant and permissible orderings of subject noun phrase, verb, and object noun phrase. Having chosen languages by these means, the task would be to spell out the likely course of development given the communicative process without *a priori* knowledge and conduct research to ascertain its validity.

What detailed investigation would show about consistency with the path to learning cannot be guessed. However, the section has presented one or two reasons for optimism as regards the learning time-scale. At least it has done this given the universality of contextually completed meaning, and this is another issue in need of further study. However, if consistency with the time-scale of learning could be guaranteed from consistency over meaning, the result would be of great interest, not just in psychology but also in linguistics. The reason is that over the years, linguists in general and Chomsky in particular (for example, Chomsky, 1968, 1975) have adduced the similarities between the natural languages as a reason additional to the learning time-scale as an argument for innateness. The most obvious of the similarities was mentioned early in Chapter 1, that all languages imply a phrase structure or transformational grammar. However, during the course of the essay, others have been introduced. What is interesting is that if contextually completed meanings are both universal and crucial, they would impose similarities on all the natural languages. Thus, it might be unnecessary to invoke innate knowledge of grammar to ensure an explanation.

IMPLICATIONS FOR DEVELOPMENTAL PSYCHOLOGY

The essay began with the convergence of interest between psychology and linguistics and it is encouraging that it can approach its conclusion in a similar vein. Despite this, it has to be recognised that convergence was not the essay's original aim. Rather, given the embarrassment to developmental theory created by the innateness hypothesis, it was to see whether there was an alternative that could seriously be considered. While the need for further research is unreservedly granted, it is to be hoped that the communicative process can now be accorded this status. However, as mentioned at the start of the chapter, seeing the communicative process as an alternative to innateness does not mean seeing it as something that would be welcome in theoretical terms. To allow this, it would be necessary to show that the communicative process without *a priori* insights into grammar does not invoke language-specific knowledge of a non-grammatical kind. Remembering how Chapter 1 criticised parallel distributed processing for precisely such knowledge, it is easy to see how it could inadvertently slip through. Thus, in this concluding section, the essay will examine the communicative process' architecture for language-specificity. It will look at what is implied by first the input mappings and second the learning procedures. Finding nothing particularly troubling, the section will end with a brief statement about the theoretical significance of what has been achieved.

The Processing of Input Mappings

It is possible to consider the communicative process' architecture from two perspectives. On the one hand, it can be viewed as a system that allows operations on a particular kind of input, namely the mappings. On the other, it can be viewed as a system that allows a particular kind of operation, namely the procedures governing the integration of mappings and the production of communicative expressions. The present section will adopt both perspectives, taking them in order. Starting then with the input mappings, the crucial point is that, stripped of their element–item content, the essence of the mappings is a hierarchy. Thus, the fundamental issue is the language-specificity or otherwise of the ability to operate on hierarchical structures. This being the case, there seems to be three sorts of evidence that might be brought to bear: (i) studies of children's performance when operating with basic, superordinate, and subordinate categories; (ii) studies of children's ascription of predicates to natural ontologies; and (iii) studies relevant to children's ability to solve class inclusion problems. All three sorts of evidence will be reviewed briefly, leading to some encouraging though not uncritical conclusions.

The distinction between basic, superordinate and subordinate categories originated in a paper by Rosch et al. (1976). In that paper, Rosch et al. define basic categories as categories at the most inclusive level at which there are attributes common to most members. Superordinate categories are categories at more inclusive levels. Subordinate categories are categories at less inclusive levels. By this definition, "chair" is a basic category, "furniture" is a superordinate, and "rocking chair" is a subordinate. This is because, on the one hand, chairs share more attributes (both perceptual and actional) than pieces of furniture, despite the latter's more inclusive status. On the other hand, chairs share as many attributes as rocking chairs, and yet include them. Rosch et al. report a series of experiments with adult subjects showing the psychological significance of the basic level. For example, basic level categories facilitated decisions about the positions of pictures in spatial arrays, the identity of picture pairs and the match-up between spoken names and depicted objects. Rosch et al. also report two studies with three- to ten-year-old children. In both studies they asked children to put together the pictures that they thought were alike. The studies differed in that one involved free sorting sixteen pictures and the other selecting a pair of pictures from a triad. Rosch et al. found that, regardless of age, performance with basic level distinctions was by far the best. However, performance with superordinates and subordinates was by no means inadequate and this could be construed as encouraging for us. Indeed, a similar point emerges from work by Daehler, Lonardo, and Bukatko (1979) with children of 22, 27, and 32 months. Daehler et al. presented a standard object and asked the children to select from an array the object that went with it. Sometimes the array contained an identical object, sometimes an object related at the basic level, sometimes an object related at the superordinate, and sometimes a complementary object. Identical objects produced the best performance followed by basic, then superordinate, and then complementary. However, performance was significantly above chance in all conditions and regardless of age. Thus, there is evidence that even before they are two, children can operate with several levels of a hierarchy.

Closely related to the work on the basic/superordinate/subordinate distinction are Keil's (1979, 1981) investigations with ontological categories. Keil believed that ontological categories are obliged by an "M-constraint" to form a hierarchical structure. His concern was whether the M-constraint is respected by children. He argued that if it is, it ought to be reflected in what children are prepared to predicate on given categories. Thus, if children are prepared to predicate "is sick" on both animals and plants but restrict "is asleep" to animals and "is wilted" to plants, it can be inferred that they have a structure in which living things are superordinate to animals and plants. To ascertain what the situation was, Keil asked a large sample of children aged three to twelve years to judge whether sentences and their opposites (for example "The car is alive" and "The car is dead") were silly or sensible. In 99.9 per cent of cases, judgements were consistent with the M-constraint and hence with a hierarchical structure.

The results are impressive, and yet there is a possible problem. The problem, which if true would apply also to the work on basic, superordinate, and subordinate categories, is that although the results show the existence of hierarchically organised knowledge, they may not show the ability to operate on the hierarchy itself. It may be that the children moved about in the hierarchy rather than took it as an object of knowledge. For purposes of the essay, we can construe making hierarchies the object of knowledge in a fairly loose fashion. There is no need, for example, to argue that the whole structure is simultaneously dealt with. Nevertheless, operating on rather than moving about has to be our concern, and this implies some anxieties about work like Keil's.

This accepted, it may be that more is to be gained from work related to class inclusion. The classic work of this kind was conducted by Inhelder and Piaget (1964). Presenting an array of flowers in which primulas, say, predominated over roses, Inhelder and Piaget would ask "Are there more flowers or more primulas?" Thus, they obliged children to quantify across levels, and by that token were undoubtedly concerned with operations on a hierarchy. The trouble is that Inhelder and Piaget found that even eight-year-olds were inclined to error, a finding amply corroborated by Hooper, Sipple, Goldman, and Swinton (1979) with a more controlled procedure and a much larger sample. Thus taken at face value, Inhelder and Piaget's results would argue against the capacity we are concerned with.

However, a mass of more recent research has suggested that a face value interpretation of Inhelder and Piaget would be overly naïve. For instance, Judd and Mervis (1979) have shown that five-year-olds can succeed on class inclusion problems if they are asked first to count the superordinate and the subordinate categories and, second, if the inconsistency between their initial responses and their counting is explained clearly. Markman (1973; Markman & Seibert, 1976) has found that five-year-olds can succeed if the problem involves a "collection". Collections, as with forests in relation to trees and bunches in relation to grapes, are organised on a part–whole basis and usually involve spatially contiguous objects. In Markman and Siebert's studies, questions like "Who would have more to eat, someone who ate the green grapes or someone who ate the bunch?" elicited performances that were above chance. Questions like "Who would have more to eat, someone who ate the green grapes or someone who ate the grapes?" elicited performances that were significantly below.

Work like Judd and Mervis' and Markman's is useful in two respects. First, it highlights the overly taxing nature of Inhelder and Piaget's procedures. Second, it demonstrates the capacity to operate on hierarchies in much younger children. Nevertheless, the children were still five years of age, and hence at the upper end of the grammar-learning range. This recognised, it is reassuring to be able to quote two further studies, the first by Smith (1979). Smith showed that children of preschool (and hence grammar-learning) age could deal with class inclusion problems phrased like "A pawpaw is a kind of fruit but not a banana. Is a pawpaw food?". The second study was by Callanan and Markman (1982) and involved two- and three-year-olds. Its major finding was that terms applying to superordinate categories like toys, animals, and cars are treated as collective, that is as akin to "forest" and "bunch". Terms applying to basic categories are not so treated. Thus, while an individual doll could be called "doll", it could not be called "toy". The important implication is that when children process sentences like "Are dolls toys?" and "Is an animal a horse?" they must be making cross-level comparisons.

The Integration and Production Procedures

Given the work of Smith and Callanan and Markman, there do seem grounds for denying the language specificity of operations by preschool children on hierarchical structures. However, the communicative process without *a priori* knowledge does not simply operate. It also performs operations of a particular kind, and the question is raised as to the uniqueness of these operations to the language system. Anyone who has struggled through the complexities of Chapters 3 and 4 could be forgiven for taking uniqueness as read. Nevertheless, while this has to be recognised, it should not be forgotten that the complexities follow from the interplay of the operations with the hierarchical mappings. Having already discussed the latter, we can discount them and focus on the operations divorced from their objects. When we do, we can see that the operations are really surprisingly simple. The procedures by which the mappings are integrated do little more than assimilate what is known, and then reorganise the knowledge to optimise the representation of what is new. The procedures by which communicative expressions are produced simply compare the options for achieving some end, and attempt to differentiate them in terms of efficacy. While the simplicity of the operations does not guarantee their generality beyond the language system, it certainly makes this more probable and warrants a review of the cognitive developmental literature with some hopes of success.

As those who have conducted such a review will already know, parallels of the operations have been invoked for a wide range of non-linguistic domains. Thus, surveying the mechanisms deployed across cognitive development as a whole, Flavell (1977) comments that: "two major classes of — processes and principles seem to be distinguishable: one class generates distinctions within cognitive entities (and) the other relates one cognitive entity to one or more others". It is easy to see why Flavell should say this, and indeed why he should quote himself as saying it several years later (Flavell, 1984). The notion of relating cognitive entities emerges from research in both the constructivist tradition of Piaget and the information processing tradition of his most ardent critics. Importantly, research in both traditions has identified "relating" in terms very similar to those used by our integration procedures. Thus, Piaget's studies of logical, spatial, and mathematical thinking have led him to construe learners as assimilating events to existing schemes, and modifying both the schemes and the overall knowledge to accommodate in as structured a fashion as possible what has proved problematic (see Piaget's (1985) discussion of beta and gamma compensations as relatively recent exposition). Likewise, Sternberg (1984) interprets "intellectual task" research as entailing "knowledge acquisition components" that compare information and combine it meaningfully. Moreover, as the interplay of the knowledge acquisition components can be mediated by feedback on (amongst other things) efficiency, combination for optimal usage is implicitly guaranteed.

As for Flavell's notion of generating distinctions within cognitive entities, it is so widespread as to be virtually truistic. It is a central feature of theorising from Werner (1948) to Fischer (1980), the latter emphasising the differentiation of "skills" into distinctive components. However, it receives its most interesting treatment in the development of "self modifying production systems". There, processes are advanced which generate distinctions within cognitive entities in a fashion that is more or less identical to how our model selects communicative expressions. As Klahr (1984) and Neeches, Langley, and Klahr (1987) explain, production systems consist of rules written in the form of condition/action pairs. Conditions are tests on the reality that the system construes. If the conditions for an action are not fulfilled, the system remains static. If the conditions for one, and only one, action are fulfilled, the system fires and the action is performed. If the conditions for more than one action are fulfilled, a state of conflict is engendered and, given a self-modifying model, conflict resolution procedures come into play. The conflict resolution procedures are particularly relevant in the present context because they are frequently construed (for example, Langley, 1987) as associating strengths with actions as a function of efficacy in usage. As strength decreases within and across contexts, actions are weeded out. As this is exactly what has been proposed for the communicative process,[2] it is reassuring to find it being invoked in a different context. This is particularly the case when the foundations of self-modifying production systems are studies of concept formation and problem solving in non-linguistic domains.

Overall then, it seems that we can give a confident answer to the question underpinning the last few paragraphs. There is nothing language-specific about the operations that the communicative process without *a priori* knowledge can perform. On the contrary, analogous processes have been invoked for a wide range of contrasting domains by researchers from a wide range of theoretical traditions. In retrospect, this should not be surprising. As Chapter 3 made clear, the communicative process without *a priori* knowledge has links with two kinds of model. The first was deemed to take an "assimilation" approach and was, as we saw in Chapter 3, heavily influenced by the work of Piaget. The second was interpreted as "accommodative", and was primarily associated with Anderson (1975, 1977, 1981). Why this is relevant is that Anderson's (1983) work on cognition in general is closely associated with the production system approach.

However, surprising or not, the analogies over processes, taken with our earlier conclusions about the processing of hierarchical structures, mean that the communicative process without *a priori* knowledge stands a good chance of meshing with a general theory of learning. What it does not mean is that the communicative process without *a priori* knowledge reduces language to general intelligence. Quite the opposite. If the communicative process without *a priori* knowledge abstracts meaning elements, as Chapter 3 suggested, the knowledge formed will be an autonomous system. The point is that the learning procedures may be general, but not the structures they form.

Linguistic Autonomy and General Learning

It is important to be clear about the distinction between general procedures and general content, for the latter is not, as regards language, a serious proposal. The need for such autonomous phenomena as syntactic form classes was amply documented in Chapter 3, and supportive evidence from other sources can readily be adduced. Fodor (1983), for example, emphasises work on speech perception to assert the "modularity" of language. He cites research showing that experiences with sentences like "Because he was afraid of electronic surveillance, the spy carefully searched the room for bugs" facilitates the processing of sentences like "Because he was afraid of electronic surveillance, the spy carefully searched the room for insects". The point Fodor makes is that "bugs" could only prime "insects" if it is divorced in perception from the meaning that its context imposes. Fodor discusses evidence of other kinds, referring briefly to recent work on language pathology. This is a topic taken up in depth by Linebarger (1989) who cites work showing that, despite well-documented difficulties in comprehension, Broca's aphasics perform well in judging grammaticality. Thus, they will acknowledge the ill-formedness of "What it is?" and the well-formedness of "What is it?" while failing to ascribe a meaning to either.

The point is that evidence like this is grist to our model's mill, for the communicative process without *a priori* knowledge is deemed to create an autonomous system. Yet, it is deemed to do this, not just using general procedures but also (remembering the mappings) from input that is not itself autonomous. This is surely interesting. Many theorists have contemplated the emergence of linguistic autonomy from something inherently grounded. However, their proposals still seem open to the criticisms that were first voiced by Roeper (1982). They are either exceedingly vague or surreptitiously constrained. Thus, there is widespread sympathy with Gleitman and Wanner's (1988) view that grounded beginnings mean discontinuous growth. It is to be hoped that the present essay has provided encouragement to those who believe things that might be otherwise. If it has, there is some chance of attention being paid to the research on which further progress depends: studies of the meanings that children learning grammar ascribe to adult speech. It is not important to know how the ascriptions are made though, as Gleitman and Wanner point out this is a major mystery. It is not even important to know why the meanings have universal features (should this prove to be the case) though from other perspectives this is a fascinating question. The crucial issue is what the meanings are like, for until it is resolved it will not be possible to say much more than the present essay about the innateness hypothesis or its developmentally more acceptable alternative.

NOTES

1. Two points need noting here. First, although the completion and polarity elements appear in (5.1), no significance should be attached to the order they are depicted in relation to the topic and predicate elements. Second, there are other possible mappings for VSO, namely: (i) a transformation that moves S rather than V; or (ii) TOPICi swung to the right of the diagram with either S or O movement.
2. When the communicative process is discussed in terms of increasing and decreasing strengths, it will be clear that links can be made with parallel distributed processing. Nevertheless, the links should not be overplayed. We are only talking about one component of the process and the criticisms raised about parallel distributed processing in Chapter 1 should not be forgotten.

References

Ackerman, B.P. (1978). Children's understanding of speech acts in unconventional directive frames. *Child Development, 49,* 311–318.

Ammon, M.S., & Slobin, D.I. (1979). A cross-linguistic study of the processing of causative sentences. *Cognition, 7,* 3–17.

Anderson, J.R. (1975). Computer simulation of a language acquisition system: A first report. In R.L. Solso (Ed.), *Information processing and cognition: The Loyola symposium.* Hillsdale, NJ: Lawrence Erlbaum Associates Inc.

Anderson, J.R. (1977). Induction of augmented transition networks. *Cognitive Science, 1,* 125–157.

Anderson, J.R. (1981). A theory of language acquisition based on general learning principles. *Proceedings of the Seventh International Joint Conference on Artificial Intelligence, Vancouver.*

Anderson, J.R. (1983). *The architecture of cognition.* Cambridge, Mass: Harvard.

Anderson, S.R. (1982). Where's morphology? *Linguistic Inquiry, 13,* 571–612.

Angiolillo, C.J., & Goldin-Meadow, S. (1982). Experimental evidence for agent-patient categories in child language. *Journal of Child Language, 9,* 627–643.

Antinucci, F., & Miller, R. (1976). How children talk about what happened. *Journal of Child Language, 3,* 167–189.

Antinucci, F., & Parisi, D. (1973). Early language acquisition: A model and some data. In C.A. Ferguson & D.I. Slobin (Eds.), *Studies of child language development.* New York: Holt, Rinehart & Winston.

Astington, J.W. (1988). Promises: Words or deeds? *First Language, 8,* 259–270.

Austin, J.L. (1962). *How to do things with words.* London: Oxford University Press.

Baker, C.L. (1979). Syntactic theory and the projection problem. *Linguistic Inquiry, 10,* 533–581.

Barnes, S., Gutfreund, M., Satterly, D., & Wells, G. (1983). Characteristics of adult speech which predict children's language development. *Journal of Child Language, 10,* 65–84.

Barrett, M.D. (1979). *Semantic development during the single word stage of language acquisition.* Ph.D. dissertation, Sussex University.

Barrett, M.D. (1982a). Distinguishing between prototypes: The early acquisition of the meanings of object names. In S.A. Kuczaj (Ed.), *Language development. Vol. 1: Syntax and semantics.* Hillsdale, NJ: Lawrence Erlbaum Associates Inc.

Barrett, M.D. (1982b). The holophrastic hypothesis: Conceptual and empirical issues. *Cognition, 11,* 47–76.

Barrett, M.D. (1983). The early acquisition and development of the meanings of action-related words. In T.B. Seiler & W. Wannenmacher (Eds.), *Concept development and the development of word meaning.* Berlin: Springer-Verlag.

Bates, E., & MacWhinney, B. (1979). A functionalist approach to the acquisition of grammar. In E. Ochs & B.B. Schieffelin (Eds.), *Developmental pragmatics.* New York: Academic Press.

Bates, E., & MacWhinney, B. (1982). Functionalist approaches to grammar. In E. Wanner & L.R. Gleitman (Eds.), *Language acquisition: The state of the art.* Cambridge: Cambridge University Press.

Bates, E., MacWhinney, B., Caselli, C., Devescovi, A., Natale, F., & Venza, V. (1984). A cross-linguistic study of the development of sentence interpretation strategies. *Child Development, 55,* 341–354.

Bavin, E.L., & Shopen, T. (1990). Cues to sentence interpretation in Warlpiri. In B. MacWhinney & E. Bates (Eds.), *The cross-linguistic study of sentence processing.* Cambridge: Cambridge University Press.

Bellinger, D. (1979). Changes in the explicitness of mothers' directives as children age. *Journal of Child Language, 6,* 443–458.

Bellugi, U. (1971). Simplification in children's language. In R. Huxley & E. Ingram (Eds.), *Language acquisition: Models and methods.* London: Academic Press.

Berko, J. (1958). The child's learning of English morphology. *Word, 14,* 150–177.

Berman, R.A. (1988). Word class distinctions in developing grammars. In Y. Levy, I.M. Schlesinger & M.D.S. Braine (Eds.), *Categories and processes in language acquisition.* Hillsdale, NJ: Lawrence Erlbaum Associates Inc.

Bernstein, M.E. (1984). Non-linguistic responses to verbal instructions. *Journal of Child Language, 11,* 293–311.

Berwick, R.C., & Weinberg, A.S. (1984). *The grammatical basis of linguistic performance: Language use and acquisition.* Cambridge, Mass: M.I.T. Press.

Bever, T.G. (1970). The cognitive basis for linguistic structures. In J.R. Hayes (Ed.), *Cognition and the development of language.* New York: John Wiley & Sons.

Bever, T.G., Fodor, J.A., & Weskel, W. (1965). On the acquisition of syntax: a critique of context generalisation. *Psychological Review, 72,* 467–482.

Bloom, L. (1970). *Language development: Form and function in emerging grammars.* Cambridge, Mass: M.I.T. Press.

Bloom, L., Lahey, M., Hood, L., Lifter, K., & Fiess, K. (1980a). Complex sentences: acquisition of syntactic connectives and the semantic relations they encode. *Journal of Child Language, 7,* 235–261.

Bloom, L., Lifter, K., & Hafitz, J. (1980b). Semantics of verbs and the development of verb inflection in child language. *Language, 56,* 386–412.

Bloom, L., Lightbown, P., & Hood, L. (1975). Structure and variation in child language. *Monographs of the Society for Research in Child Development, 40,* No.2.

Bohannon, J.N., & Stanowicz, L. (1988). The issue of negative evidence: Adult responses to children's language errors. *Developmental Psychology, 24,* 684–689.

Bowerman, M. (1973). *Early syntactic development: A cross-linguistic study with special reference to Finnish.* Cambridge: Cambridge University Press.

Bowerman, M. (1976). Semantic factors in the acquisition of rules for word use and sentence construction. In D. Morehead & A. Morehead (Eds.), *Normal and deficient child language.* Baltimore: University Park Press.

Bowerman, M. (1979). The acquisition of complex sentences. In P. Fletcher & M. Garman (Eds.), *Language acquisition: Studies in first language development.* Cambridge: Cambridge University Press.

Bowerman, M. (1987). Commentary. In B. MacWhinney (Ed.), *Mechanisms of language acquisition.* Hillsdale, NJ: Lawrence Erlbaum Associates Inc.

Bowerman, M. (1988). The 'no negative evidence' problem: How do children avoid constructing an overly general grammar. In J.A. Hawkins (Ed.), *Explaining language universals.* Oxford: Basil Blackwell.

Braine, M.D.S. (1963a). The ontogeny of English phrase structure: The first phase. *Language, 39,* 1–13.

Braine, M.D.S. (1963b). On learning the grammatical order of words. *Psychological Review, 70,* 323–348.

Braine, M.D.S. (1976). Children's first word combinations. *Monographs of the Society for Research in Child Development, 41,* No.1.

Braine, M.D.S., Brody, R.E., Fisch, S.M., Weisberger, M.J., & Blum, M. (1990). Can children use a verb without exposure to its argument structure? *Journal of Child Language, 17,* 313–342.

Braine, M.D.S., & Hardy, J.A. (1982). On what case categories there are: Why they are and how they develop. In E. Wanner & L.R. Gleitman (Eds.), *Language acquisition: The state of the art.* Cambridge: Cambridge University Press.

Braine, M.D.S. & Wells, R.S. (1978). Case-like categories in children: The actor and some related categories. *Cognitive Psychology, 10,* 100–122.

Bresnan, J. (1970). On complementisers: Towards a syntactic theory of complement types. *Foundations of Language, 6,* 297–321.

Bresnan, J. (1978). A realistic transformational grammar. In M. Halle, J. Bresnan, & G.A. Miller (Eds.), *Linguistic theory and psychological reality.* Cambridge, Mass: MIT Press.

Bridges, A. (1979). Directing two-year-old's attention: Some clues to understanding. *Journal of Child Language, 6,* 211–226.

Bridges, A. (1980). SVO comprehension strategies reconsidered: The evidence of individual patterns of response. *Journal of Child Language, 7,* 89–104.

Bridges, A. (1984). Preschool children's comprehension of agency. *Journal of Child Language, 11,* 593–610.

Bridges, A., Sinha, C., & Walkerdine, V. (1981). The development of comprehension. In G. Wells (Ed.), *Learning through interaction: The study of language development.* Cambridge: Cambridge University Press.

Broen, P.A. (1972). The verbal environment of the language-learning child. *Monographs of the American Speech and Hearing Association,* No. 17.

Bronckart, J.P., & Sinclair, H. (1973). Time, tense and aspect. *Cognition, 2,* 107–130.

Brown, B.L., & Leonard, L.B. (1986). Lexical influences on children's early positional patterns. *Journal of Child Language, 13,* 219–229.

Brown, H.D. (1971). Children's comprehension of relativised English sentences. *Child Development, 42,* 1923–1926.

Brown, P. & Levinson, S. (1978). Universals in language usage: Politeness phenomena. In E.N. Goody (Ed.), *Questions and politeness.* Cambridge: Cambridge University Press.

Brown, R. (1968). The development of the wh-question in child speech. *Journal of Verbal Learning and Verbal Behaviour, 7,* 279–290.

Brown, R. (1973). *A first language: The early stages.* London: George Allen & Unwin Ltd.

Brown, R., & Bellugi, U. (1964). Three processes in the child's acquisition of syntax. *Harvard Educational Review, 34,* 133–151.

Brown, R., Cazden, C., & Bellugi-Klima, U. (1969). The child's grammar from I to III. In J.P. Hill (Ed.), *Minnesota symposium on child psychology.* Minneapolis: The University of Minnesota Press.

Brown, R., & Fraser, C. (1964). The acquisition of syntax. In U. Bellugi & R. Brown (Eds.), *The acquisition of language.* Chicago: University of Chicago Press.

Brown, R., & Hanlon, C. (1970). Derivational complexity and order of acquisition in child speech. In J.R. Hayes (Ed.), *Cognition and the development of language.* New York: John Wiley.

Bruner, J.S. (1975). From communication to language—a psychological perspective. *Cognition, 3,* 255–287.

Cairns, H.S., & Hsu, J.R. (1978). Who, why, when and how: A development study. *Journal of Child Language, 5,* 477–488.

Callanan, M.A., & Markman, E.M. (1982). Principles of organisation in young children's natural language hierarchies. *Child Development, 53,* 1093–1101.

Camaioni, L. (1979). Child–adult and child–child conversation: An interactive approach. In E. Ochs & B.B. Schieffelin (Eds.), *Developmental pragmatics.* New York: Academic Press.

Carlson, G.N., & Tanenhaus, M.K. (1989). Introduction. In G.N. Carlson & M.K. Tanenhaus (Eds.), *Linguistic structure in language processing.* Dordrecht: Kluwer Academic.

Chapman, R.S., & Kohn, L.L. (1977). *Comprehension strategies in two and three year olds: Animate agents or probable events.* Paper presented at Stanford Child Language Research Forum, Stanford University, California.

Chomsky, C. (1969). *The acquisition of syntax in children from 5 to 10.* Cambridge, Mass: M.I.T. Press.

Chomsky, N. (1957). *Syntactic structures.* The Hague: Mouton.

Chomsky, N. (1964). The logical basis of linguistic theory. In H. Lunt (Ed.), *Proceedings of the Ninth International Congress of Linguists.* The Hague: Mouton.

Chomsky, N. (1965). *Aspects of the theory of syntax.* Cambridge, Mass: M.I.T. Press.

Chomsky, N. (1968). *Language and mind*. New York: Harcourt, Brace Jovanovich.

Chomsky, N. (1970). Remarks on nominalisation. In R.A. Jacobs & P.S. Rosenbaum (Eds.), *Readings in English transformational grammar*. Waltham, Mass: Ginn.

Chomsky, N. (1975). *Reflections on language*. New York: Pantheon.

Chomsky, N. (1981). *Lectures on government and binding*. Dordrecht: Foris Publications.

Clark, E.V. (1973). Non-linguistic strategies and the acquisition of word meanings. *Cognition, 2,* 161–182.

Clark, E.V. (1987). The principle of contrast: A constraint on language acquisition. In B. MacWhinney (Ed.), *Mechanisms of language acquisition*. Hillsdale, NJ: Lawrence Erlbaum Associates Inc.

Cohen Levine, S., & Carey, S. (1982). Upfront: The acquisition of a concept and a word. *Journal of Child Language, 9,* 645–657.

Conant, S. (1987). The relationship between age and MLU in young children: A second look at Klee and Fitzgerald's data. *Journal of Child Language, 14,* 169–173.

Cook, V. (1973). The comparison of language development in native children and foreign adults. *International Review of Applied Linguistics, 11,* 13–28.

Corrigan, R., & Odya-Weis, C. (1985). The comprehension of semantic relations by two-year olds: An exploratory study. *Journal of Child Language, 12,* 47–59.

Cromer, R.F. (1974). The development of language and cognition: The cognition hypothesis. In B. Foss (Ed.), *New perspectives in child development*. Harmondsworth, Middlesex: Penguin.

Cromer, R.F. (1976). Developmental strategies for language. In V. Hamilton & M.D. Vernon (Eds.), *The development of cognitive processes*. London: Academic Press.

Cromer, R.F. (1991). *Language and thought in normal and handicapped children*. Oxford: Basil Blackwell.

Cross, T.G. (1977). Mothers' speech adjustments: the contribution of selected child listener variables. In C.E. Snow & C.A. Ferguson (Eds.), *Talking to children: Language input and acquisition*. Cambridge: Cambridge University Press.

Cross, T.G. (1978). Mother's speech and its association with rate of linguistic development in young children. In N. Waterson & C. Snow (Eds.), *The development of communication*. Chichester: John Wiley.

Cziko, G.A. (1989). A review of the state-process and punctual-nonpunctual distinctions in children's acquisition of verbs. *First Language, 9,* 1–31.

Daehler, M.W., Lonardo, R., & Bukatko, D. (1979). Matching and equivalence judgments in very young children. *Child Development, 50,* 170–179.

Demetras, M.J., Post, K.N., & Snow, C.E. (1986). Feedback to first language learners: The role of repetitions and clarification questions. *Journal of Child Language, 13,* 275–292.

de Villiers, J.G., & de Villiers, P.A. (1973). Development of the use of word order in comprehension. *Journal of Psycholinguistic Research, 2,* 331–341.

Dore, J. (1977a). Children's illocutionary acts. In R.O. Freedle (Ed.), *Discourse production and comprehension*. Norwood, NJ: Ablex.

198   REFERENCES

Dore, J. (1977b). 'Oh them Sheriff': A pragmatic analysis of children's responses to questions. In S. Ervin-Tripp & C. Mitchell-Kernan (Eds.), *Child discourse.* New York: Academic Press.
Drach, K. (1969). The language of the parent: A pilot study. In *Working Paper No. 14: The structure of linguistic input to children.* University of California, Berkeley: Language–Behaviour Research Laboratory.
Durkin, K. (1980). The production of locative prepositions by young school children. *Educational Studies, 6,* 9–30.
Edwards, D. (1973). Sensory-motor intelligence and semantic relations in early child grammar. *Cognition, 2,* 395–434.
Edwards, D. (1978). Social relations and early language. In A.J. Lock (Ed.), *Action, gesture and symbol: The emergence of language.* London: Academic Press.
Edwards, D., & Goodwin, R. (1980). Action words and pragmatic function in early language. In S.A. Kuczaj & M.D. Barrett (Eds.), *The development of word meaning.* Berlin: Springer-Verlag.
Emonds, J. (1976). *A transformational approach to English syntax.* New York: Academic Press.
Emslie, H.C., & Stevenson, R.J. (1981). Preschool children's use of the articles in definite and indefinite referring expressions. *Journal of Child Language, 8,* 313–328.
Erbaugh, M.S. (1982). *Coming to order: Natural selection and the origin of syntax in the Mandarin-speaking child.* Ph.D. dissertation, University of California, Berkeley.
Erreich, A. (1984). Learning how to ask: Patterns of inversion in yes-no and wh-questions. *Journal of Child Language, 11,* 579–592.
Erreich, A., Valian, V., & Winzemer, J. (1980). Aspects of a theory of language acquisition. *Journal of Child Language, 7,* 157–179.
Ervin, S.M. (1964). Imitation and structural changes in children's language. In E.H. Lenneberg (Ed.), *New directions in the study of language.* Cambridge, Mass: M.I.T. Press.
Ervin-Tripp, S.M. (1970). Discourse agreement: How children answer questions. In J.R Hayes (Ed.), *Cognition and the development of language.* New York: John Wiley.
Ervin-Tripp, S.M., & Miller, W. (1977). Early discourse: Some questions about questions. In M. Lewis & L.A. Rosenblum (Eds.), *Interaction, conversation and the development of language.* New York: John Wiley.
Ewing, G. (1982). Word order invariance and variability in five children's three-word utterances: A limited scope formula analysis. In C.E. Johnson & C.L. Thew (Eds.), *Proceedings of the Second International Congress for the Study of Child Language.* Washington: University Press of America.
Fischer, K.W. (1980). A theory of cognitive development: The control and construction of hierarchies of skills. *Psychological Review, 87,* 477–531.
Flavell, J.H. (1977). *Cognitive development.* Englewood Cliffs: Prentice Hall.
Flavell, J.H. (1984). Discussion. In R.J. Sternberg (Ed.), *Mechanisms of cognitive development.* New York: W.H. Freeman & Company.
Fletcher, P. (1981). Description and explanation in the acquisition of verb-forms. *Journal of Child Language, 8,* 93–108.

Fletcher, P. (1985). *A child's learning of English*. Oxford: Basil Blackwell.

Fodor, J.A. (1983). *The modularity of mind*. Cambridge, Mass: Bradford Books.

Fodor, J.A., Bever, T.G., & Garrett, M.F. (1974). *The psychology of language: An introduction to psycholinguistics and generative grammar*. New York: McGraw-Hill.

Fodor, J.A., & Pylyshyn, Z.W. (1988). Connectionism and cognitive architecture: A critical analysis. *Cognition, 28*, 3–71.

Fouts, R.S. (1974). Capacities for language in the great apes. In *Proceedings of the 18th International Congress of Anthropological and Ethnological Sciences*. The Hague: Mouton.

Furrow, D., Nelson, K., & Benedict, H. (1979). Mothers' speech to children and syntactic development: Some simple relationships. *Journal of Child Language, 6*, 423–442.

Gardner, B.T., & Gardner, R.A. (1971). Two-way communication with an infant chimpanzee. In A.M. Schrier & F. Stollnitz, (Eds.), *Behaviour of nonhuman primates, Vol. 4*. New York: Academic Press.

Garnham, A. (1985). *Psycholinguistics*. London: Methuen.

Garvey, C. (1975). Requests and responses in children's speech. *Journal of Child Language, 2*, 41–63.

Gathercole, V.C. (1986). The acquisition of the present perfect: Explaining differences in the speech of Scottish and American children. *Journal of Child Language, 13*, 537–560.

Gazdar, G., Klein, E., Pullum, G., & Sag, I. (1985). *Generalised phrase structure grammar*. Oxford: Basil Blackwell.

Gentner, D. (1975). Evidence for the psychological reality of semantic components: the verbs of possession. In D.A. Norman & D.E. Rumelhart (Eds.), *Explorations in cognition*. San Francisco: W.H. Freeman.

Gentner, D. (1978). On relational meaning: The acquisition of verb meaning. *Child Development, 49*, 988–998.

Gleitman, L.R. (1981). Maturational determinants of language growth. *Cognition, 10*, 103–114.

Gleitman, L.R., Newport, E.L., & Gleitman, H. (1984). The current status of the motherese hypothesis. *Journal of Child Language, 11*, 43–79.

Gleitman, L.R., & Wanner, E. (1988). Current issues in language learning. In M.H. Bornstein & M.E. Lamb (Eds.), *Perceptual, cognitive and linguistic development*. Hove: Lawrence Erlbaum Associates Ltd.

Gold, E.M. (1967). Language identification in the limit. *Information and Control, 10*, 447–474.

Golinkoff, R.M., Hirsh-Pasek, K., Cauley, K.M., & Gordon, L. (1987). The eyes have it: Lexical and syntactic comprehension in a new paradigm. *Journal of Child Language, 14*, 23–45.

Goodluck, H., & Tavakolian, S. (1982). Competence and processing in children's grammar of relative clauses. *Cognition, 11*, 1–27.

Gordon, D., & Lakoff, G. (1971). Conversational postulates. *Paper from the 7th Regional Meeting of Chicago Linguistic Society*, 63–85.

Gordon, P. (1985). Evaluating the semantic categories hypothesis: The case of the count/mass distinction. *Cognition, 20*, 209–242.

Gordon, P. (1988). Count/mass category acquisition: Distributional distinctions in children's speech. *Journal of Child Language, 15*, 109–128.

Green, G.M. (1975). How to get people to do things with words: The whimperative question. In P. Cole & J.L. Morgan (Eds.), *Syntax and semantics, Vol. 3.* New York: Academic Press.

Greenberg, J.H. (1963). Some universals of grammar with particular reference to the order of meaningful elements. In J. H. Greenberg (Ed.), *Universals of language.* Cambridge, Mass: M.I.T. Press.

Greenfield, P.H., & Smith, J.H. (1976). *The structure of communication in early language development.* New York: Academic Press.

Grice, H.P. (1975). Logic and conversation. In P. Cole & J.L. Morgan (Eds.), *Syntax and semantics, Vol. 3.* New York: Academic Press.

Grieve, R., Hoogenraad, R., & Murray, D. (1977). On the young child's use of lexis and syntax in understanding locative instructions. *Cognition, 5,* 235–250.

Gropen, J., Pinker, S., Hollander, M., & Goldberg, R. (1991). Syntax and semantics in the acquisition of locative verbs. *Journal of Child Language, 18,* 115–151.

Gropen, J., Pinker, S., Hollander, M., Goldberg, R., & Wilson, R. (1989). The learnability and acquisition of the dative alternation in English. *Language, 65,* 203–257.

Halliday, M.A.K. (1975). *Learning how to mean—explorations in the development of language.* London: Arnold.

Harner, L. (1976). Children's understanding of linguistic reference to past and future. *Journal of Psycholinguistic Research, 5,* 65–84.

Harner, L. (1980). Comprehension of past and future reference revisited. *Journal of Experimental Child Psychology, 29,* 170–182.

Harner, L. (1982). Immediacy and certainty: Factors in understanding future reference. *Journal of Child Language, 9,* 115–124.

Herriott, P. (1969). The comprehension of tense by young children. *Child Development, 40,* 103–110.

Hickey, T. (1990). The acquisition of Irish: A study of word order development. *Journal of Child Language, 17,* 17–41.

Hill, A.A. (1961). Grammaticality. *Word, 17,* 1–10.

Hirsh-Pasek, K., Treiman, R., & Schneiderman, M. (1984). Brown and Hanlon revisited: Mothers' sensitivity to ungrammatical forms. *Journal of Child Language, 11,* 81–88.

Hoff-Ginsberg, E., & Shatz, M. (1982). Linguistic input and the child's acquisition of language. *Psychological Bulletin, 92,* 3–26.

Hooper, F.M., Sipple, T.S., Goldman, J.A., & Swinton, S.S. (1979). A cross-sectional investigation of children's classificatory abilities. *Genetic Psychology Monographs, 99,* 41–87.

Hopper, R. (1983). *Adult–child teasing: A preliminary conversational analysis.* Paper presented at Child Language Seminar, Strathclyde University.

Horgan, D. (1978). How to answer questions when you've got nothing to say. *Journal of Child Language, 5,* 159–165.

Howe, C.J. (1976). The meanings of two-word utterances in the speech of young children. *Journal of Child Language, 3,* 29–47.

Howe, C.J. (1981a). *Acquiring language in a conversational context.* London: Academic Press.

Howe, C.J. (1981b). Interpretive analysis and role semantics: A ten year mesalliance. *Journal of Child Language, 8,* 439–456.

Howe, C.J. (1982). The function of noun phrases in production and comprehension: some further evidence on the contribution of semantics to early grammar. In C.E. Johnson & C.L. Thew (Eds.), *Proceedings of the Second International Congress for the Study of Child Language*. Washington: University Press of America.

Howe, C.J. (1983). Concepts and methods in the study of conversation: A reply to Lynda Olsen-Fulero. *Journal of Child Language, 10,* 231–237.

Howe, C.J. (1989). Visual primacy in social attitude judgement: A qualification. *British Journal of Social Psychology, 28,* 263–272.

Hsu, J.R., Cairns, H.S., & Fiengo, R.W. (1985). The development of grammars underlying children's interpretation of complex sentences. *Cognition, 20,* 25–48.

Hurford, J.R. (1975). A child and the English question formation rule. *Journal of Child Language, 2,* 299–301.

Huttenlocher, J. (1974). The origins of language comprehension. In R.L. Solso (Ed.), *Theories in cognitive psychology: The Loyola symposium*. Hillsdale, NJ: Lawrence Erlbaum Associates Inc.

Hyams, N. (1986). *Language acquisition and the theory of parameters*. Boston: Reidel.

Ihns, M., & Leonard, L.B. (1988). Syntactic categories in early child language: Some additional data. *Journal of Child Language, 15,* 673–678.

Ingham, R. (1992). The optional subject phenomenon in young children's English: A case study. *Journal of Child Language, 19,* 133–151.

Ingram, D., & Tyack, D. (1979). Inversion of subject NP and Aux in children's questions. *Journal of Psycholinguistic Research, 8,* 333–341.

Inhelder, B., & Piaget, J. (1964). *The early growth of logic in the child*. New York: Norton.

Jackendoff, R. (1969). An interpretive theory of negation. *Foundations of Language, 5,* 218–241.

Jackendoff, R. (1977). *X-bar syntax: A study of phrase structure*. Cambridge, Mass: M.I.T. Press.

Jensen, J.T., & Stong-Jensen, M. (1984). Morphology is in the lexicon. *Linguistic Inquiry, 15,* 474–498.

Johnston, J.R., & Slobin, D.I. (1979). The development of locative expression in English, Italian, Serbo-Croatian and Turkish. *Journal of Child Language, 6,* 529–545.

Judd, S.A., & Mervis, C.B. (1979). Learning to solve class inclusion problems: The roles of quantification and recognition of contradiction. *Child Development, 50,* 163–169.

Kaplan, R.M., & Bresnan, J. (1982). Lexical-functional grammar: A formal system for grammatical representation. In J. Bresnan (Ed.), *The mental representation of grammatical relations*. Cambridge, Mass: M.I.T. Press.

Karmiloff-Smith, A. (1979). *A functional approach to child language: A study of determiners and reference*. Cambridge: Cambridge University Press.

Keenan, E.O. (1974). Conversational competence in children. *Journal of Child Language, 1,* 163–183.

Keil, F.C. (1979). *Semantic and conceptual development: An ontological perspective*. Cambridge, Mass: Harvard University Press.

Keil, F.C. (1981). Constraints on knowledge and cognitive development. *Psychological Review, 88,* 197–227.

Kernan, K.T. (1970). Semantic relations and the child's acquisition of language. *Anthropological Linguistics, 12,* 171–187.

Klahr, D. (1984). Transition processes in cognitive development. In R.J. Sternberg (Ed.), *Mechanisms of cognitive development.* New York: W.H. Freeman & Co.

Klee, T., & Fitzgerald, M.D. (1985). The relation between grammatical development and mean length of utterance in morphemes. *Journal of Child Language, 12,* 251–269.

Klima, E.S., & Bellugi, U. (1966). Syntactic regularities in the speech of children. In J.L. Lyons & R.J. Wales (Eds.), *Psycholinguistic papers.* Edinburgh: Edinburgh University Press.

Kuczaj, S.A. (1976). Arguments against Hurford's 'Aux Copying Rule'. *Journal of Child Language, 3,* 423–427.

Kuczaj, S.A. (1977). The acquisition of regular and irregular past tense forms. *Journal of Verbal Learning and Verbal Behaviour, 16,* 589–600.

Kuczaj, S.A. (1978). Why do children fail to overgeneralise the progressive inflection? *Journal of Child Language, 5,* 167–171.

Kuczaj, S.A., & Maratsos, M.P. (1975a). What children can say before they will. *Merrill-Palmer Quarterly, 21,* 89–111.

Kuczaj, S.A., & Maratsos, M.P. (1975b). On the acquisition of front, back and side. *Child Development, 46,* 202–210.

Lachter, J., & Bever, T.G. (1988). The relation between linguistic structure and associative theories of language learning—a constructive critique of some connectionist learning models. *Cognition, 28,* 195–247.

Lakoff, G. (1966). *Stative adjectives and verbs in English.* The Computational Laboratory of Harvard University Mathematical Linguistics and Automatic Translation, No. NSF-17, 1–16.

Langley, P. (1987). A general theory of discrimination learning. In D. Klahr, P. Langley, & R. Neeches (Eds.), *Production system models of learning and development.* Cambridge, Mass: M.I.T. Press.

Leech, G.N. (1983). *Principles of pragmatics.* London: Longman.

Lempert, H., & Kinsbourne, M. (1980). Preschool children's sentence comprehension: Strategies with respect to word order. *Journal of Child Language, 7,* 371–379.

Levy, Y. (1983). It's frogs all the way down. *Cognition, 15,* 75–93.

Lieberman, P. (1984). *The biology and evolution of language.* Cambridge, Mass: Harvard University Press.

Lieven, E.V.M. (1978). Conversations between mothers and young children: Individual differences and their possible implication for the study of language learning. In N. Waterson & C. Snow (Eds.), *The development of communication.* Chichester: John Wiley.

Limber, J. (1973). The genesis of complex sentences. In T.E. Moore (Ed.), *Cognitive development and the acquisition of language.* London: Academic Press.

Linebarger, M.C. (1989). Neuropsychological evidence for linguistic modularity. In G.N. Carlson & M.K. Tanenhaus (Eds.), *Linguistic structure in language processing.* Dordrecht: Kluwer Academic.

Lock, A. (1980). *The guided reinvention of language.* London: Academic Press.

Lust, B., & Mervis, C.A. (1980). Development of co-ordination in the natural speech of young children. *Journal of Child Language, 7,* 279–304.

McCawley, J.D. (1968). The role of semantics in a grammar. In E. Bach & R.T. Harms (Eds.), *Universals in linguistic theory*. New York: Holt, Rinehart & Winston.

McClelland, J.L., Rumelhart, D.E., & Hinton, G.E. (1986). The appeal of parallel distributed processing. In D.E. Rumelhart, J.L. McClelland, & the PDP Research Group (Eds.), *Parallel distributed processing: Explorations in the microstructure of cognition. Vol. 1*. Cambridge, Mass: Bradford Books.

MacLay, H., & Sleator, M.D. (1960). Responses to language: Judgments of grammaticalness. *International Journal of American Linguistics, 26*, 275–281.

Macnamara, J. (1982). *Names for things: A study of human learning*. Cambridge, Mass: M.I.T. Press.

McNeill, D. (1966). Developmental psycholinguistics. In F. Smith & G.A. Miller (Eds.), *The genesis of language: A psycholinguistic approach*. Cambridge, Mass: M.I.T. Press.

McNeill, D. (1970). *The acquisition of language: The study of developmental psycholinguistics*. New York: Harper and Row.

McPherson, L.M.P. (1991). A little goes a long way: Evidence for a perceptual basis of learning for the noun categories COUNT and MASS. *Journal of Child Language, 18*, 315–338.

McShane, J. (1980). *Learning to talk*. Cambridge: Cambridge University Press.

McTear, M. (1985). *Children's conversation*. Oxford: Basil Blackwell.

MacWhinney, B. (1975). Rules, rote and analogy in morphological formations by Hungarian children. *Journal of Child Language, 2*, 65–77.

Maratsos, M.P. (1982). The child's construction of grammatical categories. In E. Wanner & L.R. Gleitman (Eds.), *Language acquisition: The state of the art*. Cambridge: Cambridge University Press.

Maratsos, M.P., & Chalkley, M.A. (1980). The internal language of children's syntax: The ontogenesis and representation of syntactic categories. In K.E. Nelson (Ed.), *Children's language, Vol. 2*. New York: Gardner, 1980.

Maratsos, M.P., Fox, D.E.C., Becker, J.A., & Chalkley, M.A. (1985). Semantic restrictions on children's passives. *Cognition, 19*, 167–191.

Maratsos, M.P., & Kuczaj, S.A. (1978). Against the transformationalist account: A simpler analysis of auxiliary overmarkings. *Journal of Child Language, 5*, 337–345.

Maratsos, M.P., Kuczaj, S.A., Fox, D.E.C., & Chalkley, M.A. (1979). Some empirical studies in the acquisition of transformational relations: Passives, negatives and the past tense. In W.A. Collins (Ed.), *Minnesota symposium on child psychology, Vol. 12*. Hillsdale, NJ: Lawrence Erlbaum Associates Inc.

Markman, E.M. (1973). The facilitation of part-whole comparisons by use of the collective noun 'family'. *Child Development, 44*, 837–840.

Markman, E.M., & Seibert, J. (1976). Classes and collections: Internal organisation and resulting holistic properties. *Cognitive Psychology, 8*, 561–577.

Mazurkewich, I., & White, L. (1984). The acquisition of the dative alternation: Unlearning overgeneralisations. *Cognition, 16*, 261–283.

Menyuk, P. (1964). Alternation of rules in children's grammar. *Journal of Verbal Learning and Verbal Behaviour, 3*, 480–488.

Miller, J.F., & Chapman, R.S. (1981). The relation between age and mean length of utterance in morphemes. *Journal of Speech and Hearing Research, 24*, 154–161.

Miller, P. (1986). Teasing as language socialisation in a white working-class community. In B.B. Schieffelin & E. Ochs (Eds.), *Language socialisation across cultures*. Cambridge: Cambridge University Press.

Miller, W., & Ervin, S. (1964). The development of grammar in child language. In U. Bellugi & R. Brown (Eds.), *The acquisition of language*. Chicago: University of Chicago Press.

Mitchell-Kernan, C., & Kernan, K.T. (1977). Pragmatics of directive choice among children. In S.M. Ervin-Tripp & C. Mitchell-Kernan (Eds.), *Child discourse*. New York: Academic Press.

Moerk, E.L. (1972). Principles of dyadic interaction in language learning. *Merrill-Palmer Quarterly, 18,* 229–257.

Moerk, E.L. (1974). Changes in verbal child-mother interactions with increasing language skills of the child. *Journal of Psycholinguistic Research, 3,* 101–116.

Moerk, E.L. (1975). Verbal interactions between children and their mothers during the preschool years. *Developmental Psychology, 11,* 788–794.

Moerk, E.L. (1976). Processes of language teaching and training in the interactions of mother–child dyads. *Child Development, 47,* 1064–1078.

Moerk, E.L. (1978). Determiners and consequences of verbal behaviours of young children and their mothers. *Developmental Psychology, 14,* 537–545.

Moerk, E.L. (1991). Positive evidence for negative evidence. *First Language, 11,* 219–251.

Morgan, J.L., & Travis, L.L. (1989). Limits on negative information in language input. *Journal of Child Language, 16,* 531–552.

Murphy, C.M. (1978). Pointing in the context of a shared activity. *Child Development, 49,* 371–380.

Nakayama, M, (1987). Performance factors in subject-auxiliary inversion by children. *Journal of Child Language, 14,* 113–125.

Neeches, R., Langley, P., & Klahr, D. (1987). Learning, development and production systems. In D. Klahr, P. Langley, & R. Neeches (Eds.), *Production system models of learning and development*. Cambridge, Mass: M.I.T. Press.

Nelson, K. (1973). Structure and strategy in learning to talk. *Monographs of the Society for Research in Child Development, 39,* Nos. 1–2.

Nelson, K. (1976). Some attributes of adjectives used by young children. *Cognition, 4,* 13–30.

Nelson, K.E., Carskaddon, G., & Bonvillian, J.D. (1973). Syntax acquisition: impact of experimental variation in adult verbal interaction with the child. *Child Development, 44,* 497–504.

Newmeyer, F.J. (1986). *Linguistic theory in America*. Orlando: Academic Press.

Newport, E.L., Gleitman, H., & Gleitman, L.R. (1977). Mother, I'd rather do it myself: Some effects and non-effects of maternal speech style. In C.E. Snow & C.A. Ferguson (Eds.), *Talking to children: Language input and acquisition*. Cambridge: Cambridge University Press.

Ninio, A., & Bruner, J. (1978). The achievements and antecedents of labelling. *Journal of Child Language, 5,* 1–15.

Nussbaum, N.J., & Naremore, R.C. (1975). On the acquisition of present perfect 'have' in normal children. *Language and Speech, 18,* 219–226.

O'Grady, W., Peters, A.M., & Masterson, D. (1989). The transition from optional to required subjects. *Journal of Child Language, 16,* 513–529.

Olsen-Fulero, L., & Conforti, J. (1983). Child responsiveness to mother questions of varying type and presentation. *Journal of Child Language, 10*, 495–520.

Osgood, C.E. (1980). *Lectures on language performance.* New York: Springer-Verlag.

Patterson, F. (1978). The gestures of a gorilla: Sign language acquisition in another pongid species. *Brain and Language, 5*, 72–97.

Pea, R.D. (1982). Origins of verbal logic: Spontaneous denials by two- and three-year olds. *Journal of Child Language, 9*, 597–626.

Pea, R.D., & Mawby, R. (1981). *Semantics of modal auxiliary verb uses.* Paper presented at second International Congress for the Study of Child Language, Vancouver.

Penner, S.G. (1987). Parental responses to grammatical and ungrammatical child utterances. *Child Development, 58*, 376–384.

Perlmutter, D., & Postal, P. (1977). *Towards a universal characterisation of passive.* Papers from the Third Meeting of the Berkeley Linguistics Society.

Phillips, J.R. (1973). Syntax and vocabulary of mothers' speech to young children: Age and sex comparison. *Child Development, 44*, 182–185.

Piaget, J. (1929). *The child's conception of the world.* London: Routledge and Kegan Paul.

Piaget, J. (1955). *The child's construction of reality.* London: Routledge & Kegan Paul.

Piaget, J. (1985). *The equilibration of cognitive structures.* Chicago: University of Chicago Press.

Piaget, J., & Inhelder, B. (1956). *The child's conception of space.* London: Routledge & Kegan Paul.

Pinker, S. (1979). Formal models of language learning. *Cognition, 7*, 217–283.

Pinker, S. (1984). *Language learnability and language development.* Cambridge, Mass: Harvard University Press.

Pinker, S. (1989). *Learnability and cognition: The acquisition of argument structure.* Cambridge, Mass: M.I.T. Press.

Pinker, S., Lebeaux, D.S., & Frost, L.A. (1987). Productivity and constraints in the acquisition of the passive. *Cognition, 26*, 195–267.

Pinker, S., & Prince, A. (1988). On language and connectionism: Analysis of a parallel distributed processing model of language acquisition. *Cognition, 28*, 73–193.

Power, R.J.D., & Dal Martello, M.F. (1986). The use of the definite and indefinite articles by Italian preschool children. *Journal of Child Language, 13*, 145–154.

Premack, D. (1971). On the assessment of language competence in the chimpanzee. In A.M. Schrier & F. Stollnitz (Eds.), *Behaviour of non-human primates, Vol. 4.* New York: Academic Press.

Premack, D. (1985). "Gavagai!" Or the future history of the animal language controversy. *Cognition, 19*, 207–296.

Pye, C. (1983). Mayan telegraphese: Intonational determinants of inflectional development in Quiche Mayan. *Language, 59*, 583–604.

Radford, A. (1981). *Transformational syntax.* Cambridge: Cambridge University Press.

Radford, A. (1990). *Syntactic theory and the acquisition of English syntax: The nature of early child grammar.* Oxford: Basil Blackwell.

Randall, J.H. (1985). *Negative evidence from positive*. Paper presented at Child Language Seminar, Reading University.

Remick, H. (1976). Maternal speech to children during language acquisition. In W. Van Raffler-Engel & Y. Lebrun (Eds.), *Baby talk and infant speech*. Amsterdam: Swetz and Zeitlinger.

Richards, B.J. (1990). *Language development and individual differences: A study of auxiliary verb learning*. Cambridge: Cambridge University Press.

Roberts, K. (1983). Comprehension and production of word order in Stage 1. *Child Development, 54*, 443–449.

Rodd, L.J., & Braine, M.D.S. (1970). Children's imitation of syntactic constructions as a measure of linguistic competence. *Journal of Verbal Learning and Verbal Behaviour, 10*, 430–443.

Rodgon, M.M. (1976). *Single-word usage, cognitive development and the beginnings of combinational speech: A study of ten English-speaking children*. Cambridge: Cambridge University Press.

Roeper, T. (1982). The role of universals in the acquisition of gerunds. In E. Wanner & L.R. Gleitman (Eds.), *Language acquisition: The state of the art*. Cambridge: Cambridge University Press.

Rondal, J.A., Ghiotto, M., Bredart, S., & Bachelet, J-F. (1987). Age-relation, reliability and grammatical validity of measures of utterance length. *Journal of Child Language, 14*, 433–446.

Rosch, E., Mervis, C.B., Gray, W.D., Johnson, D.M., & Boyes-Braem, P. (1976). Basic objects in natural categories. *Cognitive Psychology, 8*, 382–439.

Ross, J.R. (1967). *Constraints on variables in syntax*. Ph.D. dissertation, Massachusetts Institute of Technology.

Ross, J.R. (1975). Where to do things with words. In P. Cole & J.L. Morgan (Eds.), *Syntax and semantics, Vol. 3*. New York: Academic Press.

Rumbaugh, D.M. (1977). *Language learning by a chimpanzee: The LANA project*. New York: Academic Press.

Rumelhart, D.E., & McClelland, J.L. (1987). Learning the past tenses of English verbs: Implicit rules or parallel distributed processing. In B. MacWhinney (Ed.), *Mechanisms of language acquisition*. Hillsdale, NJ: Lawrence Erlbaum Associates Inc.

Ryan, J. (1974). Early language development: Towards a communicational analysis. In M.P.M. Richards (Ed.), *The integration of a child into a social world*. Cambridge: Cambridge University Press.

Ryan, M.L. (1978). *Baby talk and intonation in adults' speech to preverbal infants*. Ph.D. dissertation, Strathclyde University.

Sachs, J. (1983). Talking about the there and then: The emergence of displaced reference in parent child discourse. In K.E. Nelson (Ed.), *Children's language, Vol. 4*. Hillsdale, NJ: Lawrence Erlbaum Associates Inc.

Sachs, J., Brown, R., & Salerno, R. (1976). Adult speech to children. In W. Van Raffler-Engel & Y. Lebrun (Eds.), *Baby talk and infant speech*. Amsterdam: Swetz & Zeitlinger.

Sacks, H., Schegloff, E.A., & Jefferson, G. (1974). A simplest systematics for the organisation of turn-taking for conversation. *Language, 50*, 696–735.

Sadock, J. (1974). *Towards a linguistic theory of speech acts*. New York: Academic Press.

Sapir, E. (1921). *Language*. New York: Harcourt, Brace & World.

Savage-Rumbaugh, E.S. (1990). Language acquisition in a nonhuman species: Implications for the innateness debate. *Developmental Psychobiology, 23,* 599–620.

Savic, S. (1975). Aspects of adult–child communication: The problem of question acquisition. *Journal of Child Language, 2,* 251–260.

Savic, S. (1978). Strategies children use to answer questions posed by adults. In N. Waterson & C. Snow (Eds.), *The development of communication.* Chichester: John Wiley.

Schaffer, H.R., & Crook, C.K. (1980). Child compliance and maternal control techniques. *Developmental Psychology, 16,* 54–61.

Schlesinger, I.M. (1971). Production of utterances and language acquisition. In D.I. Slobin (Ed.), *The ontogenesis of grammar.* New York: Academic Press.

Schlesinger, I.M. (1981). Semantic assimilation in the development of relational categories. In W. Deutsch (Ed.), *The child's construction of language.* London: Academic Press.

Schlesinger, I.M. (1982). *Steps to language: Toward a theory of native language acquisition.* Hillsdale, NJ: Lawrence Erlbaum Associates Inc.

Schlesinger, I.M. (1988). The origin of relational categories. In Y. Levy, I.M. Schlesinger, & M.D.S. Braine (Eds.), *Categories and processes in language acquisition.* Hillsdale, NJ: Lawrence Erlbaum Associates Inc.

Schneiderman, M.H. (1983). 'Do what I mean, not what I say!'. Changes in mothers' action-directives to young children. *Journal of Child Language, 10,* 357–367.

Schnur, E., & Shatz, M. (1984). The role of maternal gesturing in conversations with one-year-olds. *Journal of Child Language, 11,* 29–41.

Searle, J.R. (1969). *Speech acts: An essay in the philosophy of language.* London: Cambridge University Press.

Searle, J.R. (1975). Indirect speech acts. In P. Cole & J.L. Morgan (Eds.), *Syntax and semantics, Vol.3.* New York: Academic Press.

Seitz, S., & Stewart, C. (1975). Imitations and expansions: Some developmental aspects of mother-child conversation. *Developmental Psychology, 11,* 763–768.

Shatz, M. (1978). Children's comprehension of their mothers' question-directives. *Journal of Child Language, 5,* 39–46.

Shatz, M. (1982). On mechanisms of language acquisition: Can features of the communicative environment account for development? In E. Wanner & L.R. Gleitman (Eds.), *Language acquisition: The state of the art.* Cambridge: Cambridge University Press.

Sheldon, A. (1974). The role of parallel function in the acquisition of relative clauses in English. *Journal of Verbal Learning and Verbal Behaviour, 13,* 272–281.

Shields, M.M. (1974). The development of the modal auxiliary system in children between three and five years. *Educational Review, 26,* 180–200.

Shipley, E.F., Smith, C.S., & Gleitman, L.R. (1969). A study in the acquisition of language: Free responses to commands. *Language, 45,* 322–342.

Siegel, S. (1956). *Nonparametric methods for the behavioural sciences.* New York: McGraw Hill.

Sinclair, H., & Bronckart, J.P. (1972). SVO: A linguistic universal? A study in developmental psycholinguistics. *Journal of Experimental Child Psychology, 14,* 329–348.

Sinha, C., & Walkerdine, V. (1974). *Spatial and temporal relations in the linguistic and cognitive development of young children.* Unpublished report, Bristol University.

Slobin, D.I. (1971). *Psycholinguistics.* Glenview, Illinois: Scott Foresman & Co.

Slobin, D.I. (1973). Cognitive prerequisites for the development of grammar. In C.A. Ferguson & D.I. Slobin (Eds.), *Studies in child language development.* New York: Holt, Rinehart & Winston.

Slobin, D.I. (1977). Language change in childhood and history. In J. Macnamara (Ed.), *Language learning and thought.* New York: Academic Press.

Slobin, D.I. (1982). Universal and particular in the acquisition of language. In E. Wanner & L.R. Gleitman (Eds.), *Language acquisition: The state of the art.* Cambridge: Cambridge University Press.

Slobin, D.I. (1985). *The crosslinguistic study of language acquisition.* Hillsdale, NJ: Lawrence Erlbaum Associates Inc.

Slobin, D.I., & Bever, T.G. (1982). Children's use of canonical sentence schemas: a cross-linguistic study of word order and inflection. *Cognition, 12,* 229–265.

Slobin, D.I., & Welsh, C.A. (1973). Elicited imitation as a research tool in developmental psycholinguistics. In C.A. Ferguson & D.I. Slobin (Eds.), *Studies of child language development.* New York: Holt, Rinehart & Winston.

Smith, C.L. (1979). Children's understanding of natural language hierarchies. *Journal of Experimental Child Psychology, 27,* 437–458.

Smith, C.S. (1980). The acquisition of time talk: Relations between child and adult grammars. *Journal of Child Language, 7,* 263–278.

Smith, M.Q. (1974). Relative clause formation between 29–36 months: A preliminary report. *Stanford Papers and Reports on Child Language Development, 8,* 104–110.

Snow, C.E. (1972). Mother's speech to children learning language. *Child Development, 43,* 549–565.

Steele, S. (1978). Word order variation: A typological study. In J.H. Greenberg (Ed.), *Universals of human language.* Stanford, California: Stanford University Press.

Steffensen, M.S. (1978). Satisfying inquisitive adults: Some simple methods of answering yes/no questions. *Journal of Child Language, 5,* 221–236.

Stemmer, N. (1987). The learning of syntax: An empiricist approach. *First Language, 7,* 97–120.

Stephany, U. (1986). Modality. In P. Fletcher & M. Garman (Eds.), *Language acquisition: Studies in first language development.* (2nd ed.). Cambridge: Cambridge University Press.

Sternberg, R.J. (1984). Mechanisms of cognitive development: A componential approach. In R.J. Sternberg (Ed.), *Mechanisms of cognitive development.* New York: W.H. Freeman & Co.

Strohner, H., & Nelson, K.E. (1974). The young child's development of sentence comprehension: Influence of event probability, nonverbal context, syntactic form and strategies. *Child Development, 45,* 567–576.

Sudhalter, V., & Braine, M.D.S. (1985). How does comprehension of passives develop? A comparison of actional and experiential verbs. *Journal of Child Language, 12,* 455–470.

Sullivan, J.W., & Horowitz, F.D. (1983). The effects of intonation on infant attention: the role of the rising intonation contour. *Journal of Child Language, 10*, 521–534.

Tager-Flusberg, H., de Villiers, J.G., & Hakuta, K. (1982). The development of sentence coordination. In S.A. Kuczaj (Ed.), *Language development, Vol. 1.* Hillsdale, NJ: Lawrence Erlbaum Associates Inc.

Tavakolian, S.L. (1981). The conjoined-clause analysis of relative clauses. In S.L. Tavakolian (Ed.), *Language acquisition and linguistic theory.* Cambridge, Mass: M.I.T. Press.

Terrace, H.S. (1979). *Nim.* New York: A Knopf.

Terrace, H.S. (1981). A report to an Academy. *Annals of the New York Academy of Sciences, 364,* 94–114.

Toivainen, J. (1980). *Inflectional affixes used by Finnish-speaking children aged 1–3 years.* Helsinki: Suomalaisen Kirjallisuuden Seura.

Tyack, D., & Ingram, D. (1977). Children's production and comprehension of questions. *Journal of Child Language, 4,* 211–224.

Valian, V. (1986). Syntactic categories in the speech of young children. *Developmental Psychology, 22,* 562–579.

Valian, V. (1989). Children's production of subjects: Competence, performance and the null subject parameter. *Papers and Reports on Child Language Development, 28,* 156–163. Department of Linguistics, Stanford University.

van Riemsdijk, H., & Williams, E.(1986). *Introduction to the theory of grammar.* Cambridge, Mass: M.I.T. Press.

Wade, N. (1980). Does man alone have language? Apes reply in riddles, and a horse says neigh. *Science, 208,* 1349–1351.

Warden, D.A. (1976). The influence of context on children's use of identifying expressions and references. *British Journal of Psychology, 67,* 101–112.

Weist, R. (1986). Tense and aspect. In P. Fletcher & M. Garman, (Eds.), *Language acquisition: Studies in first language development,* (2nd ed.). Cambridge: Cambridge University Press.

Weist, R.M., Wysocka, H., Witkowska-Stadnik, K., Buczowska, E., & Konieczna, E. (1984). The defective tense hypothesis: On the emergence of tense and aspect in child Polish. *Journal of Child Language, 11,* 347–374.

Weist, R.M., Wysocka, H., & Lyytinen, P. (1991). A cross-linguistic perspective on the development of temporal systems. *Journal of Child Language, 18,* 67–92.

Wells, G. (1974). Learning to code experience through language. *Journal of Child Language, 1,* 243–269.

Wells, G. (1979). Learning and using the auxiliary verb in English. In V. Lee (Ed.), *Language development.* London: Croom Helm.

Wells, G. (1980). Adjustments in adult-child conversation: Some effects of interaction. In H. Giles, W.P. Robinson, & P.H. Smith (Eds.), *Language: Social psychological perspectives.* Oxford: Pergamon.

Werner, H. (1948). *Comparative psychology of mental development.* New York: Science Editions.

Wetstone, H.S., & Friedlander, B.Z. (1973). The effects of word order on young children's responses to simple questions and commands. *Child Development, 44,* 734–740.

Wexler, K., & Culicover, P.W. (1980). *Formal principles of language acquisition.* Cambridge, Mass: M.I.T. Press.

White, L. (1987). Children's overgeneralisations of the English dative alternation. In K.E. Nelson & A. van Kleeck (Eds.), *Children's language, Vol. 6.* Hillsdale, NJ: Lawrence Erlbaum Associates Inc.

Whorf, B.L. (1956). *Language, thought and reality.* Cambridge, Mass: M.I.T. Press.

Wilcox, S., & Palermo, D.S. (1974/75). 'In', 'on' and 'under' revisited. *Cognition, 3/3,* 245–252.

Winograd, T. (1982). *Language as a cognitive process.* Reading, Mass: Addison-Wesley.

Woods, W.A. (1970). Transition network grammars for natural language analysis. *Communications of the Association for Computing Machinery, 13,* 591–606.

Author Index

Ackerman, B.P. 45
Ammon, M.S. 177
Anderson, J.R. 28, 91, 94, 95, 98, 189, 190
Anderson, S.R. 158
Angiolillo, C.J. 153
Antinucci, F. 70, 151
Astington, J.W. 68
Austin, J.L. 66, 87
Bachelet, J-F. 150
Baker, C.L. 125
Barnes, S. 20
Barrett, M.D. 72, 140, 149, 151, 157
Bates, E. 49, 62, 154, 177
Bavin, E.L. 179
Becker, J.A. 165
Bellinger, D. 56
Bellugi-Klima, U. 20, 105
Bellugi, U. 19, 58, 59, 159
Benedict, H. 16
Berko, J. 157
Berman, R.A. 148
Bernstein, M.E. 168
Berwick, R.C. 161
Bever, T.G. 7, 49, 62, 65, 66, 101, 154, 159, 177, 183

Bloom, L. 6, 47, 64, 82, 83, 149, 151, 156, 161, 165
Blum, M. 169
Bohannon, J.N. 23
Bonvillian, J.D. 19
Bowerman, M. 23, 64, 82, 84, 149, 151, 153, 170
Boyes-Braem, P. 185
Braine, M.D.S. 5, 49, 59, 81, 82, 88, 91, 100, 106, 149, 151, 153, 164, 165, 169
Bredart, S. 150
Bresnan, J. 28, 111, 123, 158, 161
Bridges, A. 46, 48, 49, 154
Brody, R.E. 169
Broen, P.A. 14, 56, 128
Bronckart, J.P. 49, 71, 177
Brown, B.L. 149, 153
Brown, H.D. 64
Brown, P. 42, 176
Brown, R. 14, 16, 18, 19, 20, 47, 48, 53, 59, 81, 84, 105, 106, 151, 153, 165, 166, 168, 181
Bruner, J.S. 26, 57, 84
Buczowska, E. 178
Bukatko, D. 186

Palermo, D.S. 168
Parisi, D. 151
Patterson, F. 11
Pea, R.D. 72, 73
Penner, S.G. 17, 23
Perlmutter, D. 158
Peters, A.M. 163
Phillips, J.R. 15
Piaget, J. 59, 84, 89, 169, 186, 188
Pinker, S. 7, 25, 28, 29, 94, 125, 161,
    163, 169, 170, 171
Post, K.N. 19, 23
Postal, P. 158
Power, R.J.D. 168
Premack, D. 12
Prince, A. 7
Pullum, G. 10, 111, 158
Pye, C. 17
Pylyshyn, Z.W. 7
Radford, A. 10, 162
Randall, J.H. 170
Remick, H. 14, 56
Richards, B.J. 159, 168
Roberts, K. 154, 155
Rodd, L.J. 59, 106
Rodgon, M.M. 48
Roeper, T. 190
Rondal, J.A. 150
Rosch, E. 185
Ross, J.R. 55, 124
Rumbaugh, D.M. 12
Rumelhart, D.E. 6, 7
Ryan, J. 21
Ryan, M.L. 54
Sachs, J. 72
Sacks, H. 14, 54, 72
Sadock, J. 55
Sag, I. 10, 111, 158
Salerno, R. 14
Sapir, E. 176
Satterly, D. 20
Savage-Rumbaugh, E.S. 12
Savic, S. 26, 56, 57
Schaffer, H.R. 26, 44
Schegloff, E.A. 54
Schlesinger, I.M. 84, 88, 151
Schneiderman, M.H. 17, 23, 56
Schnur, E. 26, 44
Searle, J.R. 40, 41, 42, 43, 55

Seibert, J. 187
Seitz, S. 19, 59
Shatz, M. 26, 44, 46, 56
Sheldon, A. 64
Shields, M.M. 72
Shipley, E.F. 26, 44
Shopen, T. 179
Siegel, S. 75
Sinclair, H. 49, 71, 177
Sinha, C. 48, 168
Sipple, T.S. 187
Sleator, M.D. 4
Slobin, D.I. 49, 62, 98, 106, 151, 154,
    168, 177, 181, 183
Smith, C.L. 187
Smith, C.S. 26, 44, 71
Smith, J.H. 22, 48, 72, 88, 149
Smith, M.Q. 64
Snow, C.E. 15, 19, 23
Stanowicz, L. 23
Steele, S. 179
Steffensen, M.S. 60
Stemmer, N. 91
Stephany, U. 168, 178
Sternberg, R.J. 189
Stevenson, R.J. 168
Stewart C. 19, 59
Stong-Jensen, M. 158
Strohner, H. 154
Sudhalter, V. 165
Sullivan, J.W. 54
Swinton, S.S. 187
Tager-Flusberg, H. 65, 156
Tanenhaus, M.K. 159
Tavakolian, S.L. 64, 65
Terrace, H.S. 11, 12
Toivainen, J. 177
Travis, L.L. 23
Treiman, R. 17, 23
Tyack, D. 57, 159
Valian, V. 161, 162, 163, 166
van Riemsdijk, H. 10
Venza, V. 49, 154, 177
Wade, N. 12
Walkerdine, V. 48, 168
Wanner, E. 17, 191
Warden, D.A. 168
Weinberg, A.S. 161
Weisberger, M.J. 169

Subject Index